THE
EVERYTHING
LEARNING ITALIAN
BOOK

Dear Reader,

Learning a foreign language is not easy. Many people are intimidated by foreign languages and are reluctant to speak when they first start out. I can't say that it is easy; I've been a student of Italian for more than twenty-five years, and I still feel that I learn something new almost every day. Learning Italian takes time and dedication. It won't happen overnight, but you will see gradual improvements if you stick to it. Practicing isn't easy, but try to get some speaking and listening practice in wherever and whenever you can—by taking an Italian course at your local college, by having dinner in an Italian restaurant, by watching an Italian movie, by listening to Italian music, and by traveling to Italy. Practice makes perfect—and remember, you'll get out of it what you put into it!

Good luck!

Ronald Glenn Wrigley

Welcome to the EVERYTHING® Series!

These handy, accessible books give you all you need to tackle a difficult project, gain a new hobby, comprehend a fascinating topic, prepare for an exam, or even brush up on something you learned back in school but have since forgotten.

You can choose to read an *Everything®* book from cover to cover or just pick out the information you want from our four useful boxes: e-questions, e-facts, e-alerts, and e-ssentials. We give you everything you need to know on the subject, but throw in a lot of fun stuff along the way, too.

We now have more than 400 *Everything®* books in print, spanning such wide-ranging categories as weddings, pregnancy, cooking, music instruction, foreign language, crafts, pets, New Age, and so much more. When you're done reading them all, you can finally say you know *Everything®*!

QUESTION

Answers to common questions

FACT

Important snippets of information

ALERT

Urgent warnings

ESSENTIAL

Quick handy tips

PUBLISHER Karen Cooper

DIRECTOR OF ACQUISITIONS AND INNOVATION Paula Munier

MANAGING EDITOR, EVERYTHING SERIES Lisa Laing

COPY CHIEF Casey Ebert

ACQUISITIONS EDITOR Lisa Laing

ASSOCIATE DEVELOPMENT EDITOR Elizabeth Kassab

EDITORIAL ASSISTANT Hillary Thompson

THE
EVERYTHING®
LEARNING
ITALIAN BOOK

2ND EDITION

Speak, write, and understand basic
Italian in no time

Ronald Glenn Wrigley

Adamsmedia
Avon, Massachusetts

To Mom and Dad

An Everything® Series Book.
Everything® and everything.com® are registered trademarks of F+W Media, Inc.

Published by Adams Media, a division of F+W Media, Inc.
57 Littlefield Street, Avon, MA 02322 U.S.A.
www.adamsmedia.com

ISBN 10: 1-60550-092-5
ISBN 13: 978-1-60550-092-8

Printed in the United States of America.

J   I   H   G   F   E   D   C   B   A

Library of Congress Cataloging-in-Publication Data
is available from the publisher.

This publication is designed to provide accurate and authoritative information with regard to the subject matter covered. It is sold with the understanding that the publisher is not engaged in rendering legal, accounting, or other professional advice. If legal advice or other expert assistance is required, the services of a competent professional person should be sought.

—From a *Declaration of Principles* jointly adopted by a Committee of the American Bar Association and a Committee of Publishers and Associations

Many of the designations used by manufacturers and sellers to distinguish their products are claimed as trademarks. Where those designations appear in this book and Adams Media was aware of a trademark claim, the designations have been printed with initial capital letters.

This book is available at quantity discounts for bulk purchases.
For information, please call 1-800-289-0963.

Contents

Acknowledgments

This project couldn't have happened without Michael San Filippo, who wrote the first edition of this book, and to Elizabeth Kassab of Adams Media, who worked with me along the way. I would like to acknowledge all of my Italian teachers over the years—your hard work made this book possible. I couldn't have done it without you!

I owe immense gratitude to my mother and father, to my brother, and to my grandmother and grandfather, for making me who I am today, and to my wife and son for all their love and support.

Top Ten Reasons
to Study Italian

1. Penne or farfalle? You'll be able to interpret the names of the hundreds of types of pasta.

2. You won't have to rely on subtitles when watching an Italian movie.

3. You can listen to the new Zucchero CD and understand the lyrics.

4. You can read all about Italian soccer in the *Gazzetta dello Sport*.

5. You'll be able to read Dante's *La divina commedia* in Italian.

6. You can improve your SAT scores! Research shows that studying a foreign language improves analytical skills.

7. You will impress your date by ordering in Italian at an Italian restaurant.

8. Build your resume! Adding Italian to your list of skills will make your resume stand out.

9. You'll be able to converse with your Italian relatives in their native language

10. You can visit Italy and speak Italian!

Introduction

YOU'VE TAKEN THE FIRST step in learning Italian by picking up *The Everything® Learning Italian Book, 2nd Edition with CD*. The key to learning Italian—or any foreign language—is developing a strong foundation in grammar, building on that foundation through learning vocabulary, and practicing your speaking and listening skills whenever and wherever possible. This book offers a comprehensive review of Italian grammar and vocabulary for students of all levels, from beginning to advanced, and supports the student's study of the language with listening and pronunciation guides on an audio CD, interactive exercises, an Italian-English dictionary, and verb charts. From the basics of the present indicative tense through the elusive subjunctive mode, *The Everything® Learning Italian Book, 2nd Edition with CD* is a complete package resource for learners who want to develop a well-rounded foundation in the Italian language. The audio CD that accompanies *The Everything® Italian Learning Book, 2nd Edition* will enhance your learning experience. Try not to be discouraged if you don't understand the narrator; it's okay to listen again and again to get a better understanding of the audio exercises.

There is a logical progression in the way the grammar topics are presented in *The Everything® Italian Learning Book, 2nd Edition*. We begin with nouns, articles, and adjectives, then progress to various verb tenses. It is not necessary that you follow the book in order. Skipping from one chapter to another, from one concept to another, is a good way to test your knowledge of a given grammar concept.

Though this book and audio CD provide an excellent resource for improving your knowledge of Italian grammar, it is important that it not be your *only* resource. Try to practice your listening skills by watching an Italian movie or listening to Italian music. The best way to learn is, of course, to study—but also to be willing to step outside of your comfort zone!

CHAPTER 1

Basic Italian

Welcome to your introduction to the Italian language! You will get a basic idea of the language's history, its importance, and its relevance in the world today. You will probably be pleasantly surprised to find out that you already know more Italian than you think you do. This chapter highlights some of the similarities between Italian and English and gets you started down the path of discovery.

Why Learn Italian?

The Italian language is widely regarded as one of the most beautiful (if not *the* most beautiful) spoken languages in the world today. *Il parlar gentil* (the gentle language), as it is affectionately referred to by its speakers, is spoken by roughly 63 million people in the world today.

Learning Italian can open the door to a new understanding of one of the world's richest cultural traditions and most vibrant and vital contemporary societies. From the Renaissance to the Unification, Italian culture and politics have helped shape Western culture over the past 500 years.

FACT

Every year, the president of the United States signs an executive order designating October as National Italian-American Heritage Month. Coinciding with the festivities surrounding Columbus Day, the proclamation recognizes the many achievements, contributions, and successes of Italians and Italian-Americans in the United States.

So why should you study Italian? Studying a foreign language provides myriad opportunities. It will allow you to glimpse new ideas, new perspectives, new ways of thinking, and new friendships and relationships. Perhaps you're of Italian descent or you plan on traveling to Italy for business or for pleasure. Perhaps you're a college student planning on spending a semester or a year at a study abroad program in Italy. Whatever your reason, establishing a level of proficiency in the language will only enhance your experience.

Love Those Romance Languages!

What comes to mind when you hear the word "romance"? Champagne and chocolates, candlelight dinners, soft music, and Valentine's Day? Not many people will think Italian, Spanish, or Portuguese. So what are Romance languages and why is Italian part of this group? Linguistically speaking, Romance languages are descendants of the spoken form of Latin, known as Vulgar Latin. In this case, "vulgar" doesn't mean "coarse" or "off-color," but rather "common," referring to the usual, typical, everyday speech of ordinary people.

ALERT

French, Spanish, Portuguese, and other Romance languages bear a striking resemblance to Italian. But even identical twins have distinguishing characteristics, so avoid assuming that one language's grammar is identical to another's, or that similar-sounding words have the same meaning or pronunciation.

Romance languages include modern French, Italian, Spanish, Portuguese, Romanian, Catalan, the Romansch group of dialects (Switzerland), and Sardinian. Also included are such languages as Occitan and Provençal (France), Andalusian (Spain), Friulian (northeast Italy), Ladin (northern Italy), and Sicilian (southern Italy). Many Romance languages are regional dialects rather than national languages, classified together on the basis of a shared vocabulary that originated from the language of the Roman conquerors and influenced the local native languages spoken in the Mediterranean region (where the Romance languages are clustered). Today, nearly 400 million people speak Romance languages.

Italian, like the other Romance languages, is the direct offspring of the Latin spoken by the Romans and imposed by them on the peoples under their dominion. Of all the major Romance languages, Italian retains the closest resemblance to Latin.

A Brief History of the Italian Language

In the early fourteenth century, written Italian began to take form through the works of Dante Alighieri (1265–1321). A towering figure of world literature, Dante is best known for his allegorical work *La divina commedia* (*The Divine Comedy*), which he began circa 1307 and worked on until his death. *La commedia* traces Dante's imaginary journey through Hell, Purgatory, and Heaven, during which he encounters historical and mythological creatures, each symbolic of a particular fault or virtue.

Dante's Latin treatise *De vulgari eloquentia* (c. 1303) promoted vernacular Italian as a literary language fit to replace Latin. *La divina commedia*, written in Italian verse, proved Dante's argument. Dante's native Tuscan dialect was strongly influenced by the dialects of the court poets of the Sicilian School, whom Dante greatly admired. Given the dominant economic role of the Tuscan city-states in the fourteenth century, the influence of the Tuscan dialect spread. Italian, previously treated as a spoken dialect, was recognized as a language to rival Latin, and *The Divine Comedy* has remained one of the world's greatest works of literature.

L'Accademia della Crusca

In a land well-renowned for its culinary traditions, perhaps it was inevitable that the national language academy of Italy would be named for a byproduct of the bread-making process. *L'Accademia della Crusca*, or the Academy of the Chaff, was founded in Florence in 1582 to maintain the purity of the language. Still in existence today, the academy was the first such institution in Europe and the first to produce a modern national language.

ESSENTIAL

The major work of *l'Accademia della Crusca* was the compilation of A. F. Grazzini's *Vocabulario,* a dictionary of "pure" words first published in 1612 and later taken as a model by other European states.

i Crusconi

The academy developed out of the informal meetings of a group of Florentine intellectuals between 1570 and 1580. They ironically called themselves *Crusconi* (the bran flakes) with the intention of giving a jocular tone to their conversations. In 1582, the *Crusconi* gave formal status to their assembly, christening it with the name of *Accademia*. As the group continued to grow and take on new responsibilities, it was decided that each member should adopt a nickname, *motto*, and device having to do with bran and the oven.

FACT

Leonardo Salviati (*L'Infarinato*, "the floured one") joined the group at this time and gave it renewed impetus. Salviati interpreted in a new sense the name of *crusca* (bran): "As if to say that the academy should undertake a separation of the good from the bad." Together with Anton Francesco Grazzini (*Il Lasca*, "the roach"), Salviati gave the academy a new linguistic direction, setting as its goal the promotion of a Florentine language according to the model of vernacular classicism established by Pietro Bembo, who idealized the fourteenth-century Italian authors, especially Boccaccio and Petrarca. The Florentines differed from the purist Bembo to the extent that they included their national poet Dante among this privileged group.

The Question of the Language

La questione della lingua, an attempt to establish linguistic norms and codify the language, engrossed writers of all persuasions. Grammarians during the fifteenth and sixteenth centuries attempted to confer upon the pronunciation, syntax, and vocabulary of Renaissance-era Tuscan the status of a central and classical Italian speech. Eventually this classicism, which might have doomed Italian to become another dead language, was widened to include the organic changes inevitable in a living tongue.

In the dictionaries and publications of the *Accademia della Crusca*, which was accepted by Italians as the authority in Italian linguistic matters, compromises between classical purism and living Tuscan usage were successfully effected. The most important literary event of the sixteenth century did not actually take place in Florence. In 1525, the Venetian Pietro Bembo (1470–1547) set out his proposals (*Prose della volgar lingua*) for a standardized language and style. His models were Petrarca and Boccaccio, whose writings were thus elevated to the status of modern classics. It follows, then, that the language of Italian literature is modeled on the dialect spoken in Florence in the fourteenth century.

FACT

The love poetry of Francesco Petrarca (1304–1374), especially his *Canzoniere* (Song Book), had enormous influence on the poets of the fifteenth and sixteenth centuries. Giovanni Boccaccio (1313–1375) wrote the *Decameron*, 100 stories that became a model for writers of fiction and other forms of prose.

L'Accademia Today—Still Fresh

L'Accademia della Crusca is still active and vigorous today, and their affinity for symbology has not waned a bit. The academy's symbol is a flour bolter, a machine used to separate the flour from the bran in milling operations. The traditional furnishings of the academy consist of *pale* (baker's shovels), which are individual coats of arms of the members of the academy from the sixteenth to the eighteenth century. The iconography of these shovels draws on the symbolism of the cultivation of grain, the baking of bread, and other products of the flour and of the *crusca*.

There are also *gerle* (baker's baskets), which are ceremonial academic chairs in the shape of baskets. The earliest examples date from 1642. Then there are *sacchi* (sacks), cabinets where the academic secretary kept the flour—-the status, regulations, and other writings read and approved by the censorship academics.

L'Accademia: Language, Dictionaries, Linguistics

The academy has other, more serious resources too. For those interested in Italian linguistics, the history of the Italian language, and philological studies, there is the historical archive that consists of early diaries, literary manuscript texts, and correspondences from early academy members. The library at the academy consists of language texts, dictionaries, lexicons, and works devoted to the study of Italian and to linguistics in general.

Birth of a Nation and a Language

The unification of Italy in 1861 brought about sweeping social and economic reforms. Amazingly, only 2.5 percent of Italy's population could speak standard Italian at the time of unification. Mandatory schooling and the proliferation of mass communication and mass transit had an enormous impact on the formation of modern standard Italian. Local dialects, characterized as the language of the uneducated, began to fall out of favor in the decades following unification. As Benito Mussolini and his Fascist party rose to power in the early part of the twentieth century, the push toward a common language intensified. With the goal of solidifying his control over the Italian population, Mussolini outlawed the public use of Italian dialects. Modern standard Italian was by now firmly established as the sole official language of the Italian state and its people.

ESSENTIAL

Alessandro Manzoni, a nineteenth-century writer, was instrumental in the development of the Italian language. Manzoni proposed that contemporary spoken Florentine should form the basis of Italian. His masterpiece, *I promessi sposi*, served as the benchmark for literary Italian, which, after the unification of Italy in the late 1800s, became standard Italian. The *unificazione linguistica* was as important to the newly formed nation as its political structure.

A Prince of Politicians

Niccolò Machiavelli was a writer and statesman, Florentine patriot, and original political theorist, and his works included *The History of Florence*, *The Life of Castruccio Castracani*, *The Murder of Vitellozzo Vitelli*, *The Art of War*, and *La Mandragola*. However, Machiavelli is best known for *Il principe (The Prince)*, the definitive manual of modern politics. The main theme of this work is that all means may be used in order to maintain authority, and that the worst acts of the ruler are justified by the treachery of the government. Machiavelli's ideal prince was an amoral and calculating tyrant capable of unifying Italy. Over the centuries, without benefit of the historical context in which it was written, *Il principe* brought Machiavelli a reputation of amoral cynicism and immoral manipulation.

However, *Il principe* did make some interesting points. It focused on a suggested code of conduct for rulers and a description of a leader's character and personality. Machiavelli's underlying theme was that freedom is at risk when corruption is prevalent and that there is need for good laws and leaders in a free society. He also discussed a remedy for corruption, the urgent need to punish corrupt leaders, the role of the people in maintaining a good state, and how corrupt leaders discredit their governments.

FACT

Machiavelli died in Florence in 1527, and his political writings became more widely known in the second half of the sixteenth century. Ultimately considered dangerous, they were placed on the Church Index of officially banned books in 1564.

Many of Machiavelli's aphorisms, such as "it is much more secure to be feared than to be loved," have survived the centuries. Machiavelli drew upon examples from both ancient and contemporary history, and also used his own experiences. What distinguished Machiavelli's *Il principe* from other such works was the originality and practicality of his thinking. Neither the attempts to interpret Machiavelli's ideas as first steps to democratic thoughts or examples of evil reflect a balanced view of his writing. Here are a few examples of Machiavelli's thoughts from *Il principe*:

It is necessary to take such measures that, when they believe no longer, it may be possible to make them believe by force. (Chapter VI)

A man who wishes to act entirely up to his professions of virtue soon meets with what destroys him among so much that is evil. (Chapter XV)

Hence it is necessary for a prince wishing to hold his own to know how to do wrong, and to make use of it or not according to necessity. (Chapter XV)

We have not seen great things done in our time except by those who have been considered mean; the rest have failed. (Chapter XVI)

Languages of the Italian Peninsula

Though all Italians receive formal education in modern standard Italian, almost all Italians are bilingual, meaning they speak Italian and their local dialect. There are hundreds of dialects in Italy. Some differ slightly from standard Italian, while others are considered to be separate languages. Over the centuries the Italian peninsula was host to many foreign invaders, visitors, and influences—Germanic and Venetic in the north, Greek and Arab in the south—which contributed to the formation of some of the regional dialects and languages. The website *www.ethnologue.com* defines thirty-two separate and distinct languages spoken on the Italian peninsula. The number of regional dialects or accents is innumerable. For the student of Italian, pure Venetian or Sicilian will be almost incomprehensible. Rest assured speakers of these languages will almost always speak Italian as well.

FACT

In 1984, Italian musician Fabrizio De André released his most celebrated album, *Crêuza de mä* (Path to the sea). The word *crêuza* refers to a narrow road bordered by low walls, typical of Genoa and its surroundings. The album was sung entirely in the Genoese dialect, and the songs are a tribute to the traditional music from the Mediterranean coast.

Italian by the Numbers

How many people claim Italian as their *madre lingua* (mother tongue)? And where is Italian spoken? In Italy, out of a total population of 58 million people, 55 million speak Italian; some of them are bilingual in Italian and another regional dialect, and some of them use Italian as a second language. Amazingly, only 2.5 percent of Italy's population could speak standard Italian when Italy became a unified nation in 1861. Italian is also spoken by a sizable number of people in Croatia, Eritrea, France, San Marino, Slovenia, Switzerland, and the Vatican State.

Foreign Words in Italian

Because of the growing influence of American culture, especially through the media, many English words have found their way into everyday conversation. So many English words have been adopted in Italian that there's a name for them: *Itangliano* (highly anglicized Italian). These words include "club," "flirt," "shopping," "spray," and "style." It might seem as if you hear more English than Italian spoken in the tourist-heavy cities of Florence, Rome, and Venice!

ESSENTIAL

What passes for Italian in American movies, on TV shows, and between friends isn't always accurate. Many times the Italian-American lingo you may be familiar with is made up of petrified Italian words that went out of style a century ago and street slang popularized by gangster movies. All of it tends to be spoken in an anglicized, mangled pronunciation.

The Ligurian Language

The Ligurian language is spoken in Liguria in northern Italy and in parts of the Mediterranean coast of France and Monaco. Genoese is the most widely spoken dialect of the Ligurian language.

Table 1-1
The Ligurian Dialect

Ligurian Proverb	Italian Translation	English Translation
Sbaglia finn-a o præve in to dî messa.	*Sbaglia perfino il prete nel dire messa.*	Even priests make mistakes when saying mass.
Chi l'é stæto brûxòu da l'ægua cäda, à puia da freida ascî.	*Chi è stato bruciato dall'acqua calda, ha paura anche della fredda.*	One who has been burned by hot water is also afraid of cold water.

The Sicilian Language

The Sicilian language is considered distinct enough from standard Italian to be a separate language. It is spoken in Sicily and its neighboring islands, and in parts of southern Calabria. It is influenced by numerous languages, including Greek, Latin, Arabic, French, Lombard, Provençal, German, Catalan, Spanish, and, of course, Italian. The following list of words can give you an idea of the extent to which these foreign languages have influenced Sicilian.

Table 1-2
The Sicilian Dialect

Sicilian Word	English Meaning	Language of Origin
bucali	pitcher	from the Greek word *baukalion*
naca	cradle	from the Greek word *nake*
pistiari	to eat	from the Greek word *apestiein*
cafisu	measure for liquids	from the Arabic word *qafiz*
giuggiulena	sesame seed	from the Arabic word *giulgiulan*
custureri	tailor	from the French word *coustrier*

The Venetan Language

Called *veneto* in Italian, Venician or Veneton and its variants are spoken by roughly 2 million people in northeastern Italy and in Croatia and Slovenia. Many linguists consider Venetan a separate language because it contains significant structural differences when compared to modern standard Italian. The following are some examples of Venetan words:

Table 1-3
The Venetan Dialect

Venetan Word	Italian Word	English Meaning
bioto	*puro*	pure
dalundi	*lontano*	distant, far
jera	*ero*	I was
sculiero	*cucchiaio*	spoon
tosa	*ragazza*	girl

As you can see, Italian is not the only language spoken in Italy. Knowing Italian doesn't provide you with the key to one generic culture. Rather, it opens the door to thousands of different cultures, each of which has made unique contributions in the areas of the visual arts, literature, science, politics, music, cinema, cuisine, and commerce.

FACT

Venetan is spoken in Mexico! In 1882, Chipilo, Mexico, was founded by immigrants from the town of Segusino and other surrounding towns in the Italian province of Treviso. The immigrants came to Mexico to escape poverty. Their descendants still speak a variant of the Venetan language.

Italian Words You Already Know

If you've been to an Italian restaurant or watched an Italian (or an Italian-American) movie, you may already be familiar with many Italian words and expressions. There are many words related to art and architecture, music, cuisine, language and literature, politics, and science and medicine that have made their way into the English language. You probably already know more Italian words than you think! The following are some words and terms borrowed directly from the Italian language. In all cases, the English words are spelled exactly the same way in Italian.

al dente	espresso	libretto
al fresco	fantasia	madonna
alto	fettucine	maestro
antipasto	fiasco	oboe
barista	figurine	orchestra
basso	focaccia	palazzo
biscotti	forte	pasta
broccoli	gelato	pergola
calamari	gesso	piazza
cappuccino	graffiti	piano
capriccio	internedio	piccolo
chiaroscuro	intermezzo	pizza
diva	lasagna	pizzeria

prosciutto	soprano	tortellini
putto	spaghetti	trombone
ravioli	stucco	tuba
replica	studio	villa
salami	tempera	viola
segue	tempo	zucchini
solo	terra-cotta	
sonata	tiramisù	

Cognates

Learning Italian can be made easier by developing an ability to recognize cognates—words that look like English words and have a similar meaning. There are some patterns to recognize and follow in order to sharpen your ability to recognize and use cognates.

Table 1-4
Spelling Equivalents

Nouns that end in *–ia* in Italian usually end in *–y* in English.	
psicologia	psychology
autonomia	autonomy
Nouns that end in *–ica* in Italian usually end in *–ic(s)* in English.	
fisica	physics
musica	music
Nouns that end in *–tà* in Italian usually end in *–ty* in English.	
università	university
autorità	authority
Nouns that end in *–ista* in Italian usually end in *–ist* in English.	
dentista	dentist
artista	artist
Nouns that end in *–ario* in Italian usually end in *–ary* in English.	
diaro	diary
dizionario	dictionary
Nouns that end in *–ore* in Italian usually end in *–or* in English.	
professore	professor
attore	actor

Spelling Equivalents— *continued*

Nouns that end in –*ione* in Italian usually end in –ion in English.	
stazione	station
religione	religion
Nouns that end in –*za* in Italian usually end in –ce in English.	
importanza	importance
indipendenza	independence
Adjectives ending in –*ale* in Italian usually end in –al in English.	
speciale	special
locale	local
Adjectives ending in –*oso* usually end in –ous in English.	
religioso	religious
amoroso	amorous

False Friends

There are thousands of cognates between Italian and English, but some of them can be false friends! Make sure you know the true meaning of a word before working it into your spoken language. The following section will help you to avoid many common mistakes. It is important to keep in mind that not all words that look alike mean the same thing. There are numerous false friends in Italian and English! False friends are words that look alike but have different meanings.

> *annoiato* ≠ annoyed; *annoiato* = bored
> *argomento* ≠ argument; *argomento* = subject
> *assistere* ≠ to assist; *assistere* = to attend
> *attendere* ≠ to attend; *attendere* = to wait
> *attualmente* ≠ actually; *attualmente* = currently
> *bravo* ≠ brave; *bravo* = good/clever
> *camera* ≠ camera; *camera* = room
> *caldo* ≠ cold; *caldo* = hot
> *collegio* ≠ college; *collegio* = boarding school
> *cocomero* ≠ cucumber; *cocomero* = watermelon
> *editore* ≠ editor; *editore* = publisher

educato ≠ educated; *educato* = polite
eventualmente ≠ eventually; *eventualmente* = possibly, if necessary
fabbrica ≠ fabric; *fabbrica* = factory
fattoria ≠ factory; *fattoria* = farm
parente ≠ parent; *parente* = relative
largo ≠ large; *largo* = wide
libreria ≠ library; *libreria* = bookstore
lussuria ≠ luxury; *lussuria* = lust
magazzino ≠ magazine; *magazzino* = warehouse
patente ≠ patent; *patente* = driver's license
preservativo ≠ preservative; *preservativo* = condom
romanza ≠ romance; *romanza* = novel

The Best Way to Learn Italian

The Italian national soccer team, known as *gli Azzurri* because of the blue of their jerseys, has for years ranked among the top teams in the world. Italy has won the World Cup three times, Italian-born players routinely sign multimillion-dollar contracts for European teams, and the Italian soccer leagues offer some of the most talented competition anywhere. The overriding reason for their success? Practice, practice, practice. And that's the secret to learning Italian or any other foreign language. Exercise your language muscles every day, and soon you too will be competing with the best of them. Just remember that you can't learn everything at once! Go slow and be thorough.

ESSENTIAL

The eighteenth-century *Palazzo Gallenga Stuart* is headquarters for the *Università per Stranieri di Perugia*, the world's oldest and most prestigious center of Italian language education. State-of-the-art language labs and highly flexible course programs make this school an irresistible choice for anyone wanting to study in Italy.

The quickest and most effective way to learn Italian is the total-immersion method. This means traveling to Italy for an extended period, studying at any of the thousands of schools throughout the country, and speaking only Italian. Many programs include a home-stay component that enhances the cultural exchange. You literally eat, breathe, and dream in Italian.

Unfortunately, not everyone has the opportunity to spend weeks or months in Florence, Rome, or other Italian towns sipping *espresso*, touring ancient ruins, and taking language classes. There are other ways to learn Italian without leaving your hometown, wherever that may be.

FACT

Many cable companies in the United States offer Italian programming through the *Rai* channel. Watching an Italian movie, news, or television show can help you develop an ear for the language. Check with your local cable provider to see if it's available in your area.

You've already taken the most important step to learning Italian when you picked up this book, because the most important thing is to start studying! And any method is appropriate, whether it's reading an Italian textbook, taking a language course at a university or local language school, completing workbook exercises, listening to a tape or CD, or conversing with a native Italian speaker. Spend some time every day reading, writing, speaking, and listening to Italian to become accustomed to the target language. Slowly but surely, your confidence will grow, your vocabulary will expand, and you'll be communicating in Italian.

Things to Remember

Try to avoid negative thinking. With time and effort, you will begin to put together the foundation for a wonderful learning experience. Don't be discouraged by what you can't do—focus on what you *can* do, and do it! When you start to put the language into practice, set reasonable expectations for yourself. Asking someone to repeat something can only help you understand. One of your goals should be to use the language as frequently as possible. Be vocal and don't be afraid to make mistakes!

CHAPTER 2

One Letter, One Sound

Italian is widely considered to be one of the most beautiful languages in the world. The key to understanding pronunciation is the "one letter, one sound" rule. Every letter has a unique sound, and it is always pronounced in the same way. Although some exceptions do exist, learning each letter's unique sound will take you a long way in pronouncing Italian words.

The Italian ABCs

In this chapter, you'll use the "one letter, one sound" rule to begin the foundation of learning *la bella lingua* (the beautiful language). For example, in most cases the letter *a* in Italian is always pronounced in the same way (as in the English word *car*). This is not the case with English, where pronunciation follows few rules and often involves guesswork or memorization. Let's look at the letter *a* again—but this time in English. It has several different pronunciations. The words *cat*, *date*, and *park* all contain the letter *a*, and it is pronounced differently in each one. As you develop an ear for the Italian language, you will gain a better understanding of the slight variations in pronunciation of the letter *a*. For the student of Italian, mastering pronunciation basics is easy. It just takes a little bit of practice!

TRACK 1

Table 2-1

L'alfabeto **(The Italian Alphabet)**

Letter	Italian Pronunciation	Letter	Italian Pronunciation
a	ah	*o*	oh
b	bee	*p*	pee
c	chee	*q*	koo
d	dee	*r*	EHR-reh
e	eh	*s*	EHS-seh
f	EHF-feh	*t*	tee
g	jee	*u*	oo
h	AHK-kah	*v*	voo/vee
i	ee	*w*	doppia-voo
l	EHL-leh	*x*	iks
m	EHM-meh	*y*	ypsilon
n	EHN-neh	*z*	TSEH-tah

Table 2-2

The Italian Alphabet Pronunciation Key

Italian Letter(s)	English representation	Comparable English Pronunciation	Example in Italian
A	ahh	as in far	*alta*
B	b	as in boy	*bello*
C	chi	as *ch* in children when followed by *e* or *i*	*cina, Gucci*
	k	as *k* in keep when followed by *he* or *hi*	*chi, bruschetta*
	k	as *kee* in keep when followed by *a, o,* or *u*	*caro, scopo, scuba*
	k	as *kee* in keep when followed by a consonant	*criminale*
	sh	as *sh* in she when preceded by *s* and followed by *i* or *e*	*scelta, sci*
D	d	as in David	*dormo*
E	e	as in elf	*elefante*
F	f	as in father	*fare*
G	j	as *j* in gem or jeep when followed by *e* or *i*	*gelato, giorno*
	g	as *g* in go when followed by *he* or *hi*	*spaghetti, paghi*
	g	as *g* in go when followed by *a, o,* or *u*	*gastronomia, lago, Gucci*
	lli	as *lli* in million when followed by *l*	*figlio, aglio, famiglia*
	ni	as *ni* in onion when followed by *n*	*gnocchi, ognuno, signore*
H		always silent	*spaghetti, hotel, hanno*
I	ee	as in meet	*Italia*
L	l	as in love	*Lucca*
M	m	as in meet	*Marco*
N	n	as in nice	*Napoli*
O	o	as in loan	*Como*
P	p	as in Peter	*pizza*
Q	qu	as *qu* in quick	*questo*
R	r	as in ladder	*raro*

The Italian Alphabet Pronunciation Key—*continued*

S	s/z	as in hose when it is between two vowels	*casa*
	s/z	as in hose when it begins a word and is immediately followed by *b, d, g, l, m, n, r,* or *v*	*sbadiglio, smettere*
	s	as in sky, elsewhere	*sasso, sentire*
T	t	as in time	*teatro*
U	oo	as *oo* in cool	*uno*
V	v	as in victory	*vittoria*
Z	ts	as *tz* in pretzel	*pizza*
	ds	as *ds* in lads	*zero*

Italian Vowels

The pronunciation of the Italian vowel is rather straightforward. The following is a basic pronunciation guide.

The Vowel A

In Italian, the vowel *a* is pronounced as in the English word *father.*

TRACK 2

Table 2-3

Pronunciation of the Vowel A

Italian	English
gatto	cat
malato	sick
fata	fairy
Maria	Maria
banana	banana

E: The Short/Open Vowel E

In Italian, the short vowel *e* is pronounced as in the English word *pen*.

TRACK 3

Table 2-4
Practice Pronunciation of the Short/Open Vowel E

Italian	English	Italian	English
penna	pen	*sette*	seven
Ecco!	Here it is!	*sorelle*	sisters

E: The Long/Closed Vowel E

In Italian, the long vowel *e* is pronounced like the vowel pair *ai* in the English word *air*.

TRACK 4

Table 2-5
Practice Pronunciation of the Long/Closed Vowel E

Italian	English	Italian	English
vede	she/he sees	*fede*	faith
beve	she/he drinks	*mele*	apples

The Vowel I

In Italian, the vowel *i* is pronounced like the vowel pair *ea/ee* in the English words *tree* or *tea*, or like the long *i* in words like *machine* or *trampoline*.

TRACK 5

Table 2-6
Practice Pronunciation of the Vowel I

Italian	English
libri	books
vini	wines
bambini	children

O: The Open/Short Vowel O

The open/short vowel *o* is pronounced as in the English word lost.

TRACK 6

Table 2-7
Practice Pronunciation of the Open/Short Vowel O

Italian	English	Italian	English
posta	mail	*porta*	door
corda	rope	*cosa*	thing

O: The Closed/Long Vowel O

The closed/long vowel *o* is pronounced as in the English word chose.

TRACK 7

Table 2-8
Practice Pronunciation of the Closed/Long Vowel O

Italian	English	Italian	English
solo	alone	*volo*	flight
nome	name	*ora*	hour/now

The Vowel U

The vowel *u* is pronounced as in the English word rude, or like the vowel pair *oo* in the word food.

TRACK 8

Table 2-9
Practice Pronunciation of the Vowel U

Italian	English	Italian	English
uno	one	*bruno*	brown
lungo	long	*profumo*	perfume

Double Consonants

Native speakers of English often have great difficulty in mastering the pronunciation of double consonants in Italian. One rule to keep in mind in learning correct pronunciation is that every letter in an Italian word must be pronounced. It logically follows that double consonants are pronounced longer than single consonants.

Say the sentence "I met Tim," focusing on the final T of met, and the first T of Tim. If you can pick up on the sound of the two consonants, you're on your way to understanding the correct pronunciation of double consonants in Italian.

TRACK 9

Table 2-10
Practice Pronunciation of Double Consonants

Single Consonant	Double Consonant	Single Consonant	Double Consonant
sano	*sanno*	*fata*	*fatta*
lego	*leggo*	*papa*	*pappa*

The Letter R

The letter *r* (and the double *rr*) are perhaps the most difficult letters for non-native speakers of Italian to master. It is interesting to note that the English *r* is also very difficult for non-native speakers of English! Say the following English words aloud, focusing on the motions made by your mouth and tongue:

- roar
- rice
- car
- hair
- roam
- right
- ring
- rack

You will notice that the English *r* is formed in the back of the mouth with the back of the tongue and that it is a soft, round sound. On the contrary, the Italian *r* is formed using the tip of the tongue on the upper palate behind the front teeth. Try pronouncing these English words, paying close attention to the placement of the tip of the tongue when pronouncing the letter *d*.

- dog
- dinner
- dart
- duck

Table 2-11
Pronunciation Exercise: The Letter R

Italian	English	Italian	English
raro	rare	reggere	to support
Roma	Rome	forno	oven
caro	dear/expensive	ritornare	to return
foro	forum	furbo	shrewd
povero	poor	futuro	future

Table 2-12
Pronunciation Exercise: The Letters RR

Italian	English	Italian	English
carro	cart	vorrei	I would like
burro	butter	berresti	you would drink
sorriso	smile	porre	to place/to put
birra	beer	tradurre	to translate
corretto	correct	correre	to run

Exercise 2-1

Practice your Italian by reading the following sentences aloud.

1. *Mario vorrebbe una birra Peroni.* — **Mario would like a Peroni (beer).**
2. *Vorrebbero sorridere.* — **They would like to smile.**
3. *La signora comprò una parrucca.* — **The woman bought a wig.**
4. *Vorrei correre perché ho parecchia fretta.* — **I would like to go because I'm in a hurry.**
5. *Non riesco a tradurre la lettera da Roma.* — **I can't translate the letter from Rome.**

The Letters L and GL

In Italian, the letter *l* is pronounced as in the English word "like."

TRACK 12

Table 2-13
Pronunciation Exercise: The Letter L

Italian	English
lago	lake
lento	slow
libro	book
locale	place
lungo	long

The *gl* in Italian is pronounced like the *–lli* in the English "million." Practice saying the word million, trying to focus on the position of the tongue as you're saying the *–lli* combination.

TRACK 13

Table 2-14
Pronunciation Exercise: The Letters GL

Italian	English	Italian	English
famiglia	family	*figli*	sons
moglie	wife	*aglio*	garlic

Exercise 2-2

Practice your Italian by reading the following sentences aloud.

1. *Gli studenti l'hanno letto.*   **The students read it.**
2. *I figli fanno gli spaghetti all'aglio e olio.*   **The sons are making spaghetti with garlic and oil.**
3. *Vogliamo leggere il libro.*   **We want to read the book.**
4. *La Sicilia è un'isola in un clima caldo.*   **Sicily is an island in a warm climate.**
5. *Quella bella ragazza è la figlia del signor Luigi Miglia.*   **That beautiful girl is Mr. Luigi Miglia's daughter.**

The Letters S and Z

The letter *s* has two distinct sounds. The difference is similar to the difference present in the two English words rice (here there is a distinct *s* sound) and rise (here there is more of a *z* sound). When the letter *s* appears at the beginning of a word, it has the same sound S sound as in rice, house, snake, or sip.

TRACK 14

Table 2-15
Pronunciation Exercise: The Letter S

Italian	English	Italian	English
salame	salami	*soldi*	money
secolo	century	*subito*	right away
sicuro	certain		

When the letter *s* is followed by *ca, co, cu, che, chi, f, p, qu,* or *t,* it has the same S sound as in rice, house, snake, or sip.

TRACK 15

Table 2-16
Pronunciation Exercise: S + Consonant

Italian	English		
scaffale	shelf	*scheda*	card/file
sconsigliare	to advise against	*schiacciare*	to flatten
scultore	sculptor		

When the letter *s* is doubled (*ss*), it has the same *s* sound as in rice, house, snake, or sip.

TRACK 16

Table 2-17
Pronunciation Exercise: SS

Italian	English
nessuno	no one
passa	she/he passes
pessimo	worst
sassofono	saxophone
stesso	same

When the letter *s* is followed by the consonants *b, d, g, l, m, n, r,* or *v,* it has the same *z* sound as in rise, wise, lies, or pies.

TRACK 17

Table 2-18
Pronunciation Exercise: S + Consonant

Italian	English
sbadigliare	to yawn
sdegno	disdain
sgarbato	impolite
sbagliato	wrong
smalto	enamel

When the letter *s* occurs between two vowels, it has the same *z* sound as in rise, wise, lies, or pies.

TRACK 18

Table 2-19
Pronunciation Exercise: Intervocalic S

Italian	English
casa	house
misi	I put
peso	weight
visito	I visit
base	base

When followed by *–ce, –ci, –cia, –cie, –cio,* or *–ciu,* the *s* is pronounced as the *sh* in the English words ship, shine, and harsh.

TRACK 19

Table 2-20
Pronunciation Exercise: S + Consonant

Italian	English
sciare	to ski
scienza	science
sciopero	strike
sciupare	to damage
asciugare	to dry

The Letter Z

In Italian the letter *z* has two sounds: like the *ts* in cats, bits, and rots and like the *ds* in cards, bids, and rods. The difference in pronunciation is mostly regional, but most Italians seem to prefer the *ds* sound.

TRACK 20

Table 2-21
Pronunciation Exercise: Z *(ds)*

Italian	English
zaino	backpack
zucchero	sugar
zero	zero
zucchini	zucchini
zuppa	soup

However, there are some exceptions. The words in the following exercise are invariably pronounced using the *ts* sound of cats, hats, and mats.

TRACK 21

Table 2-22
Pronunciation Exercise: Z *(ts)*

Italian	English	Italian	English
pizza	pizza	pezzi	pieces
mozzarella	mozzarella	bellezza	beauty

Developing an ear for these two distinct sounds can be difficult. To learn the subtle differences between the two, try to be aware of the sounds whenever you hear Italian being spoken!

Exercise 2-3

TRACK 22

First, read the following sentences aloud, paying close attention to the pronunciation of the *s* and *z* sounds. Then listen to the track to see how your pronunciation matches up. Highlight any words you pronounced incorrectly and focus on learning the sounds that give you trouble.

1. *Se non mi sbaglio, il prosciutto costa sessanta dollari al kilo.*   **If I'm not mistaken, the prosciutto costs $60 a kilo.**

2. *Il pizzaiolo fa la pizza a mezzogiorno.* The pizzamaker makes pizza at noon.

3. *Ha scelto la sciarpa azzurra.* She chose the blue scarf.
4. *Le scarpe sono nell'asciugatrice.* The shoes are in the dryer.
5. *Ha smesso di aspettare.* He stopped waiting.
6. *Ha messo lo zucchero nel caffè a colazione.* He put sugar in the coffee at breakfast.
7. *Legge* **La Gazzetta dello sport** *per sapere notizie sulla sua squadra.* He reads the *Gazzetta dello sport* to find out news about his team.
8. *Sai se Stefano si è sposato con Isela?* Do you know if Stefano married Isela?
9. *Mi sono sbagliato.* I made a mistake.
10. *La stazione di Salerno è sempre stata nello stesso posto.* Salerno's station has always in the same place.

The Letters C and G

In Italian, the letter *c* has two distinct sounds, like the hard *k* sound in the English word key and like the softer *ch* sound in the English word child. The letter *g* also has two distinct sounds, like the hard *g* sound of the English word gardens, and like the softer *j* sound of the English word jar.

The Consonant C

C is pronounced as a hard *k* sound when followed by *a, o, u, he,* or *hi.*

TRACK 23

Table 2-23
Pronunciation Exercise: C

Italian	English
cameriere	waiter
amico	friend
cura	cure
che	that
chi	who

The Italian *c* is pronounced as the *ch* in child when it is followed by *e* or *i*.

Table 2-24
Pronunciation Exercise: CH

Italian	English
cucinare	to cook
amici	friends
cento	100
celebrare	to celebrate
ciao	hello/goodbye

The Consonant G

The Italian *g* is pronounced as a hard *g* sound when followed by *a, o, u, he, hi,* or *r*.

Table 2-25
Pronunciation Exercise: G

Italian	English	Italian	English
gatto	cat	ghetto	ghetto
gonfiare	to inflate	ghiaccio	ice
guscio	shell	grasso	fat

The Italian *g* is pronounced as the *j* in jar when it is followed by *e* or *i*.

Table 2-26
Pronunciation Exercise: G

Italian	English
gettare	to throw
genio	genius
Gino	Gino
pagina	page
cugino	cousin

Exceptions to the Rule

One letter equals one sound. That's the general rule in Italian, but there are some rebellious letter combinations.

Diphthongs

Let's take the name Maria as an example. In this word, the *i* is stressed. The one-letter, one-sound rule needs to be qualified by saying that when one of the two vowels of a two-vowel combination is stressed—as in *Maria*, *leone*, or *trattoria*—we must articulate both vowel sounds. However, there is an exception to this rule in the form of diphthongs. A dipthong is a combination of two vowels that produce a single vowel sound. In Italian, diphthongs occur when an unstressed *i* or *u* is either preceded by or followed by *a*, *e*, or *o*.

TRACK 27

Table 2-27
Pronunciation Exercise: Diphthongs

Italian	English	Italian	English
lei	she	*vorrei*	I would like
più	more	*autobus*	bus
hai	you have	*tabaccaio*	tabacconist

Foreign Letters

There are five foreign letters that are used in words borrowed from other languages.

Table 2-28

Italian Letter(s)	Italian Pronunciation	Comparable English Pronunciation	Example in Italian
J	*i lunga*	as *j* in joy	*jolly*
K	*cappa*	*k* in key	*kiwi*
W	*doppia vu*	*w* in whiskey	*whiskey*
X	*ics*	*x* in extra	*mixer*
Y	*ipsilon*	*y* in yogurt	*yogurt*

Accent/Stress

Most words in Italian are pronounced with the stress falling on the next-to-last syllable.

am*i*co   mang*ia*re   cartol*i*na   vol*e*re

There is also a group of words that are pronounced with the stress falling in the last syllable. All of these words have a written accent.

TRACK 28

Table 2-29
Accented Vowel

Italian	English	Italian	English
università	university	*venerdì*	Friday
perché	why/because	*virtù*	virtue

Many words are pronounced with the stress on the third-to-last or fourth-to-last syllable. There is no rule governing the placement of the stress in these cases. As you develop an ear for the language you will learn which pronunciation sounds better.

TRACK 29

Table 2-30
Which Syllable?

Italian	English
facile	easy
portabile	portable
aspettano	they wait
mangiare	to eat
accademia	academy

Italian Dictionaries

There are hundreds of English–Italian Dictionaries on the market. With so many to choose from, it's tough to know which will suit your needs. There are several very good online dictionaries. The Italian publisher Garzanti has an excellent online resource at *www.garzantilinguistica.it*. It requires registration, but you can access the dictionaries for free.

Punctuation and Orthography

Now that you've worked so hard to master the alphabet and pronunciation, you'll need orthographic marks and punctuation to make it all come together. Orthography is the representation of the sounds of a language by written or printed symbols, usually accent marks. Punctuation marks are those dots, dashes, and marks that denote pauses, questions, and other patterns of speech. Mastering orthography and punctuation isn't easy, and while you may not use all of these on a regular basis, being able to refer to them in Italian will get you that much closer to fluency.

Punctuation Marks	Italian Names	Punctuation Marks	Italian Names
,	la virgola	!	il punto esclamativo
( )	le parentesi tonde	?	il punto interrogativo
.	il punto; punto fermo	'	l'apostrofo
[ ]	le parentesi quadre	—	la lineetta
;	il punto e virgola	" "	le virgolette
}	le sgraffe	:	due punti
*	l'asterisco	. . .	i puntini di sospensione
´	l'accento acuto (upward-pointing accent)	`	l'accento grave (downward-pointing accent)
-	il trattino	/	la sbarretta
@	la chiocciola		

CHAPTER 3

Grammar Basics: Nouns, Articles, and Adjectives

Nouns, articles, and adjectives are the building blocks of any language. Following are the basic grammatical rules you need to know to start to build your foundation in Italian. There are some major differences between the fundamentals of the English and Italian languages. In Italian, nouns and adjectives are associated with a gender, and this is one of the most difficult concepts for English-speakers to grasp. This chapter will break down all the differences and similarities to help you start building your vocabulary.

Kinds of Nouns

Nouns—*i nomi*—are words we use to describe people, places, things, or ideas. They are one of the most fundamental parts of any language, and Italian is no exception. The most curious thing about Italian nouns is that they have endings that change depending on their gender and number.

Common Nouns

A common noun is a word that refers to a person, place, thing, event, substance, quality, or idea.

Table 3-1
Common Nouns

Italian	English	Italian	English
libro	book	*penna*	pen
anno	year	*compleanno*	birthday
amica	(female) friend	*letto*	bed

Proper Nouns

A proper noun is a word used to name an individual, event, or place.

Table 3-2
Proper Nouns

Italian	English	Italian	English
Venezia	Venice	*Capodanno*	New Year
Marco	Mark	*il dottor Savastano*	Doctor Savastano
Natale	Christmas	*la professoressa Romeo*	Professor Romeo

Masculine Nouns

In Italian, a gender (masculine or feminine) is attributed to each and every noun. As a general rule, all nouns that end in *–o* are masculine.

Table 3-3

Masculine Nouns

Italian	English	Italian	English
ufficio	office	*fratello*	brother
negozio	store	*cugino*	(male) cousin
telefono	telephone	*amico*	(male) friend

Feminine Nouns

As a general rule, nouns ending in –*a* are feminine.

Table 3-4

Feminine Nouns

Italian	English	Italian	English
amica	(female) friend	*macchina*	car
sorella	sister	*strada*	street
casa	house	*chiesa*	church

Exercise 3-1

Say each noun aloud to practice your pronunciation. Pay close attention to the final vowel sound. Write the noun's gender in the blank provided.

1. *casa* _____
2. *libro* _____
3. *bottiglia* _____
4. *macchina* _____
5. *figlio* _____

Nouns Ending in –*e*

You may have noticed that there are many nouns that end in –*e* in their singular form, not–*o* or –*a*. Nouns that end in –*e* can be either masculine or feminine. There are a few cues to look for in determining the gender of nouns ending in –*e*.

Table 3-5

Nouns ending in *–ORE* are masculine

Italian	English	Italian	English
dottore	doctor	*fiore*	flower
professore	professor	*odore*	odor
favore	favor	*autore*	author

Nouns ending in *–IONE* are feminine

Italian	English	Italian	English
stazione	station	*conversazione*	conversation
ragione	reason	*televisione*	television
lezione	lesson	*situazione*	situation

Nouns Ending in a Consonant

Nouns ending in a consonant are masculine. These words are almost always borrowed from another language. Some examples include the following words.

- *film*
- *bar*
- *sport*
- *hobby*
- *tram*
- *autobus*

Nouns Ending in an Accented Vowel

There are several common words that end in an accented vowel. Correct pronunciation of these words can be tricky. Make sure to stress the last syllable!

Table 3-6

Nouns ending in *–È, –Ì,* or *–Ò* are masculine

Italian	English
caffè	coffee
tassì	taxi
casinò	casino

Nouns ending in –à or –ù are feminine

Italian	English
città	city
gioventù	youth

Exercise 3-2

Say each noun aloud to practice your pronunciation. Pay close attention to the final syllable sound. Is the noun masculine or feminine? Write each noun's gender in the blank provided.

1. *dottore* _____
2. *stazione* _____
3. *film* _____
4. *fiore* _____
5. *religione* _____

Plurals of Nouns

In Italian, a noun is made plural by changing the final vowel of the noun.

Singular Nouns that End in –o

As a general rule, a singular noun ending in –o changes to –i in the plural.

Table 3-7

Singular	Plural
libro	*libri*
amico	*amici*
aeroporto	*aeroporti*
fratello	*fratelli*
teatro	*teatri*

Singular Nouns That End in –*a*

A singular noun ending in –*a* changes to –*e* in the plural.

Table 3-8

Singular	Plural
sorella	sorelle
pizza	pizze
casa	case
ragazza	ragazze
macchina	macchine

Singular Nouns That End in –*e*

Singular nouns ending in –*e*, whether masculine or feminine, change to –*i* in the plural.

Table 3-9

Singular	Plural
dottore	dottori
stazione	stazioni
fiore	fiori
televisione	televisioni
autore	autori

Nouns With Irregular Endings

Though the general rule of forming plurals is easy to follow, there are a few important exceptions to bear in mind. Many of these exceptions affect commonly used nouns. First, a singular noun ending in –*io* changes to –*i* in the plural.

Table 3-10

Singular	Plural	Singular	Plural
calendario	calendari	diario	diari
stadio	stadi	figlio	figli

However, if the *i* of the *io* pair is stressed, as in the word *zio*, the plural is made by changing the *o* to an *i*. *Zio* becomes *zii*.

Singular nouns ending in *–co*, *–go*, *–ca*, and *–ga* add an *h* before the final vowel to preserve the hard sound of the *c* or *g*.

Table 3-11

Singular	Plural	Singular	Plural
tedesco	tedeschi	amica	amiche
albergo	alberghi	maga	maghe

There are some exceptions to this rule. There are no rules for which nouns add an *h* and which simply change to an *i*, so you'll just have to memorize the exceptions.

Table 3-12

Singular	Plural
amico	amici
politico	politici
medico	medici

Singular nouns that end in an accented vowel are invariable, meaning they do not change from the singular to the plural.

Table 3-13

Singular	Plural	Singular	Plural
città	città	tassì	tassì
caffè	caffè	tribù	tribù

Nouns that end in consonants are invariable and do not change from the singular to the plural.

Table 3-14

Singular	Plural
sport	sport
bar	bar
yogurt	yogurt

Nouns that are commonly used in their truncated form do not change from the singular to the plural.

Table 3-15

Singular	Plural
cinema (short for cinematografo)	cinema
auto (short for automobile)	auto
moto (short for motocicletta)	moto

Exercise 3-3

TRACK 30

Repeat the nouns after the narrator. Pay close attention to the final syllable sound. Is the noun masculine or feminine? Singular or plural? Circle the correct answers.

1. *amici*   masculine or feminine?   singular or plural?
2. *stazioni*   masculine or feminine?   singular or plural?
3. *maghe*   masculine or feminine?   singular or plural?
4. *bar*   masculine or feminine?   singular or plural?
5. *religione*   masculine or feminine?   singular or plural?

Introduction to Articles

In English, there are two types of articles—indefinite and definite. *A* and *an* are indefinite articles. They are used before singular nouns and don't refer to anything specific (a city, an eagle). *The* is a definite article. It is used before a singular noun and refers to a specific noun (the game, the king). Articles are a little more complicated in Italian, but they're easy to keep straight with a little practice.

FACT

In Italian, the correct formation of the indefinite article is determined by the gender (masculine or feminine) of the noun that it precedes. The correct formation of the definite article depends on the number (singular or plural) and gender (masculine or feminine) of the noun that it precedes.

Indefinite Articles

The indefinite article, the equivalent of *a* or *an* in English, has the form *un* or *uno* for masculine nouns, and *un'* and *una* for feminine nouns. Look at the first letter of the word in order to come up with the correct form of the indefinite article.

Table 3-16

If the first letter of the noun is . . .	Masculine	Feminine	
a consonant	*un ragazzo*	*una casa*	
a vowel	*un amico*	*un'amica*	
s+consonant	*uno stadio*	*una studentessa*	
z	*uno zero*	*una zebra*	

Definite Articles

The formation of the definite article (corresponds to the word *the* in English) is a bit more complicated. There are seven forms of the definite article in Italian. *Il*, *l'*, *lo*, *i*, and *gli* are all masculine, and *la*, *l'*, *le* are all feminine. In order to determine the correct form of the definite article, look at the initial letter of the noun, and its gender (masculine or feminine) and number (singular or plural).

Table 3-17
Masculine Articles

If the first letter of the word is . . .	Singular	Plural	
a consonant	*il lago*	*i laghi*	
a vowel	*l'amico*	*gli amici*	
s + consonant	*lo studente*	*gli studenti*	
the letter z	*lo zero*	*gli zeri*	

Table 3-18
Feminine Articles

If the first letter of the word is . . .	Singular	Plural	
a consonant	*la ragazza*	*le ragazze*	
a vowel	*l'amica*	*le amiche*	

Exercise 3-4

TRACK 31

To practice your spoken Italian and to develop an ear for recognizing definite and indefinite articles, repeat the articles and nouns after the narrator. Is there a definite or indefinite article preceding the noun? Circle the correct answer.

1. *il calendario*   definite or indefinite article
2. *un'amica*   definite or indefinite article
3. *gli sport*   definite or indefinite article
4. *la macchina*   definite or indefinite article
5. *un telefono*   definite or indefinite article

A Word on Adjectives

An adjective modifies or describes a noun. In Italian, an adjective must agree in number (singular or plural) and gender (masculine or feminine) with the noun that it modifies.

Italian Adjectives

There are two categories of adjectives in Italian. The first category is comprised of adjectives whose masculine singular form ends in *–o*. These adjectives have four possible endings:

Mario è bravo. (Mario = **masculine, singular;** *bravo* = **masculine, singular)** Mario is good.

Maria è brava. (Maria = **feminine, singular;** *brava* = **feminine, singular)** Maria is good.

Mario e Marco sono bravi. (Mario e Marco = **masculine, plural;** *bravi* = **masculine, plural)** Mario and Marco are good.

Maria e Marla sono brave. (Maria e Marla = **feminine, plural;** *brave* = **feminine, plural)** Maria and Marla are good.

The second category is comprised of adjectives whose masculine singular form ends in *–e*. These adjectives have two possible endings.

*Mario è intelligente. (Mario = **masculine, singular;** intelligente = **masculine, singular**)* Mario is intelligent.

*Maria è intelligente. (Maria = **feminine, singular;** intelligente = **feminine, singular**)* Maria is intelligent.

*Mario e Marco sono intelligenti. (Mario e Marco = **masculine, plural;** intelligenti = **masculine, plural**)* Mario and Marco are intelligent.

*Maria e Marla sono intelligenti. (Maria e Marla = **feminine, plural;** intelligenti = **feminine, plural**)* Maria and Marla are intelligent.

Placement of Adjectives—After the Noun

We've already determined that adjectives must agree in number and gender with the nouns they modify. When paired with a noun, most adjectives follow the noun.

Giulio è un ragazzo intelligente.	**Giulio is an intelligent young man.**
I bambini italiani giocano nel parco.	**The Italian children play in the park.**

Adjectives of Nationality

Adjectives that denote nationality always follow the noun that they modify. The following is a list of adjectives in their neutral, singular form. As an exercise, try to change them to plural.

Table 3-19

English	Italian	English	Italian
African	*africano*	Italian	*italiano*
American	*americano*	Japanese	*giapponese*
Australian	*australiano*	Mexican	*messicano*

English	Italian	English	Italian
Belgian	*belgo*	Indian	*indiano*
Brazilian	*brasiliano*	Moroccan	*marocchino*
Canadian	*canadese*	New Zealander	*neozelandese*
Chinese	*cinese*	Polish	*polacco*
Dutch	*olandese*	Portuguese	*portoghese*
English	*inglese*	Russian	*russo*
Egyptian	*egiziano*	Scottish	*scozzese*
European	*europeo*	Spanish	*spagnolo*
French	*francese*	Swedish	*svedese*
German	*tedesco*	Swiss	*svizzero*
Irish	*irlandese*		

FACT

Adjectives denoting nationality are not capitalized in Italian. I am American is *Sono americano* or *Sono americana*. Nouns denoting nationalities are capitalized in Italian—as in *gli Italiani*, *gli Americani*, *i Cinesi* (the Italians, the Americans, the Chinese). The names of countries are also capitalized.

When travelling around Italy you will certainly hear these terms used to describe an Italian's regional provenance ("He is Calabrian," for example).

Table 3-20

Region	Adjective Form
Abruzzo	*abruzzese*
Basilicata	*lucano*
Calabria	*calabrese*
Campania	*campano*
Emilia-Romagna	*emiliano, romagnolo*
Friuli-Venezia Giulia	*friulano, giuliano*
Lazio	*una persona del Lazio*
Liguria	*ligure*
Lombardia	*lombardo*
Marche	*marchigiano*

Region	Adjective Form
Molise	molisano
Piemonte	piemontese
Puglia	pugliese
Sardegna	sardo
Sicilia	siciliano
Toscana	toscano
Trentino-Alto Adige	trentino, altoatesino
Umbria	umbro
Valle d'Aosta	valdostano
Veneto	veneto

Adjectives of Color

Adjectives that denote color always follow the noun they modify. The following is a list of adjectives in their neutral, singular form. The adjectives *blu*, *marrone*, *arancione*, *rose*, and *viola* are invariable, and therefore they don't change to reflect the number and gender of the nouns they modify.

Table 3-21

English	Italian	English	Italian
black	nero	orange	arancione
(dark) blue	blu	pink	rosa
(pale) blue	azzurro	purple, violet	viola
brown	marrone	red	rosso
gray	grigio	white	bianco
green	verde	yellow	giallo

Placement of Adjectives—Before the Noun

Although most adjectives follow the noun they modify, there are some exceptions. The following is a group of commonly used adjectives that usually precede the nouns they modify. There is no way to tell if an adjective comes before or after a noun simply by looking at it. The best way to learn the correct placement of an adjective is to develop and ear for them!

Table 3-22

Italian	English	Italian	English
altro	other	lungo	long
bello	beautiful, nice	molto	many
bravo	good, capable	nuovo	new
brutto	ugly	piccolo	small
buono	good	primo	first
caro	dear	stesso	same
cattivo	bad	ultimo	last
giovane	young	vecchio	old
grande	big	vero	true

Io abito in una piccolo casa.	I live in a small house.
L'ho visto l'altro giorno.	I saw him the other day.
Elena è una bella ragazza.	Elena is a beautiful girl.
Ho dei vecchi amici.	I have some old friends.
Maria ha molte cugine.	Maria has many cousins.

Buono (Good) and *Bello* (Beautiful, Nice)

The adjectives *buono* and *bello* are two commonly used adjectives that follow their own specific rules. Unlike most adjectives, which have either two or four possible endings, *buono* has six possible endings and *bello* has seven possible endings. When it is paired with a noun, the adjective *buono* has several different endings, most of which are similar in structure to the endings of the indefinite article in the singular and regular endings in the plural.

Table 3-23

Italian	English	Italian	English
un libro	a book	un buon libro	a good book
uno studente	a student	un buono studente	a good student
un'amica	a (female) friend	una buon'amica	a good (female) friend
una studentessa	a (female) student	una buona studentessa	a good (female) student
due ragazzi	two boys	due buoni ragazzi	two good boys
due ragazze	two girls	due buone ragazze	two good girls

When *buono* follows the noun it modifies or the verb *essere* (covered in Chapter 4), it has four forms.

È un ragazzo buono.	**He's a good boy.**
La pizza è buona.	**The pizza is good.**
Ho amici buoni.	**I have good friends.**
Le torte sono buone.	**The cakes are good.**

In regular usage, certain adjectives—*buono* and *bello* included—normally precede the nouns they modify. These adjectives can be used after a noun for emphasis.

Exercise 3-5

Write the correct form of *buono* in each line provided.

1. _____ *studentesse*
2. _____ *ragazzi*
3. *una* _____ *amica*
4. *un* _____ *vino*
5. *un* _____ *albergo*

The adjective *bello* (beautiful, handsome, nice) also has several different endings, all of which are similar in structure to the endings of the definite article.

Table 3-24

il libro	the book	*un bel libro*	a beautiful book
l'amico	the (male) friend	*un bell'amico*	a handsome (male) friend
lo studente	the (male) student	*il bello studente*	the handsome (male) student
la ragazza	the girl	*la bella ragazza*	the beautiful girl
le ragazze	the girls	*le belle ragazze*	the beautiful girls
l'amica	the (female) friend	*una bell'amica*	a beautiful (female) friend
i libri	the books	*i bei libri*	the beautiful (or nice) books
gli studenti	the students	*i begli studenti*	the beautiful students

Exercise 3-6

Write the correct form of *bello* in the following sentences.

1. *Che* _____ *casa!*
2. *Che* _____ *giorno!*
3. *Che* _____ *ragazzi!*
4. *Che* _____ *amiche!*
5. *Che* _____ *uffici!*

Quantitative, Possessive, Demonstrative, and Interrogative Adjectives

Quantitative, possessive, demonstrative, and interrogative adjectives all precede the nouns they modify.

- Quantitative adjectives: *molto, tanto, troppo, poco* (much, so much, too much, little)
- Possessive adjectives: *il mio, il tuo, il suo* (my, your, his/her)
- Demonstrative adjectives: *questo, questi* (this, these)
- Interrogative adjectives: *che, quale* (what, which)

Quantitative Adjectives

The most common quantitative adjectives are *molto* (much, many), *tanto* (so much, so many), *troppo* (too much, too many), and *poco* (little, few). As adjectives (modifying a noun), each has four forms.

Table 3-25

molto	tanto	troppo	poco
molta	tanta	troppa	poca
molti	tanti	troppi	pochi
molte	tante	troppe	poche

Io bevo molto vino.	**I drink a lot of wine.**
Io bevo tanta birra.	**I drink so much beer.**
Io leggo troppi libri.	**I read too many books.**
Io leggo poche riviste.	**I read few magazines.**

Possessive Adjectives

Possessive adjectives are used to express ownership or relations with family members. As adjectives, they must agree in number and gender with the noun that they modify. It is important to notice that the definite article almost always precedes the possessive adjective in Italian!

Table 3-26

Subject	Possessor	Masculine Singular	Masculine Plural	Feminine Singular	Feminine Plural
io	my	il mio	la mia	i miei	le mie
tu	your (informal, singular)	il tuo	la tua	i tuoi	le tue
lui	his	il suo	la sua	i suoi	le sue
lei	hers	il suo	la sua	i suoi	le sue
Lei	your (formal, singular)	il Suo	la Sua	i Suoi	le Sue
noi	our	il nostro	la nostra	i nostri	le nostre
voi	your (informal, plural)	il vostro	la vostra	i vostri	le vostre
loro	their	il loro	la loro	i loro	le loro
Loro	your (formal, plural)	il Loro	la Loro	i Loro	le Loro

Exercise 3-7

Translate the expressions into Italian. Don't forget the definite article!

1. their book _____
2. our friends _____
3. your (singular, formal) house _____
4. your (plural, informal) birthday _____
5. his books _____

The definite article is omitted from the possessive adjective when it is used to express a relationship to a family member in the singular (except when using the *loro* possessive adjective).

mio fratello   *il loro fratello*

tua sorella   *i miei cugini*

nostro zio

Exercise 3-8

Circle the correct way of expressing possession.

1. *il mio libro/mio libro*
2. *la loro sorella/loro sorella*
3. *i nostri amici/nostri amici*
4. *il nostro cugino/nostro cugino*
5. *il suo ragazzo/suo ragazzo*

Demonstrative Adjectives *Questo* and *Quello*

The demonstrative adjective *questo* (this, these) precedes the noun, and has five forms:

questo ragazzo	quest'amico	queste riviste
questa donna	questi amici	

Quello (that, those) also precedes the noun, but it has more endings. Repeat the nouns after the narrator. Pay close attention to the form of *quello* that is being used.

TRACK 32

Table 3-27

Italian	English	Italian	English
quel vestito	that suit (dress)	*quei libri*	those books
quell'onore	that honor	*quegli uomini*	those men
quello zaino	that backpack	*quelle scarpe*	those shoes
quella donna	that woman		

Interrogative Adjectives

There are three interrogative adjectives in Italian: *quale, che,* and *quanto.* All three precede the noun to which they refer.

Quale has two forms—*quale* and *quali. Quale* is used before singular nouns and *quali* is used before plural nouns.

Quale libro?	**Which book?**
Quali ragazzi?	**Which boys?**

In written and spoken Italian you will see (and hear) that the singular form of *quale* contracts before third-person forms of the verb *essere* (to be).

Qual' è il suo libro?	**Which book is hers?**

Che is invariable and can be used with singular or plural nouns. *Che* has the same meaning as the word *quale*, but it is considered to be more colloquial. In everyday spoken Italian, *che* is increasingly preferred to *quale*. It is generally used in questions to request specific information.

Che ore sono?	**What time is it?**
Che macchina hai?	**What kind of car do you have?**
Che vuoi?	**What do you want?**

In their singular forms, *quanto* and *quanta* mean "how much?" In their plural forms, *quanti* and *quante* mean "how many?"

Quanto costa la macchina?	**How much does the car cost?**
Quanta pasta vuoi?	**How much pasta do you want?**

Repeat the questions aloud after they are read by the narrator to practice your pronunciation. Pay close attention to the form of interrogative adjective.

TRACK 33

Table 3-28

Italian	English	Italian	English
Quale libro?	Which book?	*Che vuoi?*	What do you want?
Quali ragazzi?	Which boys?	*Che libro hai?*	What (or which) book do you have?
Qual' è il suo libro?	Which is his book?	*Quanto costa la macchina?*	How much does the car cost?
Che ore sono?	What time is it?	*Quanta pasta vuoi?*	How much pasta do you want?
Che macchina hai?	What (kind of) car do you have?	*Quanti amici hai?*	Ho many friends do you have?

CHAPTER 4

Verbs:
Avere and *Essere*

The verbs *avere* (to have) and *essere* (to be) are two of the most commonly used verbs in Italian. They are essential for compound verb formations, idiomatic expressions, and many other grammatical constructions. In this chapter we will examine these verbs in the present tense and scrutinize their uses in idiomatic expressions. We will also examine informal versus formal ways of addressing people.

Subject Pronouns

Subject pronouns (personal pronouns) are used to indicate the subject of a verb. It is acceptable to omit the subject pronoun from a sentence. *Io ho una macchina./Ho una macchina.* (I have a car.)

Table 4-1

Singular				Plural			
io	I	*lui, lei*	he, she	*noi*	we	*loro*	they
tu	you (informal)	*Lei*	you (formal)	*voi*	you (informal)	*Loro*	you (formal)

TRACK 34

Listen to each of the subject pronouns spoken by the narrator. Repeat each one to practice your pronunciation.

Table 4-2

io	I	*lui, lei*	he, she	*noi*	we	*loro*	they
tu	you (informal)	*Lei*	you (formal)	*voi*	you (informal)	*Loro*	you (formal)

When Are Subject Pronouns Required?

There are a few cases in which subject pronouns are required in Italian.

- **For contrast:** *Noi lavoriamo e tu ti diverti.* (We work and you amuse yourself.)
- **For emphasis:** *Lo pago io.* (I'll pay for it.)
- **After the words *almeno, anche, magari, neanche, nemmeno, neppure:*** *Neanche noi andiamo al cinema.* (We aren't going to the cinema either.)
- **When the subject pronoun stands by itself:** *Chi voule giocare? Io!* (Who wants to play? I do!)

Exercise 4-1

Provide the correct subject pronoun for each of the following nouns or pronouns. Then check your answers in the Answer Key.

1. *Io e tu:* _____
2. *Marco:* _____

3. *Giorgio e Maria:* _____

4. *Tu e lei:* _____

5. *Gli studenti:* _____

6. *Cinzia:* _____

The Verb *Avere*: To Have

The verb *avere* (to have) is a commonly used auxiliary verb in Italian. It can be used to show possession (for example, I have a new car), and it is used in many useful idiomatic expressions. *Avere* is an irregular verb (*un verbo irregolare*); it does not follow a predictable pattern of conjugation. Even though most forms of *avere* begin with the letter *h*, that letter is never pronounced. Commit to memory the present indicative tense (*il presente*) form of *avere*. You will see it used in many Italian grammatical constructions.

FACT

The present tense is also referred to as the present indicative tense. It is the tense that "indicates" or states action at the present, a state of being, a habitual action, or an occurrence in the (very) near future.

Table 4-3

Present Indicative Tense Conjugation of *AVERE*

Singular		Plural	
io ho	I have	*noi abbiamo*	we have
tu hai	you (informal) have	*voi avete*	you (informal) have
lui ha	he has	*loro hanno*	they have
lei ha	she has	*Loro hanno*	you (formal) have
Lei ha	you (formal) have		

When you use *avere* in sentences, you can almost always leave out the subject pronoun. If you are taking about a person and want to mention his or her name, you would place it immediately before the conjugated form of *avere*.

Hai cugini in California?	**Do you have cousins in California?**
Ho tre cugini in California.	**I have three cousins in California.**
Ha una villa in campagna.	**He has a house in the country.**
Maria ha un vestito nuovo.	**Maria has on a new dress.**

Listen to each of the sentences spoken by the narrator. Repeat each one to practice your pronunciation.

TRACK 35

Table 4-4

Italian	English
Io ho buoni amici.	I have good friends.
Tu hai una nuova macchina.	You have a new car.
Lei ha una Ferrari rossa.	She has a red Ferrari.
Noi abbiamo una casa in campagna.	We have a house in the country.
Voi non avete pazienza.	You do not have patience.
Loro hanno una buon'idea.	They have a good idea.

Exercise 4-2

Rewrite the sentences using the subject provided.

1. *Io ho una nuova macchina.*
   Io e Davide _____.
2. *Abbiamo molti amici in Italia.*
   Tu e Eugenio _____.
3. *Tu hai fame.*
   Michele e Mario _____.
4. *Marco ha una buon'idea.*
   Tu _____.
5. *Voi avete caldo.*
   Io _____.

The Verb *Essere*: To Be

The verb *essere* (to be) is another commonly used auxiliary verb in Italian. It can be used to describe someone or something (for example, "he is intelligent" or "the book is interesting"). It is a very important verb—expect to see it throughout this book!

Table 4-5
Present Indicative Tense Conjugation of *ESSERE*

Singular		Plural	
io sono	I am	*noi siamo*	we are
tu sei	you (informal) are	*voi siete*	you (informal) are
lui è	he is	*loro sono*	they are
lei è	she is	*Loro sono*	you (formal) are
Lei è	you (formal) are		

TRACK 36

Listen to each of the sentences spoken by the narrator. Repeat each one to practice your pronunciation.

Io sono americano.	**I am American.**
Tu sei di Boston.	**You are from Boston.**
Lei è una buona persona.	**She is a good person.**
Noi non siamo studenti.	**We are not students.**
Voi siete allegri.	**You are happy.**
Loro sono italiani.	**They are Italian.**

Essere Used to Show Possession

Essere + *di* + proper name indicates possession. In Italian there is no "apostrophe + s" construction to signal possession.

È di Marco.	**It is Marco's. Literally:**
	It is of Marco.

To find out who owns something, ask *Di chi è . . . ?*

Di chi è questo libro?   **Whose book is this?**
Di chi sono questi libri?   **Whose books are these?**

Exercise 4-3

Read each question aloud. After you've read each question, go back and answer each question on the line provided.

1. *Di dove sei?* _____.
2. *Hai molti amici?* _____.
3. *Gli amici sono simpatici?* _____.
4. *Che macchina hai?* _____.
5. *È nuova la macchina?* _____.

FACT

To find out where someone is from, ask the question, *Di dove sei?* (informal) or *Di dov'è?* (formal). The answer is easy: *Sono di Providence.* (I am from Providence.) OR *Sono americana.* (I am American.).

Exercise 4-4

Complete the following statements below with the appropriate form of *essere*.

Maria è di Roma. Io non _____ *di Roma. Marco e suo fratello* _____ *di Roma. Anche noi* _____ _____ *di Roma. Paola* _____ *di Napoli. E tu, di dove* _____? *Voi* _____ _____ *di Venezia.*

    Tu sei americana. Giuseppe _____ *americano? Io e mia moglie* _____ *americani, ma Massimo non* _____ *americano:* _____ *italiano.*

QUESTION

The Present Indicative Tense and Questions

The present indicative tense in Italian has several equivalents in English.

Io ho	**I have/I do have/I am having**
Maria ha	**Maria has/Maria does have/Maria is having**

In English, declarative statements have a different word order than interrogative statements.

Declarative:	**Maria is a student.**
Interrogative:	**Is Maria a student?**

There are three ways to form a question in Italian. In the first example that follows, you will see that the subject is moved to the end of the sentence. In the second, the word order does not change. In all cases, the inflection of the voice changes so that the pitch rises at the end of the sentence, thereby forming a question.

1. Subject stays at the beginning of the sentence, before the verb: *Maria è una studentessa?*
2. Subject moves to the end of the sentence: *È una studentessa Maria?*
3. Subject moves to precede the verb (the least frequent option): *È Maria una studentessa?*

To negate a sentence (to make it negative), we place the word *non* before the conjugated verb:

Maria non è una studentessa.

TRACK 37

Listen to the following declarative and interrogative statements. Notice the change in inflection that denotes a question. Repeat each one after it is spoken to practice your pronunciation.

1. *Ha 39 anni Marcello?*
2. *Hanno freddo i bambini?*
3. *Non ho molta fame.*
4. *È in gamba Gabriella?*
5. *Mio zio è sano come un pesce.*

Idiomatic Expressions

An idiomatic expression is an expression whose meaning cannot be translated literally from one language into another. Native speakers of English are able to deduce the figurative meaning of the expression "It's raining cats and dogs." For non-native speakers of English, this expression can be puzzling, if not downright scary! In order to understand the expression and others like it, a person must develop an understanding of the culture in which it is used.

QUESTION

How can I ask someone's age?
The idiomatic expression *Quanti anni hai?* (literally, "How many years do you have?") is used to ask the question "How old are you?" Use the expression *Io ho* (number) *anni* (I'm [number] years old) to respond. Not that you would travel throughout Italy asking people their age, but it's helpful to know!

The verbs *avere* and *essere* are used with many idiomatic expressions in Italian. The key to understanding these idiomatic expressions is to not let your knowledge of English get in your way—try not to get into the habit of translating the expressions word for word!

Table 4-6

Idiomatic expressions with avere			
avere fame	to be hungry	*avere voglia di*	to want, to feel like
avere sete	to be thirsty	*avere ragione*	to be right, correct
avere sonno	to be sleepy	*avere torto*	to be wrong, incorrect
avere caldo	to be warm (hot)	*avere* + number + *anni*	to be . . . years old
avere freddo	to be cold	*avere a che fare con*	to deal with
avere fretta	to be in a hurry	*avercela con*	to have it in for
avere paura di	to be afraid of	*aversela a male*	to feel bad
avere bisogno di	to need, have need of		

Though not as common as idiomatic expressions with *avere*, there are a few useful idiomatic expressions using the verb *essere*.

Table 4-7

Italian	English
essere al verde	to be broke
essere in gioco	to be at stake
essere nelle nuvole	to daydream, to have one's head in the clouds
essere sano come un pesce	to be fit as a fiddle
essere buono come il pane	to be worth one's weight in gold
essere una buona forchetta	to be a hearty eater
essere ricco sfondato	to be filthy rich
essere sazio	to be full
essere un morto di fame	to be a nobody or a nothing
essere sciupato	to have gotten skinnier
essere in gamba	to be on the ball

Table 4-8

Io ho sonno.	I am sleepy.
Tu hai caldo.	You are hot.

Table 4-9

Marco ha freddo.	Marco is cold.
Giovanni ha fretta.	Giovanni is in a hurry.
Noi siamo al verde.	We are broke.
Il nostro onore è in gioco.	Our honor is at stake.
Marco e Carlo sono sempre nelle nuvole.	Marco and Carlo are always daydreaming.
Quanto sei sciupato!	How skinny you've gotten!

C'è, Ci Sono, and *Ecco!*

C'è (there is) and *ci sono* (there are) are used to indicate the existence of something. *C'è*, meaning "there is," is singular, and therefore it must be used with a singular subject. *Ci sono*, or "there are," is plural and must be used with a plural subject.

C'è un bancomat qui vicino?	**Is there an ATM around here?**
Ci sono molti ristoranti italiani a Boston.	**There are many Italian restaurants in Boston.**

Ecco is used to point out the existence of something that is in sight. It is invariable and can be used with singular or plural nouns.

Ecco il ristorante cinese!	**Here's the Chinese restaurant!**

Com'è? and *Come sono?*

Com'è? (What is it like?) and *Come sono?* (What are they like?) are used when you want to ask someone to describe what someone or something is like.

Io ho una macchina.	**I have a car.**
Com'è la macchina?	**What's the car like?**
È una Ford rossa.	**It's a red Ford.**

Ho due cugine in Florida.	**I have two cousins in Florida.**
Come sono?	**What are they like?**
Sono alte e bionde come	**They're tall and blonde like**
la loro madre.	**their mother.**

Exercise 4-5

Answer the following questions about your city.

1. *C'è un ristorante cinese a* (your city)?_____
   _____.

2. *Quanti abitanti ci sono a* (your city)? _____
   _____.

3. *C'è un'università a* (your city)? _____
   _____.

4. *Ci sono ristoranti italiani a* (your city)? _____
   _____.

5. *C'è una biblioteca pubblica a* (your city)? _____
   _____.

Language Basics

The following vocabulary forms the foundation of any conversation. Learning how to say "yes" or "no" and the valuable question words—"who," "what," "when," "where," and "why"—will help get any conversation started!

yes	*sì*	and	*e*	okay	*d'accordo*
no	*no*	or	*o*	what	*che*
when	*quando*	why	*perché*	where	*dove*
how	*come*	who	*chi*		

Be Polite

You'll notice that Italian verbs have both a formal (*Lei*) and informal (*tu*) conjugations. Native speakers of English may find it difficult to gauge when the formal way of speaking should be used. As a general rule, the formal way of speaking should be used when meeting people for the first time, when greeting elders, and in business situations. Italians may tell you when it's time to use the informal by saying *Diamoci del tu.* (Let's address each other informally.) In any event, when you're not sure which to use, it's always safe to go with the formal. Though this may be too much to learn for the casual traveler, the following "polite" words can go a long way!

please	per favore/per piacere/per cortesia	it is my pleasure	piacere mio
thank you	grazie	pardon me	mi scusi
thank you very much	mille grazie	I'm sorry	mi dispiace
you're welcome	prego		

TITLES

Sir, Mr.	Signore
Ma'am, Mrs.	Signora
Miss	Signorina

Greetings

This section introduces you to some valuable expressions that you can use to greet people and get the conversation started. Remember, when introducing yourself, be confident and polite!

ALERT!

Many of us are familiar with the word *ciao.* It does indeed mean both hello and goodbye, but it is considered to be very informal. You would use it with friends, but be careful using it in other, more formal, situations. You would not use it, for example, in a formal business meeting when addressing potential business partners!

Ice Breakers

These are the essentials!

Good morning.	*Buona mattina.*
Good day.	*Buon giorno.*
Good evening.	*Buona sera.*
Good night.	*Buona notte.*
Hello! (formal)	*Salve!*
Hi! (informal)	*Ciao!*

Conversation Starters

Once you get past the greetings, you may want to get the conversation rolling. The following table contains some useful conversation starters.

Conversation Starters			
How are you?	*Come stai?*	I am from . . .	*Sono di . . .*
Fine, thanks.	*Bene, grazie.*	I come from . . .	*Vengo da . . .*
Excellent!	*Ottimo!*	. . . the United States.	*gli Stati Uniti.*
Yes.	*Sì.*	. . . England.	*l'Inghilterra.*
No.	*No.*	. . . Australia.	*l'Australia.*
My name is . . .	*Mi chiamo . . .*	. . . Canada.	*la Canada.*
What's your name? (formal)	*Come si chiama Lei ?*	. . . France.	*la Francia.*
What's your name? (informal)	*Come ti chiami?*	. . . Spain.	*la Spagna.*
His name is . . .	*Lui si chiama . . .*	. . . China.	*la Cina.*
Her name is . . .	*Lei si chiama . . .*	. . . Japan.	*il Giappone.*
I am . . .	*Sono . . .*	Thank you.	*Grazie.*
Where are you from?	*Di dove sei?*	Please (Here you are).	*Prego.*
You're welcome.	*Non c'è di che.*	. . . in an hour.	*. . . tra un'ora.*
May I introduce you to . . . ?	*Posso presentarti . . . ?*	. . . later.	*. . . più tardi.*

Conversation Starters			
Nice to meet you.	*Piacere di conoscerti.*	Do you speak . . . (informal)	*Parli . . .*
Bye!	*Arrivederci.*	Do you speak . . . (formal)	*Parla . . .*
Good-bye (for good).	*Addio.*	. . . English?	*. . . inglese?*
See you . . .	*Ci vediamo . . .*	. . . German?	*. . . tedesco?*
. . . tomorrow.	*. . . domani.*	. . . French?	*. . . francese?*
. . . this afternoon.	*. . . questo pomeriggio.*	. . . Spanish?	*. . . spagnolo?*
. . . this evening.	*. . . stasera.*	Where is . . . ?/ Where are . . . ?	*Dov'è . . . ?/Dove sono . . . ?*
. . . next week.	*. . . la settimana prossima.*	Can you tell me . . . ? (informal)	*Puoi dirmi . . . ?*
Can you show me . . . ? (informal)	*Puoi mostrarmi . . . ?*	Can you tell me . . . ? (formal)	*Può dirmi . . . ?*
Can you show me . . . ? (formal)	*Può mostrarmi . . . ?*		

CHAPTER 5

Numbers, Time, Dates, and Seasons

This chapter introduces you to numbers (cardinal and ordinal), which will be useful when you want to buy bus tickets, pay for your meal, decide whether that leather bag at the outdoor market is really such a good deal, or need to arrive on time for an opera performance. You'll learn to tell time and talk about dates, seasons, and many other useful terms and expressions.

Cardinal Numbers from 0 to 1,000

The cardinal numbers in Italian follow a spelling pattern. Be careful, spelling can be tricky!

Table 5-1

1 uno	11 undici	21 ventuno	31 trentuno	101 centouno
2 due	12 dodici	22 ventidue	32 trentadue	150 centocinquanta
3 tre	13 tredici	23 ventitrè	33 trentatrè	200 duecento
4 quattro	14 quattordici	24 ventiquattro	40 quaranta	300 trecento
5 cinque	15 quindici	25 venticinque	50 cinquanta	400 quattrocento
6 sei	16 sedici	26 ventisei	60 sessanta	500 cinquecento
7 sette	17 diciassette	27 ventisette	70 settanta	600 seicento
8 otto	18 diciotto	28 ventotto	80 ottanta	700 settecento
9 nove	19 diciannove	29 ventinove	90 novanta	800 ottocento
10 dieci	20 venti	30 trenta	100 cento	900 novecento
1.000 mille				

Writing Numbers in Italian

All of these numbers are invariable except *zero* and *uno*. The number *uno* has the same forms as the indefinite article. *Un amico* can mean a friend or one friend, depending on the context. The plural of *zero* is *zeri*.

Ci sono due zeri nel numero di telefono.	**There are two zeros in the phone number.**

When *–tre* is the last digit of a number larger than twenty, the final *–e* of *–tre* is accented.

ventitrè, trentatrè, quarantatrè

Numbers from *venti* to *novanta* drop their final vowel before adding *uno* or *otto*.

ventuno, trentotto, novantuno

The numbers *ventuno, trentuno,* and all the way up to *novantuno* usually drop the final *–o* when followed by a noun.

Mio fratello ha quarantun anni.   **My brother is forty-one years old.**

When followed by the word *anni,* the numbers *venti, trenta,* and all the way up to *novanta* usually drop the final vowel.

Mio nonno ha ottant'anni.   **My grandfather is eighty years old.**

Cardinal Numbers from 1,001 to 999,999

In Italian, cardinal numbers are written as one word, except when *mille* or *mila* is followed by numbers smaller than 100 or by multiples of 100 (*trecento, quattrocento,* etc.). In these instances the conjunction word *e* (and) is placed between the two words.

Table 5-2

Italian	English
mille e tre	one thousand three
mille e otto	one thousand eight
mille e quaranta	one thousand forty
mille e duecento	one thousand two hundred
mille e novecento	one thousand nine hundred
But . . .	
millecentouno	one thousand one hundred and one
millecentonove	one thousand one hundred and nine
millecentoventotto	one thousand one hundred and twenty-eight
millequattrocentonovantadue	one thousand four hundred and ninety-two
milleottocentosessantuno	one thousand eight hundred and sixty-one

From 1,000 to 999,999

Mille means one thousand (not simply thousand): its multiples are therefore made of number + *mila* (the plural of *mille*):

From 1,000 to 999,999

Table 5-3

Italian	English
duemila	two thousand
tremila	three thousand
quattromila	four thousand
cinquemila	five thousand
diecimila	ten thousand
undicimila	eleven thousand
dodicimila	twelve thousand
ventimila	twenty thousand
trentamila	thirty thousand
centomila	one hundred thousand
centocinquantamila	one hundred and fifty thousand
cinquecentomila	five hundred thousand
novecentonovantanovemila	nine hundred ninety-nine thousand

Period or Comma?

When writing numbers, Italian uses periods where English would use commas and vice versa.

Table 5-4

English	Italian
1,000	1.000
1.25%	1,25%

When spoken, the word *virgola* (comma) is used.

1.5% *(one point five percent)*   **1,5%** *(uno virgola cinque percento)*

The indefinite article is not used with *cento* (hundred) and *mille* (thousand), as it is in English.

cento dollari	**a hundred dollars**
mille dollari	**a thousand dollars**

Cento has no plural form. *Mille* has the plural form *mila*.

cento dollari	**one hundred dollars**
duecento dollari	**two hundred dollars**
mille dollari	**one thousand dollars**
duemila dollari	**two thousand dollars**

Repeat each number after it is read by the narrator to practice your pronunciation.

TRACK 38

uno	*quattro*	*mille*	*trentamila*
due	*cinque*	*duemila e otto*	*quarantamila*
tre	*cento*		

Ordinal Numbers

Ordinal numbers are used to put things into an order—for example, the third chapter or the first person. The ordinal number is commonly expressed with a Roman numeral when following the name of a pope (Benedict XVI or Benedetto Sedicesimo) or monarch (Vittorio Emanuele III or Vittorio Emanuele Terzo).

Table 5-5

English	Italian	English	Italian
first	*primo*	twelfth	*dodicesimo*
second	*secondo*	thirteenth	*tredicesimo*
third	*terzo*	fourteenth	*quattordicesimo*
fourth	*quarto*	twentieth	*ventesimo*
fifth	*quinto*	twenty-first	*ventunesimo*
sixth	*sesto*	twenty-second	*ventiduesimo*
seventh	*settimo*	twenty-third	*ventitreesimo*
eighth	*ottavo*	thirtieth	*trentesimo*
ninth	*nono*	one hundredth	*centesimo*
tenth	*decimo*	thousandth	*millesimo*
eleventh	*undicesimo*	millionth	*milionesimo*

Use of Ordinal Numbers

The first ten ordinal numbers each have a distinct form. After *decimo*, they are formed by dropping the final vowel of the cardinal number and adding *–esimo*. Numbers ending in *–trè* and *–sei* retain the final vowel of the cardinal number before adding *–esimo*.

- *undici—undicesimo*
- *ventitrè—ventitreesimo*
- *trentasei—trentaseiesimo*

FACT

There's no widely accepted term for the twenty-first century that follows the pattern in Table 5-6. We can say *il secolo ventunesimo*, which is perhaps the most popular term for the new millennium (*il nuovo millennio*).

Ordinal numbers, like adjectives, agree in number and in gender with the nouns they modify. Ordinal numbers normally precede the noun.

la seconda settimana	**the second week**
il cinquantesimo anniversario	**the fiftieth anniversary**

When written as numbers, the number is followed by a small° (masculine) or ª (feminine).

il 10° capitolo　　**the tenth chapter**　　*la 5ª pagina*　　**the fifth page**

TRACK 39

Repeat each ordinal number after it is read by the narrator to practice your pronunciation.

primo	*quarto*	*settimo*	*nono*
secondo	*quinto*	*ottavo*	*decimo*
terzo	*sesto*		

In Italian, the following terms are used to refer to the centuries. These terms are often used in connection with art, literature, and history.

Table 5-6

Italian	English
il Duecento (il secolo tredicesimo)	thirteenth century
il Trecento (il secolo quattordicesimo)	fourteenth century
il Quattrocento (il secolo quindicesimo)	fifteenth century
il Cinquecento (il secolo sedicesimo)	sixteenth century
il Seicento (il secolo diciassettesimo)	seventeenth century
il Settecento (il secolo diciottesimo)	eighteenth century
l'Ottocento (il secolo diciannovesimo)	nineteenth century
il Novecento (il secolo ventesimo)	twentieth century

Note that these substitute forms are usually capitalized.

la letteratura italiana del Quattrocento	**Italian literature of the fifteenth century**
l'arte religiosa del Trecento	**religious art of the fourteenth century**

Che ora è? Che ore sono? Telling Time in Italian

The questions *Che ora è?* and *Che ore sono?* both mean "What time is it?" and can be used interchangeably.

Che ora è? Sono le due e trenta.	**What time is it? It's two-thirty.**
Che ore sono? Sono le due e trenta.	**What time is it? It's two-thirty.**

The expression *Sono le* is used to express all times from two o'clock on:

Sono le due.	**It's two o'clock.**
Sono le quattro e quindici.	**It's four-fifteen.**
Sono le otto meno due.	**It's seven-fifty-eight. (literally, It's eight o'clock minus two.)**
Sono le dodici e venti.	**It's twelve-twenty.**

È l'una is used to express all times using the one o'clock hour.

È l'una.	**It's one o'clock.**
È l'una e dieci.	**It's one-ten.**
È l'una meno cinque.	**It's twelve-fifty-five. (literally, It's one o'clock minus five.)**
È l'una e quarantacinque.	**It's one-forty-five.**

It is common in Italy to see the twenty-four-hour clock used for scheduling purposes, including train or plain schedules, conference schedules, and television programming.

Il treno per Bari parte dal binario sei alle diciannove e venti.	**The train for Bari leaves from track six at seven-twenty.**

È . . . is used with the following time expressions:

È mezzogiorno.	**It's noon.**	*È mezzanotte.*	**It's midnight.**

The expression *A che ora . . . ?* is used to ask "At what time . . . ?"

A che ora vai alla festa?	**At what time are you going to the party?**
A che ora torni stasera?	**At what time are you returning this evening?**

FACT

When using numbers to express time, we use a period in Italian where we use a colon in English. In Italian, 5:15 would be written as *5.15.*

TRACK 40

Repeat each time expression after it is read by the narrator.

Sono le 5.17.   *È l'1.15.*
Sono le 3.08.   *È mezzogiorno.*
Sono le 2.24.

The Metric System: Distance, Volume, and Weight

Italy uses the metric system for measuring. Metric units and their American-system equivalents appear in the following tables.

Table 5-7
Distance

Non-metric to Metric	Metric to Non-metric
1 inch = 25.4 millimeters	1 millimeter = 0.0394 inches
1 inch = 2.54 centimeters	1 centimeter = 0.3937 inches
1 foot = 0.3048 meters	1 meter = 3.281 feet
1 yard = 0.9144 meters	1 meter = 1.094 yards
1 mile = 1.609 kilometers	1 kilometer = 0.6214 miles

Table 5-8
Volume

Non-metric to Metric	Metric to Non-metric
1 pint = 0.5682 liters	1 liter = 1.76 pints
1 U.S. pint = 0.47311 liter	1 liter = 2.114 U.S. pints
1 U.S. gallon = 3.785 liters	1 liter = 0.26 U.S. gallons

Table 5-9
Weights

Non-metric to Metric	Metric to Non-metric
1 ounce = 28.35 grams	1 gram = 0.03527 ounces
1 pound = 453.6 grams	1 gram = 0.002205 pounds
1 pound = 0.4536 kilograms	1 kilogram = 2.205 pounds
1 ton = 1016.05 kilograms	1 kilogram = 0.0009842 tons

un litro di benzina	**a liter of gas**
mezzo kilo di pasta	**a half a kilogram of pasta**
cento grammi di farina	**100 grams of flour**

The Days of the Week

The Italian calendar begins with Monday and ends with the weekend days of Saturday and Sunday. Days of the week, months of the year, and names of seasons are not capitalized in Italian unless, of course, they are at the beginning of the sentence. The singular definite article is used before the day of the week to express a habitual action. *Il lunedì* means on Mondays or every Monday, and *la domenica* means on Sundays or every Sunday. Repeat each day of the week after the narrator to practice your pronunciation.

TRACK 41

DAYS OF THE WEEK

Monday	*lunedì*	Friday	*venerdì*	
Tuesday	*martedì*	Saturday	*sabato*	
Wednesday	*mercoledì*	Sunday	*domenica*	
Thursday	*giovedì*			

FACT

You may notice that the months *settembre*, *ottobre*, *novembre*, and *dicembre* look similar to the words for seven (*sette*), eight (*otto*), nine (*nove*), and ten (*dieci*). This interesting phenomenon has its roots in the Roman calendar, which began in March; September, October, November, and December were the seventh, eighth, ninth, and tenth months of the Roman year.

Months

You'll notice some similarities between the English names for months and the Italian names for months. Repeat each month after the narrator to practice your pronunciation.

TRACK 42

MONTHS OF THE YEAR

January	*gennaio*	July	*luglio*
February	*febbraio*	August	*agosto*
March	*marzo*	September	*settembre*
April	*aprile*	October	*ottobre*
May	*maggio*	November	*novembre*
June	*giugno*	December	*dicembre*

Here's a useful rhyme to remember how many days are in each month:

Trenta giorni ha novembre
con aprile, giugno, e settembre,
di ventotto ce n'è uno,
tutti gli altri ne hanno trentuno.

Dates

In English, when we want to express the date we use ordinal numbers—February 21st, March 13th, October 25th, etc. In Italian it is important to keep in mind that only the first day of the month is expressed with an ordinal number (*il primo luglio* = July 1); the rest of the months use the cardinal numbers and are preceded by the definite article.

il 13 (tredici) marzo, 2007 (duemilasette)
il 21 (ventun) febbraio, 1975 (millenovecentosettantacinque)
il 25 (venticinque) ottobre, 1968 (millenovecentosessantotto)

milleottocento	**1800**	*millenovecento ottanta*	**1980**
millenovecento	**1900**	*duemila*	**2000**
millenovecentosettantacinque	**1975**		

Repeat each of the following useful expressions after it is read by the narrator to practice your pronunciation.

TRACK 43

Che giorno è oggi?	**What day is it today?**
Oggi è martedì, 13 marzo.	**Today is Tuesday, March 13.**
Quanti ne abbiamo oggi?	**What's today's date?**
Ne abbiamo dodici.	**Today is the twelfth.**

Holidays in Italy

One thing to remember if you visit Italy: Check the calendar. Not only are there holidays that are part of the government calendar, but many towns and cities celebrate saints' days and local festivals. The tourist board should have this information available, but the following are the country's official national holidays. On these dates, everything shuts down—including museums, public buildings, and many retail shops.

Table 5-10

National Holidays in Italy		
January 1	*Capodanno*	New Year's Day
January 6	*Epifania*	Feast of the Epiphany
Easter Monday	*Pasquetta*	Little Easter
April 25	*Festa della Resistenza*	Liberation Day
May 1	*Festa dei Lavoratori*	Labor Day
August 15	*Ferragosto*	Feast of the Assumption
November 1	*Ognissanti*	All Saints' Day
December 8	*Immacolata Concezione*	Immaculate Conception of the Blessed Virgin Mary
December 25	*Natale*	Christmas
December 26	*Festa di Santo Stefano*	St. Stephen's Day

Seasons

If you are talking about more general periods of time, it is helpful to know the names of the seasons.

spring	*la primavera*	**autumn**	*l'autunno*
summer	*l'estate*	**winter**	*l'inverno*

Weather Words

The weather in Italy varies greatly from region to region and from season to season. The climate of southern Italy can be described as Mediterranean— hot summers and mild winters. As you move up the Italian peninsula during *l'inverno*, there can be ice storms and below-freezing temperatures. Many consider the spring (April-May) and autumn (September-October) to be the best times to visit Italy. The weather is mild and there are fewer tourists. The following words and expressions will come in useful when you are having a conversation about the weather.

How's the weather?	*Che tempo fa?*	**It's snowy.**	*Nevica.*
It's sunny.	*C'è il sole.*	**It's raining.**	*Piove.*
It's nice.	*Fa bel tempo.*	**It's windy.**	*Tira vento.*
It's cold.	*Fa freddo.*	**It's foggy.**	*C'è la nebbia.*
It's hot.	*Fa caldo.*		

Table 5-11
Weather Words

English	Italian	English	Italian
storm	*il temporale*	rainstorm	*il temporale*
lightning	*il lampo*	cloudy	*nuvoloso*
changeable	*variabile*	dusk	*il crepuscolo*
air	*l'aria*	fog	*la nebbia*
rain	*la pioggia*	frost	*il gelo*
barometer	*il barometro*	hail	*la grandine*
to rain	*piovere*	ice	*il ghiaccio*
blizzard	*la tormenta*	mist	*la foschia*
snow	*la neve*	weather report	*il bollettino meteorologico*
climate	*il clima*	cloud	*la nuvola*
storm	*la tempesta*	sun	*il sole*

Useful Expressions and Constructions: Cold

Fa freddo means "It's cold." This idiomatic expression is used only in reference to weather or room temperatures. When talking about a person's reaction to the cold: or to someone or something being cold, use the following expressions.

avere freddo	**to be cold**
Mia madre ha sempre freddo.	**My mother is always cold.**

essere freddo	**to be cold**
La birra è fredda.	**The beer is cold.**
Mio fratello è freddo con me.	**My brother is cold toward me.**

Sports and Activities

Now that you know the days of the week, the months of the year, and the seasons, it's time to learn the words and terms associated with indoor and outdoor activities. Soccer, by far the most popular sport in Italy (and in most countries in the world!), is by no means the only sport in Italy. You will find numerous sports, games, and activities available for your recreational pleasure.

Golf has become increasingly more popular over the past few years in Italy. Golf courses are widely available, but greens fees can be expensive. Driving ranges are an inexpensive way to keep your swing in top form!

Commonly Heard

Some words are common to all sports and games. Whether you're reading about it in the newspaper, watching it on TV, or observing from the audience, you're bound to hear the following words sooner or later.

Table 5-12

Sports Words					
ball	*il pallone*	player	*il giocatore*	entertaining	*divertente*
championship	*il campionato*	popular	*popolare*	team	*la squadra*
competition	*la gara*	race	*la gara*	fan	*il tifoso*
defeat	*la sconfitta*	to prefer	*preferire*	free time	*il tempo libero*
to enjoy oneself	*divertirsi*	spectators	*gli spettatori*	game	*la partita*
sport	*lo sport*	to win	*vincere*	to lose	*perdere*
entertainment	*il divertimento*	victory	*la vittoria*		

Outdoor Activities

What do you do in your free time? The following are some useful terms and expressions associated with outdoor activities.

Table 5-13

Outdoor Activities			
l'alpinismo	mountain climbing	*il ciclismo*	bicycling
il campeggio	camping	*la corsa nautical*	boat racing
la caccia	hunting	*la corsa automobilistica*	auto racing
il canotaggio	rowing	*l'equitatazione*	horseback riding
l'excursionismo	hiking	*la pallamano*	handball
il footing	jogging	*la pallanuoto*	water polo
la ginnastica	gymnastics	*la pallavolo*	volleyball
il gioco dei birilli	bowling	*il pugilato*	boxing
il patinaggio	skating	*lo sci di discesa*	downhill skiing
il nuoto	swimming	*lo sci di fondo*	cross-country skiing
lo sci nautico	water skiing	*gli sport*	sports

In Italian, there are two words (used interchangeably) for soccer: *il calcio* and *il football*. Football as we know it in the United States is called *football americano* in Italy. When friends want to get together for a pickup game, they will often refer to it as *pallone* (similar to the way Americans say "Let's play some ball.").

The Name of the Game

Italians play all sorts of sports, not just soccer! There are many amateur hockey, baseball, and basketball leagues all over Italy.

Table 5-14

Popular Games					
baseball	baseball	*football americano*	American football	*calcio*	soccer
biliardi	pool	*nascondino*	hide-and-seek	*carte*	cards
bocce	bocce ball	*pallacanestro*	basketball	*dardi*	darts
pallavolo	volleyball	*pallamano*	handball	*golf*	golf
pallone	ball	*scacchi*	chess	*tennis*	tennis

Soccer

If you're visiting Italy in soccer season, try to catch a game. Most all large cities have a professional team, and you'll find semi-professional and amateur games everywhere. For the uninitiated, soccer can be confusing. The following are some terms you might come across when watching a soccer match.

Table 5-15

Soccer Terminology			
bicycle kick	*la rovesciata*	half-way line	*la linea di metà campo*
to cheat	*barare*	header	*il colpo di testa*
corner flag	*la bandierina d'angolo*	to kick	*calciare*
crossbar	*la traversa*	linesman	*il guardalinee*
dribble	*il dribbling*	midfield player	*il centrocampista*
field	*il campo di calcio*	obstruction	*l'ostruzione*
foul	*il fallo*	offside	*il fuorigioco*
free kick	*il calcio di punizione*	pass	*il passaggio*
goal kick	*il calcio di rinvio*	penalty area	*l'area di rigore*
goal line	*la linea di fondo*	post	*il palo*
goalkeeper	*il portiere*	to score a goal	*fare un gol*
referee	*l'arbitro*	shirt (jersey)	*la maglia*
short pass	*il passaggio corto*	tie score	*il pareggio*
sweeper	*il libero*	touch line	*la linea laterale*
throw-in	*la rimessa laterale*		

Other Hobbies

What to do with all that free time? Here's a short list of some hobbies and pastimes practiced throughout the world.

Table 5-16

Hobbies			
art	*l'arte*	horse racing	*l'ippica*
art exhibit	*la mostra d'arte*	to listen to music	*ascoltare la musica*
ballet	*il balletto*	literature	*la letteratura*
book	*il libro*	novel	*il romanzo*
cinema	*il cinema*	opera	*l'opera*
crossword puzzle	*il cruciverba*	to paint	*dipingere*
to dance	*ballare*	paintbrush	*il pennello*
dancing	*il ballo*	painting	*la pittura*
to draw	*disegnare*	pastime	*il passatempo*
drawing	*il disegno*	to read	*leggere*
photography	*la fotografia*	sculpture	*la scultura*
poetry	*la poesia*	theater	*il teatro*

More Leisure Activities

The following is a list of useful *–are* verbs associated with indoor activities. Note that the verb *giocare* (to play) is followed by the preposition *a* (at) when followed by the name of a sport or game.

Table 5-17

–are Verbs

ascoltare	to listen (to)	*guardare*	to watch, to look at
ballare	to dance	*improvvisare*	to improvise
barare	to cheat	*nuotare*	to swim
calciare	to kick	*raccontare*	to tell a story, tale
cantare	to sing	*recitare*	to recite; to perform, to act; to play (the part of)
disegnare	to draw	*suonare a orecchio*	to play by ear
fare un gol	to score a goal	*suonare a prima vista*	to sight-read, to play at sight
giocare	to play	*suonare il pianoforte*	to play the piano
giocare a calcio	to play football	*suonare la chitarra*	to play the guitar
giocare a carte	to play cards	*tirare i dadi*	to throw the dice
giocare a golf	to play golf	*giocare a tennis*	to play tennis

CHAPTER 6

First-Conjugation (*–are*) Verbs

There are three primary groups of verbs in Italian, and this chapter will deal with the first-conjugation group: those verbs that end in *–are*. Most Italian verbs belong to this group, and they follow a highly uniform pattern. Once you learn how to conjugate one *–are* verb, you've essentially learned hundreds of them.

An Introduction to Italian Verbs

There are three categories of verbs in Italian, and they are divided by their infinitive form—that is, their unconjugated form. In English, examples of the infinitive include to eat, to drink, and to sleep. In Italian, verbs are broken into three main groups.

Table 6-1

Italian Verbs	
–are	first-conjugation verbs
–ere	second-conjugation verbs
–ire	third-conjugation verbs

This chapter will introduce you to the present tense of –are verbs.

Regular –are Verbs

Most all –are verbs are regular: they follow a pattern of conjugation. Once you learn this pattern, conjugating almost any other –are verb is easy.

Table 6-2

–ARE Verbs			
abitare	to live	lavorare	to work
aspettare	to wait	imparare	to learn
parlare	to speak		

To conjugate these –are verbs, remove the –are ending and replace it with a different ending for each subject.

Table 6-3

Conjugation of the verb PARLARE (to speak)

Singular	Plural
io parlo	noi parliamo
tu parli	voi parlate
lui parla	loro parlano
lei parla	loro parlano
Lei parla	Loro parla

The present indicative tense in Italian can carry different meanings in English, depending on the context.

Io parlo italiano.	**I speak Italian./I am speaking Italian./ I do speak Italian.**
Io non parlo italiano.	**I don't speak Italian./I am not speaking Italian.**

The present indicative tense in Italian can also be used to express an action that will take place in the future.

Stasera guardo la televisione.	**I will watch TV this evening.**

Conjugating –are verbs

Listen to the track. Repeat each sentence to practice your pronunciation.

TRACK 44

1.	*Io parlo italiano.*	**I speak Italian.**
2.	*Marco, tu parli inglese?*	**Marco, do you speak English?**
3.	*Mio fratello non parla francese.*	**My brother does not speak French.**
4.	*Io e mia moglie parliamo spagnolo.*	**My wife and I speak Spanish.**
5.	*Tu e Giuseppe non parlate giapponese.*	**You and Giuseppe do not speak Japanese.**
6.	*I miei figli parlano durante film.*	**My sons speak throughout the film.**

Verbs Ending in *–ciare*, *–giare*, and *–sciare*

There are a small number of commonly used first conjugation verbs that end in *–ciare*, *–giare*, and *–sciare*. These are conjugated like other *–are* verbs with the exception of two forms—the *noi* and *tu* forms. To conjugate these verbs you must drop the *–iare* of the infinitive before adding the *–i (tu)* and *–iamo (noi)*.

Table 6-4

Conjugation of the verb *INCOMINCIARE* (to begin)

Singular	Plural
io incomincio	noi incominciamo
tu incominci	voi incominciate
lui incomincia	loro incominciano
lei incomincia	loro incominciano
Lei incomincia	Loro incominciano

The following are more verbs in this category:

assaggiare (**to taste**)	*parcheggiare* (**to park**)
cominciare (**to start**)	*racconciare* (**to fix, to mend**)
invecchiare (**to grow old, to age**)	*strisciare* (**to creep, to crawl**)
marciare (**to march**)	*noleggiare* (**to rent**)
viaggiare (**to travel**)	

Verbs Ending in *–care* and *–gare*

There are a small number of commonly used first-conjugation verbs that end in either *–care* or *–gare*. To conjugate these verbs you must add an *h* before the *–i (tu)* and *–iamo (noi)*:

Table 6-5

giocare	to play
io gioco	noi giochiamo
tu giochi	voi giocate
lui gioca	loro giocano
lei gioca	Loro giocano
Lei gioca	

Verbs Ending in *–gliare* and *–gnare*

Verbs ending in *–gliare (tagliare, pigliare)* drop the *i* of the root only before the vowel *i*.

Table 6-6
Conjugating *TAGLIARE* (to cut)

person	singular	person	plural
io	taglio	noi	tagliamo
tu	tagli	voi	tagliate
lui, lei, Lei	taglia	loro, Loro	tagliono

The following are other verbs that belong to this category:

aggrovigliare **(to entangle)**   *regnare* **(to rule, to reign)**
agognare **(to long for, to crave)**   *sbagliare* **(to make a mistake, to err)**
avvinghiare **(to clutch, to grip)**   *sognare* **(to dream)**
pigliare **(to take)**

Exercise 6-1

Complete each sentence with the present indicative tense form of the indicated verbs.

1. *La regina* _____. (*regnare*)
2. *Io e Marco* _____ *per molte ore.* (*marciare*)
3. *Io* _____ *la zuppa.* (*assaggiare*)
4. *Tu* _____ *forte.* (*avvinghiare*)
5. *Lei* _____ *molto.* (*invecchiare*)
6. *Voi* _____ *la macchina.* (*noleggiare*)
7. *Marco* _____ *la motocicletta.* (*parcheggiare*)
8. *Loro* _____ *i pantaloni.* (*racconciare*)

Ascoltare, Aspettare, Guardare

In Italian, the verbs *ascoltare* (to listen or to listen to), *aspettare* (to wait or to wait for), and *guardare* (to watch or to look at) do not take a preposition, as they do in English.

Io ascolto la musica.   I listen *to* music.
Noi aspettiamo l'autobus.   We are waiting *for* the bus.
Loro guardano le foto.   They are looking *at* the pictures.

Table 6-7
Commonly Used –*are* Verbs

Italian Infinitive	English Infinitive	Italian Infinitive	English Infinitive
abitare	to live	lavorare	to work
arrivare	to arrive	mandare	to send
ascoltare	to listen (to)	mangiare	to eat
aspettare	to wait (for)	nuotare	to swim
ballare	to dance	pagare	to pay
cambiare	to change	parlare (a/di)	to speak
cantare	to sing	passare	to pass
cercare	to look for	pensare (a/di)	to think
chiamare	to call	portare	to bring
comprare	to buy	ricordare	to remember
desiderare	to want	spiegare	to explain
dimenticare	to forget	studiare	to study
domandare	to ask	telefonare	to phone
entrare	to enter	tornare	to return
frequentare	to attend	trovare	to find
giocare	to play	usare	to use
guardare	to look (at)	visitare	to visit
guidare	to drive	insegnare (a+infinitive)	to teach
imparare (a+infinitve)	to learn	incontrare	to meet
incominciare (a+infinitive)	to begin	lavare	to wash

Exercise 6-2

Say each verb conjugation aloud to practice your pronunciation. Write the infinitive form of each verb in the space provided.

1. *io gioco* _____
2. *voi telefonate* _____
3. *pensiamo* _____
4. *tu e Michele abitate* _____
5. *i bambini pensano* _____

You will often see the verb *pensare* followed by a preposition. Depending on which preposition is used, the verb takes on a slightly different meaning. *Pensare a* + noun = to think about someone or something:

Io penso a mio fratello. **I'm thinking about my brother.**

Pensare di + infinitive = to think about doing something:

Io penso di mangiare con i miei amici. **I'm thinking about eating with my friends.**

Double Verb Constructions

When using a double verb construction, the first verb is conjugated and the second is left in its infinitive form:

Io desidero mangiare fuori stasera. **I want to eat out this evening.**

Following is a list of *–are* verbs that are followed by a preposition when used in a double verb construction.

Table 6-8

Verb	Italian	English
insegnare a	*Insegno a sciare.*	I teach skiing.
andare a	*Vado a studiare.*	I am going to study.
aiutare a	*Aiuto mio figlio a fare i compiti.*	I help my son do homework.
cercare di	*Cerco di imparare.*	I am trying to learn.
cominciare a	*Comincia a fare caldo.*	It's starting to get hot.
continuare a	*Continuo a studiare.*	I continue studying.
imparare a	*Imparo a parlare l'italiano.*	I am learning to speak Italian.
iniziare a	*Inizio a capire.*	I am starting to understand.

TRACK 45

Repeat each sentence after it is read by the narrator.

1. *Io studio perché desidero imparare.*   **I study because I want to learn.**
2. *Dove aspettate l'autobus?*   **Where do you wait for the bus?**
3. *Penso a mio fratello. Lui è al verde.*   **I'm thinking about my brother. He's broke.**
4. *Io non lavoro il sabato.*   **I don't work on Saturdays.**
5. *Noi giochiamo a tennis oggi.*   **We're playing tennis today.**

Exercise 6-3

Translate the following sentences into Italian. Choose from among the *are* verbs provided. Some idiomatic expressions with *avere* may be needed as well.

pensare (a/di)	*parlare*	*mangiare*
desiderare	*abitare*	*giocare (a)*
incominciare	*imparare (a)*	*spiegare*

1. I am learning to speak Italian._____.
2. They are starting to work on Friday._____.
3. We are thinking of eating in the new restaurant._____.
4. The boys want to explain the situation. _____.
5. The professor is speaking with a student. _____.
6. John lives in Boston. _____.
7. Do you play tennis? _____.
8. He is afraid of the other children._____.
9. We feel like eating the pizza._____.
10. You and John do not need the computer today._____.

Irregular *–are* Verbs: *andare, fare, stare, dare*

Andare (to go), *fare* (to do), *dare* (to give), and *stare* (to stay, to feel) are irregular verbs. As such they do not follow a pattern of conjugation.

Table 6-9

	andare	fare	dare	stare
io	vado	faccio	do	sto
tu	vai	fai	dai	stai
lui, lei, Lei	va	fa	dà	sta
noi	andiamo	facciamo	diamo	stiamo
voi	andate	fate	date	state
loro, Loro	vanno	fanno	danno	stanno

Andiamo a teatro stasera.	**We are going to the theater tonight.**
Faccio gli spaghetti alla carbonara.	**I am making spaghetti alla carbonara.**
Come stai? Sto bene, grazie.	**How are you? I am fine, thanks.**
Io do una bottiglia di vino a mio cognato.	**I am giving a bottle of wine to my brother-in-law.**

The verb *fare* (to do, to make) is often shortened to *far* when the first letter of the word that follows it begins with a consonant. For example, *Voglio far colazione* means "I want to have breakfast." This is done for pronunciation purposes.

TRACK 46

Here are some examples of *andare*, *fare*, *dare*, and *stare* being used in sentences. Repeat each one after it is read to practice your pronunciation.

1. *Io vado a un concerto stasera.*	**I am going to a concert tonight.**
2. *Che cosa volete fare stasera?*	**What do you want to do tonight?**

3. *Dove andiamo noi per le vacanze?*   **Where are we going for vacation?**

4. *Marcello, come stai tu?*   **Marcello, how are you doing?**
5. *Loro danno le informazioni ai turisti.*   **They give the information to the tourists.**

Exercise 6-4

Complete each sentence with the most appropriate verb (*andare, fare, dare,* or *stare*).

1. *Come _____ Loro oggi?*
2. *Che cosa _____, tu?*
3. *Io _____ a mangiare in un ristorante.*
4. *La madre _____ soldi a suo figlio.*

FACT

Be careful not to confuse the third person singular conjugation of the verb *dare* (*Anna dà la chiave a Maria* = Anna gives the key to Maria) with the preposition *da* (from). The accented vowel is pronounced more abruptly, but other than that the pronunciation is almost identical. However, the meaning is totally different!

Idiomatic Expressions with Irregular Verbs

As you will see, there are many commonly used idiomatic expressions using the irregular verbs. Try not to translate these expressions literally from one language to the other!

Idiomatic Expressions with *Fare*

The verb *fare* expresses the basic idea of doing or making, as in *fare gli esercizi* (to do the exercises) and *fare il letto* (to make the bed), but it is also used in many idioms.

Table 6-10

Idiomatic Expressions with Fare			
fare amici	to make friends	*fare una domanda*	to ask a question
fare attenzione	to pay attention	*fare un errore*	to make a mistake
fare il bagno	to take a bath	*far fingere*	to pretend
fare il biglietto	to buy a ticket	*fare una foto(grafia)*	to take a picture
fare i compiti	to do homework	*fare freddo*	to be cold (weather)
fare caldo	to be hot (weather)	*fare una gita*	to take a short trip
fare la coda/la fila	to stand in line	*fare un giro*	to go for a ride
fare colazione	to have breakfast	*fare la guerra*	to wage war
fare la doccia	to take a shower	*fare male*	to ache, to hurt
fare passare	to let (someone) pass	*fare la spesa*	to go food shopping
fare una passeggiata	to take a walk	*fare le spese*	to go shopping
fare una pausa	to take a break	*fare di tutto*	to do all in one's power
fare il pieno	to fill up the gas tank	*fare vedere*	to show something to someone
fare la prenotazione	to make a reservation	*fare un viaggio*	to take a trip
fare del proprio meglio	to do one's best	*fare un regalo*	to give a gift
fare alla romana	to split the check		

Exercise 6-5

Read each sentence aloud to practice your pronunciation. Each sentence contains an idiomatic expression with the verb *fare*.

1. *Gli studenti non fanno attenzione.* — **The students aren't paying attention.**
2. *Fai la doccia alle otto di mattina.* — **You take a shower at eight o'clock in the morning.**
3. *Io e mia moglie facciamo colazione.* — **My wife and I are having breakfast.**

4. *I ragazzi fanno alla romana in pizzeria.* — **The kids split the check in the pizzeria.**

5. *I turisti fanno molte fotografie.* — **The tourists are taking many pictures.**

Idiomatic Expressions with *Dare*

There are a handful of commonly used idiomatic expressions using the verb *dare*.

Table 6-11

dare da mangiare a	to feed	*dare noia a*	to bother
dare del Lei	to address someone formally	*dare retta a*	to listen to/to pay attention to
dare del tu	to address someone informally	*dare torto a*	to blame
dare la caccia a	to chase	*dare un calcio a*	to kick
dare fastidio a	to bother	*dare un pugno a*	to punch

Idiomatic Expressions with *Stare* and *Andare*

The verbs *stare* and *andare* are used in many idiomatic expressions as well. *Stare* has different English equivalents according to the adjective or adverb that accompanies it.

Table 6-12

stare attento/a/i/e	to be careful	*starsene da parte*	to stand aside, to be on one side
stare bene/male	to be well/not well	*stare su*	to stand/sit up straight
stare zitto/a/i/e	to keep quiet	*stare a cuore*	to matter, to have at heart
stare fresco	to be mistaken/to kid oneself	*stare con*	to live with
stare fuori	to be outside	*stare in piedi*	to be standing
stare in guardia	to pay attention		

The verb *andare* is commonly used with means of transportation—for instance, *andare in macchina* means "to go by car." Like *stare*, *andare* may be combined with other words to take on new meanings.

Table 6-13

andare a cavallo	to go on horseback
andare in moto	to go on a motorcycle
andare in aereo	to go by plane
andare a piedi	to go by foot
andare in bicicletta	to ride a bicycle
andare in treno	to go by train
andare in macchina	to go by car

Table 6-14

andare avanti	to proceed, to go on	andare indietro	to back up
andare con	to accompany, to take, to go with	andare lontano	to go far away
andare dentro	to enter, to go in	andare per terra	to fall
andare fuori	to go out	andarsene	to go away, to leave

Exercise 6-6

Which verb makes the most sense? Choose among the four irregular verbs (*andare, fare, dare, stare*). Write the correct form in the space provided.

1. *Noi _____ attenzione quando parla.*
2. *Tu e Mario _____ a casa oggi?*
3. *Dove _____ noi per le vacanze?*
4. *Loro _____ informazioni ai turisti.*
5. *Come _____ Loro oggi?*
6. *Che cosa _____, tu?*
7. *Io _____ a mangiare in un ristorante.*
8. *La madre _____ soldi a suo figlio.*

Exercise 6-7

Read each expression aloud to practice your pronunciation.

Fanno colazione.   *Andiamo in macchina.*
Andiamo avanti!   *Facciamo un regalo a Marcello.*
Sto bene.   *Stai male.*

Interrogative Expressions

Interrogative words and expressions are used to ask questions. You will see that their function and placement are similar to their English counterparts.

Table 6-15

Italian	English	Italian	English
Chi?	Who? or Whom?	*Quando?*	When?
Che (cosa)?	What?	*Quale/i?*	Which?
Come?	How? What?	*Perché?*	Why?
Dove?	Where?	*Quanto/a/i/e?*	How much? How many?

Chi sei? — **Who are you?**

Che cosa fai? — **What are you doing?**

Come va? — **How's it going?**

Dove mangi stasera? — **Where are you going to eat this evening?**

Quando comincia il semestre? — **When does the semester begin?**

Quale macchina? — **Which car?**

Perché non vai al cinema? — **Why aren't you going to the movies?**

Quanto costa? — **How much does it cost?**

Exercise 6-8

Complete the following sentences with the appropriate interrogative word or expression.

1. _____ *stai?* (how)
2. _____ *vai stasera?* (where)
3. _____ *libri desideri comprare?* (how many)
4. _____ *fai così?* (why)
5. _____ *film desideri vedere questo fine settimana?* (which)

CHAPTER 7

Second- and Third-Conjugation (*–ere* and *–ire*) Verbs

First-conjugation verbs are the most common in Italian. This chapter will help you to expand your knowledge of verbs in the present indicative tense. Though there are many similarities among the conjugations of first-, second-, and third-conjugation verbs, it's important to be able to tell them apart.

–ere and *–ire* Verbs in the Present Indicative Tense

Second- and third-conjugation verbs are verbs whose infinitive forms end in *–ere* and *–ire*, respectively. You will notice from the conjugations below that *–ere* and *–ire* verbs differ from each other only in the *voi* forms.

Table 7-1

rispondere (to respond)		partire (to leave)	
io rispondo	noi rispondiamo	io parto	noi partiamo
tu rispondi	voi rispondete	tu parti	voi partite
lui risponde	loro rispondono	lui parte	loro partono
Lei risponde	Loro rispondono	Lei parte	Loro partono
lei risponde		lei parte	

There are more irregular second- and third-conjugation verbs than first-conjugation verbs. Irregular second- and third-conjugation verbs will be presented as such in Chapter 8.

Table 7-2

Regular *–ERE* verbs					
assistere	to attend	correre	to run	mettere	to put
chiedere	to ask	credere	to believe	perdere	to lose
chiudere	to close	decidere (di)	to decide (to do something)	ripetere	to repeat
conoscere	to know	discutere (di)	to discuss (something)	rispondere	to answer
leggere	to read	ricevere	to receive	scrivere	to write
prendere	to take	vivere	to live	vedere	to see
vendere	to sell	spendere	to spend		

Repeat the conjugations of the second conjugation verb *prendere*.

TRACK 47

Table 7-3

Verb Conjugation

io prendo	Mia moglie ed io prendiamo
tu prendi	Tu e Pietro prendete
Marco prende	i tuoi fratelli prendono

ESSENTIAL

While the infinitive forms of both first- and third-conjugation Italian verbs always have the accent on the second-to-last syllable (*domandare* = doh-mahn-DAH-ray; *dormire* = door-MEE-ray), second conjugation verbs are often pronounced with the accent on the third-to-last syllable, as in *comprendere* (kohm-PREHN-deh-ray, "to comprehend") or *aggiungere* (ah-JOON-jeh-ray, "to add").

Exercise 7-1: Working with –ere Verbs

Complete each sentence with the present indicative tense conjugation of the *–ere* verb in parentheses.

1. *Tu e Elena* _____ *alle miei lettere. (rispondere)*
2. *Giovanni e Mario* _____ *di sport nel bar. (discutere)*
3. *Io* _____ *la mia macchina. (prendere)*
4. *Mia sorella* _____ *sempre le chiavi di casa. (perdere)*
5. *Lui* _____ *la porta perché tira vento. (chiudere)*

Table 7-4

Useful *–IRE* verbs			
aprire	to open	*partire (da)*	to leave (from)
dormire	to sleep	*seguire*	to follow
offrire	to offer	*servire*	to serve
sentire	to hear		

TRACK 48

Repeat the conjugations of the third-conjugation verb *dormire*.

Table 7-5

Verb Conjugation

io dormo	*Mia moglie ed io dormiamo*
tu dormi	*Tu e Pietro dormite*
Marco dorme	*i tuoi fratelli dormono*

–gnere, *–cere*, and *–gliere* Verbs

Many second-conjugation verbs have irregular conjugations and interesting phonetic rules to be aware of. There are many second-conjugation verbs that do not follow a pattern of conjugation. Here are some that do follow a pattern. Pronunciation can be tricky!

Table 7-6
Verbs Ending in –gnere, *spegnere* (to turn off, to put out)

io spengo	noi spegniamo
tu spegni	voi spegnete
lui spegne	loro spengono

As you can see, *spegnere* has two irregular forms: in the *io* and *loro/Loro* forms, where the soft *gn* switches to the hard *ng*. Repeat the conjugations of the verb *spegnere* to practice your pronunciation.

Verbs Ending in *–cere*

Another verb group that undergoes a spelling change includes verbs that end in *–cere*, like *dispiacere* (to displease).

Table 7-7
***dispiacere* (to displease)**

io dispiaccio	noi dispiacciamo
tu dispiaci	voi dispiacete
lui dispiace	loro dispiacciono

Repeat the conjugations of the verb *dispiacere* to practice your pronunciation. The following are more verbs that belong to this category.

compiacere (to gratify, to please)
giacere (to lie down)
nuocere (to harm, to injure)
piacere (to please)
tacere (to be quiet)

Verbs Ending in *–gliere*

Verbs in this category are very similar to verbs that end in *–gnere*. That is, they undergo a spelling change in the *io* and *loro/Loro* forms, where two consonants switch places—in this case, from *gl* to *lg*. For example, take a look at the conjugation of *togliere* (to remove).

TRACK 51

Table 7-8
Conjugating *TOGLIERE* (to remove)

io tolgo	lei toglie	voi togliete
tu togli	noi togliamo	loro tolgono

Repeat the conjugations of the verb *togliere* to practice your pronunciation.

The following are more verbs conjugated like *togliere*.
accogliere (to give hospitality to, to welcome)
cogliere (to pick)
raccogliere (to harvest, to gather)
sciogliere (to undo, to untie, to loosen)

–ire/–isc Verbs

There are a good number of third-conjugation verbs that add an *–isc* between the stem and ending in all forms except the *noi* and *voi* forms. There is no foolproof method to distinguish the *–isc* verbs from the regular *–ire* verbs. To memorize them is to learn them!

Table 7-9
capire (to understand)

io capisco	noi capiamo
tu capisci	voi capite
lui capisce	loro capiscono
lei capisce	Loro capiscono
Lei capisce	

The following examples are other verbs that follow this pattern of conjugation.

costruire	to build	*riferire*	to report, to relate
finire	to finish	*spedire*	to send
preferire	to prefer	*suggerire*	to suggest, to recommend
pulire	to clean	*ubbidire*	to obey
restituire	to give back		

Exercise 7-2

Read each of the following sentences below aloud.

Giovanni spedisce il pacco.
Tu restituisci il libro a Giovanni.
Davide e Marco suggeriscono un buon film.

Modal Verbs: *Dovere*, *Potere*, and *Volere*

Modal verbs are verbs that are used to express possibility, ability, need, or intention. The modal verbs *dovere* (must, to have to), *potere* (can, to be able to), and *volere* (to want to, to want) are irregular in the present indicative tense. They are most often followed by an infinitive. In limited instances, *dovere* and *volere* may be followed by a noun. When followed by a noun, *dovere* means "to owe." When followed by a noun, *volere* means "to want," as in *Voglio un caffè* (I want a coffee).

Table 7-10
***VOLERE* (to want to)**

Singular	*Plural*
io voglio	noi vogliamo
tu vuoi	voi volete
lui vuole	loro vogliono
lei vuole	Loro vogliono
Lei vuole	

Table 7-11
POTERE (can, to be able to)

Singular	Plural
io posso	noi possiamo
tu puoi	voi potete
lui può	loro possono
lei può	Loro possono
Lei può	

Table 7-12
DOVERE (must, to have to)

Singular	Plural
io devo	noi dobbiamo
tu devi	voi dovete
lui deve	loro devono
lei deve	Loro devono
Lei deve	

Io voglio andare in vacanza in Messico.	**I want to go on vacation in Mexico.**
Non posso andare in vacanza in Messico perché devo lavorare tutta l'estate.	**I can't go on vacation in Mexico because I have to work all summer.**
Io non posso andare a teatro stasera perché devo studiare.	**I can't go to the theater tonight because I have to study.**
Io devo cinque dollari a Stefano.	**I owe Stefano five dollars.**
Io voglio un caffè.	**I want a coffee.**
Io voglio bere un caffè.	**I want to drink a coffee.**

Exercise 7-3

Say each of the following sentences aloud to practice your pronunciation.

Tu vuoi comprare una nuova macchina.	**You want to buy a new car.**
Davide e Maria vogliono fare un viaggio in Inghilterra	**Davide and Maria want to take a trip to England.**

I miei amici vogliono andare al cinema.	**My friends want to go to the movies.**
Lui vuole ascoltare la musica.	**He wants to listen to music.**
Io e Elena vogliamo visitare Venezia.	**Elena and I want to visit Venice.**

Exercise 7-4

The following people want to do certain things. State that they are unable to do these things and state a reason why, using the verbs *potere* and *dovere*, as in the example. *Marco vuole fare una passeggiata. Non può fare una passeggiata perché deve studiare.* **Marco wants to take a walk. He can't take a walk because he has to study.**

1. *Tu vuoi comprare una nuova Mercedes.*

   _____.

2. *Davide e Maria vogliono fare un viaggio in Inghilterra.*

   _____.

3. *I miei amici vogliono andare al cinema.*

   _____.

4. *Lui vuole ascoltare la musica.*

   _____.

5. *Io e Elena vogliamo visitare Venezia.*

   _____.

Time Expressions

The following vocabulary will help you express events that happen rarely, often, now, later, or at some point in the past.

Table 7-13

puntuale	punctual	*a volte*	sometimes
in anticipo	early	*qualche volta*	sometimes
in ritardo	late	*di quando in quando*	every now and then

ogni volta	each (every) time	*di rado*	rarely
una volta . . .	once . . .	*ogni giorno/settimana/ mese/anno*	every day/week/ month/year
. . . al giorno	. . . a day	*di solito*	usually
. . . alla settimana	. . . a week	*di tanto in tanto*	every now and then
. . . al mese	. . . a month	*tutti i giorni*	every day
. . . all'anno	. . . a year	*tutte le sere*	every evening
due volte . . .	twice . . .	*ogni tanto*	every now and then

Exercise 7-5

Read each sentence aloud to practice your pronunciation.

1. *Gli aeroplani partono tardi dall'aeroporto di Boston.* **The airplanes leave late from the airport in Boston.**
2. *Telefono a mia madre una volta alla settimana.* **I call my mother once a week.**
3. *Ogni tanto leggo un libro.* **I read a book every now and then.**
4. *Guardo la televisione tutte le sere.* **I watch television every night.**
5. *Ogni anno vado in vacanza in Europa.* **I go on vacation in Europe every year.**

Adverbs

An adverb is a part of speech that can modify a verb, an adjective, another adverb, a phrase, or a clause. It indicates manner, time, place, cause, or degree and can answer questions such as how, when, where, and how much. In English, it is common for adverbs to end in –ly, such as quickly, easily, and particularly. In Italian, the suffix *–mente* corresponds to the English –ly suffix. To form an adverb, the *–mente* suffix is added to the feminine singular form of the adjective.

Table 7-14

Adjective	Feminine Singular Form	Adverb
libero	*libera*	*liberamente*
tranquillo	*tranquilla*	*tranquillamente*

Adjective	Feminine Singular Form	Adverb
attento	*attenta*	*attentamente*
rapido	*rapida*	*rapidamente*

Adjectives whose singular forms end in –*e* add the suffix –*mente* without changing the final vowel.

Table 7-15

Adjective	Adverb
intelligente	*intelligentemente*
triste	*tristemente*

Adjectives whose singular forms end in –*le* or –*re* drop the final –*e* before adding the suffix –*mente*.

Table 7-16

Adjective	Adverb
probabile	*probabilmente*
particolare	*paricolarmente*

FACT

Be careful! *Molto*, *tanto*, *troppo*, and *poco* can be used as both adjectives (*Io ho molti amici* = I have many friends) and adverbs (*I suoi amici sono molto simpatici* = His friends are very nice). As adjectives, they agree in number and gender with the noun they modify; as adverbs they do not.

Exercise 7-6

Rewrite the following adjectives as adverbs.

1. *facile* _____
2. *raro* _____
3. *disperato* _____
4. *recente* _____
5. *difficile* _____

Exercise 7-7

TRACK 52

Listen to each sentence. Underline the adverb in each sentence.

1. *Andrea Bocelli canta molto bene.*
2. *Noi ascoltiamo attentamente.*
3. *Mio fratello parla poco.*
4. *Giovanni cerca disperatamente le chiavi della macchina.*

Not all adverbs are formed by adding the suffix –*mente*. The following is a list of common adverbs that don't follow a spelling change pattern. The only way to learn the exceptions is to memorize them.

Table 7-17

Italian	English	Italian	English
ancora	still	*(non) . . . mai*	never
attorno	around, about	*(non) . . . più*	no longer, not anymore
bene	well	*oltre*	beyond
contro	against	*presto*	soon, before long
dentro	in, inside	*sempre*	always
dietro	behind, at the back of	*sopra*	above, on top
dopo	then, afterwards	*sotto*	underneath, below
fuori	outside	*vicino*	nearby, close by
già	already	*insieme*	together
inoltre	moreover	*male*	badly

See Chapter 12 for more information about negative adverbs.

Adverbs always precede the adjective or adverb they modify, and they generally follow a simple verb form. For example: *Ceniamo sempre alle otto.* (We always have dinner at 8:00.) In sentences with compound tenses, most adverbs are placed after the participle. For example: *Sono arrivato tardi al museo.* (I arrived late at the museum.) However, certain common adverbs such as *già, ancora, sempre, (non) . . . mai,* and *(non) . . . più* are inserted between the auxiliary verb and the past participle of the compound form, as in the examples on the following page.

Maria è sempre venuta in orario.	**Maria always came on time.**
Non ho ancora finito i miei compiti.	**I still haven't finished my homework.**

Useful Expressions and Constructions: To Return

There are several different ways to state the verb *tornare* (to return). There is a distinction between to return to a place and to return an object to its owner.

Table 7-18

to return	*tornare*	
to go back/to come back to a place	*ritornare*	
to turn back	*tornare indietro*	
to give back	*restituire, rendere*	

Torno in Italia l'anno prossimo.	**I am returning to Italy next year.**
Torniamo indietro perché non abbiamo più soldi.	**We're turning back because we don't have any more money.**
Restituiscono il libro alla biblioteca.	**They are returning the book to the library.**

CHAPTER 8

Irregular *-ere* and *-ire* Verbs

We have seen a handful of irregular verbs already. In this chapter we will expand our knowledge of verbs by taking a look at more irregular conjugations. You will see that some of the irregular verbs here follow a pattern and can be categorized, while others can't. The best way to learn them is to study and practice them!

Irregular *–ere* verbs

Presented here are some commonly used irregular *–ere* (second-conjugation) verbs. They do not follow a pattern of conjugation in the present tense. To memorize them is to learn them!

Table 8-1

beve	to drink
compiere	to finish, to complete
promuovere	to promote
rimanere	to remain, to stay
sedere	to sit
tenere	to keep, to remain, to stay
valere	to be worth

Table 8-2

Present Indicative Tense Conjugation of *Bere* (to drink)

Singular	*Plural*
io bevo	noi beviamo
tu bevi	voi bevete
lui beve	loro bevono
lei beve	Loro bevono
Lei beve	

Present Indicative Tense Conjugation of *Compiere* (to finish, to complete)

Singular	*Plural*
io compio	noi compiamo
tu compi	voi compiete
lui compie	loro compiono
lei compie	Loro compiono
Lei compie	

Present Indicative Tense Conjugation of *Promuovere* (to promote)

Singular	*Plural*
io promuovo	noi promoviamo/promuoviamo
tu promuovi	voi promovete/promuovete
lui promuove	loro promovono
lei promuove	Loro promovono
Lei promuove	

Present Indicative Tense Conjugation of *Rimanere* (to stay, to remain)

Singular	*Plural*
io rimango	noi rimaniamo
tu rimani	voi rimanete
lui rimane	loro rimangono
lei rimane	Loro rimangono
Lei rimane	

Present Indicative Tense Conjugation of *Sedere* (to sit)

Singular	*Plural*
io siedo/seggo	noi sediamo
tu siedi	voi sedete
lui siede	loro siedono/seggono
lei siede	Loro siedono/seggono
Lei siede	

Present Indicative Tense Conjugation of *Tenere* (to keep)

Singular	*Plural*
io tengo	noi teniamo
tu tieni	voi tenete
lui tiene	loro tengono
lei tiene	Loro tengono
Lei tiene	

Table 8-3

The following verbs are all conjugated like the verb *tenere*.

Italian	English
appartenere	to belong
mantenere	to keep, to maintain
ottenere	to obtain, to get
ritenere	to hold, to detain
sostenere	to support, to uphold, to sustain

Exercise 8-1

Conjugate the irregular *-ere* verb *valere* in the present indicative tense. *Valere* is used in a very common idiomatic expression: *Vale la pena.* (It is worthwhile). It is a useful expression—you're sure to hear it often!

Valere (to be worth)

io_____	noi _____
tu _____	voi _____
lui_____	loro _____
lei _____	Loro _____
Lei_____	

Exercise 8-2

Underline the sentence with correct spelling of the verb conjugation.

1. *Marco non tiene l'anello.*   *Marco non tene l'anello.*
2. *Tutti i miei amici si sedono al banco.*   *Tutti i miei amici si siedono al banco.*
3. *Davide e Maria andano al mare.*   *Davide e Maria vanno al mare.*
4. *Tu, come stai?*   *Tu, come sti?*
5. *Mi da dei consigli?*   *Mi dà dei consigli?*

Exercise 8-3

Read each conjugation of the verb *tenere* aloud.

Tenere (to keep)

io tengo	noi teniamo
tu tieni	voi tenete
Elena tiene	tutti i ragazzi tengono

Exercise 8-4

Conjugate the verb *sostenere* in the spaces provided.

1. *io* _____
2. *tu* _____
3. *Elena* _____
4. *noi* _____
5. *voi* _____
6. *tutti i ragazzi* _____

To Know: *Sapere* and *Conoscere*

Both *sapere* and *conoscere* correspond to the verb "to know" in English. The verb *sapere* means to know a fact or to know how to do something. *Sapere* is an irregular verb in the present indicative tense.

Table 8-4
Present Indicative Tense Conjugation of *Sapere*

Singular

io so	tu sai	lui sa	lei sa	Lei sa

Plural

noi sappiamo	voi sapete	loro sanno	Loro sanno	

Io so che Giovanni è intelligente.	**I know Giovanni is intelligent.**
Loro sanno che il museo chiude alle nove.	**They know the museum closes at nine o'clock.**
Voi non sapete sciare? È facilissimo!	**You don't know how to ski? It's easy!**

Conoscere is a regular second conjugation verb. It means to know or to be familiar with a person, a place, or a thing. It can also mean to meet someone for the first time.

Table 8-5
Present Indicative Tense Conjugation of *Conoscere*

Singular

io conosco	tu conosci	lui conosce	lei conosce	Lei conosce

Plural

noi conosciamo	voi conoscete	loro conoscono	Loro conoscono	

Exercise 8-5

Write the correct form of *sapere* or *conoscere* according to the context .

1. *Giovanni non _____ che io vengo alla festa.*
2. *Matteo ed Elena _____ bene la città di Boston.*
3. *Massimo vuole _____ la mia amica.*

4. *Io _____ sciare ma non _____ giocare a tennis.*
5. *Tutti gli studenti _____ parlare inglese.*

Irregular *–ire* Verbs

We've already seen some irregular *–ire* verbs, those that have an *–isc* ending. The following verbs don't follow a pattern of conjugation.

Dire, Uscire, and *Venire*

Dire, uscire, and *venire* are three commonly used third conjugation verbs that are irregular in the present indicative tense.

Table 8-6
Present Indicative Tense Conjugation of *Dire* (to say)

Singular	Plural
io dico	noi diciamo
tu dici	voi dite
lui dice	loro dicono
lei dice	Loro dicono
Lei dice	

The list on the following page are verbs that are conjugated like *dire*.

Table 8-7

Italian	English	Italian	English
benedire	to bless	indire	to announce publicly, to declare
contraddire	to contradict	interdire	to prohibit
disdire	to retract, to cancel	maledire	to curse

Table 8-8
Present Indicative Tense Conjugation of *Uscire* (to go out)

Singular	Plural
io esco	noi usciamo
tu esci	voi uscite
lui esce	loro escono
lei esce	Loro escono
Lei esce	

The verb *riuscire* (to succeed) is conjugated like the verb *uscire.*

Table 8-9

Present Indicative Tense Conjugation of *Venire* (to come)

Singular	Plural
io vengo	noi veniamo
tu vieni	voi venite
lui viene	loro vengono
lei viene	Loro vengono
Lei viene	

The verbs *svenire* (to faint) and *convenire* (to suit, to be necessary) are conjugated like the verb *venire.*

Exercise 8-6

Rewrite each sentence with the new subject provided.

1. *Elena e Caterina escono stasera.* **Io e Marco** _____.
2. *Tu e Mario venite alla festa.* **Gabriella** _____.
3. *Io dico la verità.* **I ragazzi** _____.
4. *Io e gli altri ragazzi usciamo insieme.* **Loro** _____.
5. *Il signor Giacomo non viene con noi.* **Tu** _____.

More Irregular −*ire* Verbs

Study the following common −*ire* verbs to get a better grasp on conjugating them.

Table 8-10

Present Indicative Tense Conjugation of *Salire* (to ascend, to climb)

Singular	Plural
io salgo	noi saliamo
tu sali	voi salite
lui sale	loro salgono
lei sale	Loro salgono
Lei sale	

Present Indicative Tense Conjugation of *Morire* (to die)

Singular	*Plural*
io muoio	noi moriamo
tu muori	voi morite
lui muore	loro muoiono
lei muore	Loro muoiono
Lei muore	

Present Indicative Tense Conjugation of *Comparire* (to appear)

Singular	*Plural*
io compaio/comparisco	noi compariamo
tu compari/comparisci	voi comparite
lui comparisce/compare	loro compariscono/compaiono
lei comparisce/compare	Loro compariscono/compaiono
Lei comparisce/compare	

Present Indicative Tense Conjugation of *Riempire* (to fill)

Singular	*Plural*
io riempio	noi riempiamo
tu riempi	voi riempite
lui riempie	loro riempiono
lei riempie	Loro riempiono
Lei riempie	

Present Indicative Tense Conjugation of *Udire* (to hear)

Singular	*Plural*
io odo	noi udiamo
tu odi	voi udite
lui ode	loro odono
lei ode	Loro odono
Lei ode	

Exercise 8-7

TRACK 53

Repeat each sentence after the narrator reads it to practice your pronunciation. Rewrite each sentence with the new subject provided.

1. *Io e Elena udiamo il grido.*
New subject: *Tu e Marco*_____.
2. *Caterina riempie il vaso di acqua.*
New subject: *I ragazzi* _____.
3. *Lorenzo muore dalla voglia di sapere la verità.*
New subject: *Io* _____.
4. *I bambini salgono le scale.*
New subject: *Noi due* _____.

Verbs Ending in –arre, –orre, and –urre

Verbs ending in *–arre* (*trarre*), *–orre* (*porre*), and *–urre* (*tradurre*) derive from their Latin cousins (*trahere, ponere, traducere*).

Table 8-11

Italian Verb	Latin Verb	English Meaning
trarre	trahere	to draw, to pull
porre	ponere	to put, to place
tradurre	traducere	to translate

Table 8-12
Present Indicative Tense of *Trarre* (to pull, to draw out)

Singular	Plural
io traggo	noi traiamo
tu trai	voi traete
lui trae	loro traggono
lei trae	loro traggono
Lei trae	Loro traggono

Other verbs conjugated like *trarre* include *distrarre* (to distract), *contrarre* (to contract), and *sottrarre* (to subtract). There are also quite a few verbs that end in *–orre*, the most common of which is *porre* (to place, to set down).

Table 8-13
Present Indicative Tense Conjugation of *Porre* (to place, to set down)

Singular	*Plural*
io pongo	noi poniamo
tu poni	voi ponete
lui pone	loro pongono
lei pone	Loro pongono
Lei pone	

Some other verbs that are conjugated like *porre* include the following:

Table 8-14

Italian	English	Italian	English
comporre	to compose	opporre	to oppose
disporre	to arrange, to set out	posporre	to place or put after
esporre	to exhibit, to display	proporre	to propose, to put
imporre	to impose	riporre	to put back, to replace

Finally, you need to remember verbs that end in *–urre*, like *tradurre*.

Table 8-15
Present Indicative Tense Conjugation of *Tradurre* (to translate)

Singular	*Plural*
io traduco	noi traduciamo
tu traduci	voi traducete
lui traduce	loro traducono
Lei traduce	Loro traducono

Some other verbs that are conjugated like *tradurre* include the following:

Table 8-16

Italian	English	Italian	English
condurre	to take, to lead	produrre	to produce, to yield
indurre	to inspire, to infuse	ridurre	to reduce, to curtail
introdurre	to introduce, to show		

Useful Expressions and Constructions

There are a few different ways to state the verb "to succeed" and "to leave."

Table 8-17

Italian	English
succedere a	to succeed in order, to come next
riuscire a	to be successful, to succeed in doing something
riuscire	to be successful

Chi succede alla regina?	**Who will succeed the queen?**
Non riesco a capire.	**I can't understand.**
Mio fratello riesce in tutto.	**My brother succeeds in all that he does.**

Table 8-18

Italian	English	Italian	English
lasciare	to leave someone or something	*andare via*	to leave, to go away
partire	to leave, to depart	*uscire da*	to leave from, to go out of

Lascio le chiavi sulla scrivania.	**I am leaving my keys on the desk.**
Il treno parte alle nove.	**The train is leaving at nine o'clock.**
Vai via!	**Go away!**
Gli studenti escono dall'aula.	**The students are going out of the classroom.**

Exercise 8-8

Answer the questions in full sentences in Italian.

1. *Quale ristorante preferisci: il ristorante italiano o il ristorante cinese?*
   _____.

2. *Che cosa fai la sera quando finisci di lavorare?* _____
   _____.

3. *Tu capisci l'italiano?* _____.
4. *Puoi suggerire un film italiano?* _____.
5. *A che ora finisci di lavorare il venerdì pomeriggio?* _____
   _____.

CHAPTER 9

Prepositions

This chapter introduces prepositions, which are used to indicate the location, time, position, or direction of an object in relation to the verb. For example: "The gift is FOR John." For the most part, the usage of prepositions in Italian is pretty straightforward, and your knowledge of the proper use of prepositions in English should be helpful. There are some cases where prepositions are used in idiomatic expressions; in these cases, the best way to learn them is through practice.

Simple Prepositions

Prepositions are commonly known as linking words. They connect nouns, verbs, and other vital words.

Table 9-1
Common Italian Prepositions

a	at, in, to	in	at, in, into	da	by, from	su	on
con	with	per	for	di	about, from, of	tra/fra	between

Pepositions in Italian don't always have a single equivalent to their English counterparts.

Articulated Prepositions

The prepositions *a, da, di, in,* and *su* can be combined with a definite article to form one word. These are called contractions or articulated prepositions.

Vado a+il negozio. = Vado al negozio. **I am going to the store.**
Sono i libri di+gli studenti. = Sono i libri degli studenti. **They are the students' books.**

Table 9-2
Prepositional Articles

	IL	LO	L'(masc.)	LA	L'(fem.)	I	GLI	LE
A	al	allo	all'	alla	all'	ai	agli	alle
DI	del	dello	dell'	della	dell'	dei	degli	delle
DA	dal	dallo	dall'	dalla	dall'	dai	dagli	dalle
SU	sul	sullo	sull'	sulla	sull'	sui	sugli	sulle
IN	nel	nello	nell'	nella	nell'	nei	negli	nelle

The prepositions *con, per,* and *tra* do not form a contraction when they are followed by a definite article.

Mio padre parla con il mio amico. **My father is speaking with my friend.**
Il libro d'italiano è tra il dizionario e il calendario. **The Italian book is between the dictionary and the calendar.**

The Preposition *a*

The preposition *a* can mean to, at, or in, depending on its context. You will need the preposition *a* to express destination or location. It must also be used before an indirect object, after certain verbs, and in many idiomatic expressions.

Destination or Location

The preposition *a* is used to indicate a destination or a location.

Oggi andiamo all'università.	**We are going to the university today.**
Vado al mercato il lunedì.	**I go to the market every Monday.**
Abito a Boston.	**I live in Boston.**

ALERT

Be careful! The preposition *a* is used before the names of cities and towns. For example, *abito a Boston* means "I live in Boston." However, the preposition *in* is used with larger geographical areas, such as states, large islands, countries, and continents. *Vado in Italia l'anno prossimo* means "I am travelling to Italy next year."

Before an Indirect Object

As we know, an indirect object is a noun (or pronoun) that receives the action of the verb, usually by way of the prepositions "to" or "for," as in "I give the book **to John**" or "I read **to my son** every evening." Indirect objects are often introduced by the preposition *a* in Italian.

Mando un email a mio fratello.	**I am sending an e-mail to my brother.**
Devo dare questa lettera a Pietro.	**I have to give this letter to Peter.**
Telefono agli amici.	**They are phoning their friends.**

Verbs and the Preposition *a*

The preposition *a* is used after several verbs that are followed by a noun (verb + *a* + noun). In many cases the use of the preposition in Italian does not parallel its use in English.

Table 9-3

assistere a	to attend	Assisto alla conferenza.	I am attending the conference.
assomigliare a	to resemble	Davide assomiglia ad Eugenio.	David resembles Eugene.
credere a	to believe in	Non credo all'astrologia.	I don't believe in astrology.
giocare a	to play	Gioco a calcio con mio fratello.	I play soccer with my brother.
partecipare a	to participate in	Giovanni non partecipa al concorso.	Giovanni is not participating in the contest.
pensare a	to think about	I ragazzi non pensano al futuro.	The boys aren't thinking about their future.

The preposition *a* is also used after several verbs when they are followed by an infinitive (verb + *a* + infinitive form of verb).

Table 9-4

andare a	to go to	Vado a sciare.	I am going skiing.
aiutare a	to help to	Ti aiuto a fare i compiti.	I am helping you do your homework.
cominciare a	to start/to begin to	Comincio a capire l'italiano.	I am beginning to understand Italian.
continuare a	to continue	Stefano continua a mangiare.	Stefano keeps on (continues) eating.
imparare a	to learn to	I bambini imparano a scrivere.	The children are learning to write.
insegnare a	to teach to	Ti insegno a nuotare.	I am teaching you to swim.
provare a	to try to	Carmelo prova a suonare la chitarra.	Carmelo is trying to play the guitar.
riuscire a	to manage to	Caterina non riesce a risolvere il problema.	Caterina can't manage to resolve the problem.

Other Uses of the Preposition a

The preposition *a* is used in many idiomatic expressions. There's no real pattern to its usage in these expressions, so learning them will take practice.

Ho visto il programma **alla televisione**.   **I saw the show on television.**
Ho sentito la canzone **alla radio**.   **I heard the song on the radio.**

*Stasera andiamo **a teatro**.*	**We are going to the theater tonight.**
*Vuoi andare **al cinema** domani sera?*	**Do you want to go to the movies tomorrow night?**
*Si va **a piedi**?*	**Shall we go by foot?**
*Studiano **all'estero**.*	**They are studying abroad.**
*Marco non è **a casa**.*	**Marco isn't home.**
*I bambini non vanno **a scuola** la domenica.*	**The children don't go to school on Sundays.**
*I miei genitori vanno **a letto** presto.*	**My parents go to bed early.**

ESSENTIAL

As you probably already know, Italians are very passionate about their food. Food is to be savored in Italy, and dinner is an important and integral social activity. The expression *A tavola!* is commonly used to call people "to the table." In American English, we use the expression "Dinner's ready!"

Exercise 9-1

The following are some examples of the use of the preposition *a*. Read each sentence aloud to practice your pronunciation.

Davide assomiglia ad Eugenio.	Davide resembles Eugenio.
Non credo all'astrologia.	I don't believe in astrology.
Ti aiuto a fare i compiti.	I will help you to do your homework.
I bambini imparano a scrivere.	The children are learning to write.
Ho visto il programma alla televisione.	I saw the program on television.
Vuoi andare al cinema domani sera?	Do you want to go to the movies tomorrow night?
Si va a piedi?	Can we walk?
Marco non è a casa.	Marco isn't home.
Tutti a tavola!	Everyone to the table!

Exercise 9-2

Fill in the blank with the correct preposition.

1. *Marcello abita _____ Roma.*
2. *Il fratello _____ Massimo si chiama Adriano.*
3. *Gli studenti studiano _____ biblioteca.*
4. *Telefono _____ mia madre ogni domenica.*
5. *Non mi piace la pizza _____ acciughe.*

The Preposition *da*

The Italian preposition *da* is most commonly used to indicate origin or source, in which case it corresponds to the preposition "from" in English.

Parto da Boston.	**I am leaving from Boston.**
È un regalo dai miei genitori.	**It is a gift from my parents.**
Pietro viene dalla Sicilia.	**Pietro comes from Sicily.**

However, *da* is also used in time expressions, in which case you may translate it as "since" or "for." Italian uses the construction of present tense + *da* + time expression to indicate an action that began in the past and is still going on in the present.

Da quanto tempo leggi questa rivista?	**How long have you been reading this magazine?**
Leggo questa rivista da molto tempo.	**I've been reading this magazine for a long time.**

Da is also used to express the equivalent of the English phrase "at the (house, office, place) of . . . "

Mangio da Massimo.	**I'm eating at Massimo's house.**
Andiamo dai signori Rossi.	**We're going to the Rossi's house.**
Vado dal dentista.	**I am going to the dentist's (office).**
Porto la macchina dal meccanico.	**I am bringing the car to the mechanic's (garage).**

The preposition *da* can indicate for what or for whom something is intended:

un campo da calcio	**a soccer field**
un campo da golf	**golf course**
scarpe da ginnastica	**gym shoes, sneakers**
bicicletta da uomo	**man's bicycle**

It is also used in the following idiomatic constructions:

Non c'è niente da fare.	**There is nothing to do.**
Cosa c'è da mangiare?	**What is there to eat?**
È una cosa da poco.	**It's nothing, it's of no importance.**
una persona da poco	**a worthless person**

ALERT

In English we have the luxury of adding an apostrophe and the letter *s* to the end of a noun when we want to show possession. This does not work in Italian. In Italian we must use the preposition *di. Il libro di Giovanni* means Giovanni's book (literally, "the book of Giovanni").

Exercise 9-3

Read each sentence aloud to practice your pronunciation.

Parto da Boston.	I am leaving from Boston.
È un regalo dai miei genitori.	It's a gift from my parents.
Da quanto tempo leggi questa rivista?	How long have you been reading this magazine?
Leggo questa rivista da molto tempo.	I've been reading this magazine for a while.
Vado dal dentista.	I'm going to the dentist's.
Porto la macchina dal meccanico.	I am bringing the car to the mechanic's.
Cosa c'è da mangiare?	What's there to eat?
È una cosa da poco.	It's no big deal.

The Preposition *di*

The preposition *di* means "of" or "from" and is used in the following situations:

- to show possession
- to show what something is made of
- after certain verbs (verb + *di* + infinitive form of verb)

- to indicate origin
- to make comparisons

Possession

The following examples using the preposition *di* show possession:

Di chi sono questi libri?	**Whose books are these?**
Sono i libri del professore d'italiano.	**They are the Italian professor's books.**

What's It Made Of?

The preposition *di* can be used to describe what something is made of.

Compro una giacca di cuoio.	**I am buying a leather jacket.**
Elena ha orecchini d'oro.	**Ellen has gold earrings.**

ESSENTIAL

When you meet someone for the first time, it's considered more polite to use the formal form of speaking. The expression *Di dove sei?* is appropriate in informal situations, but use the formal form *Di dov'è Lei?* when you meet someone for the first time or in situations that require more formality.

Origin

Di is used with the verb *essere* to indicate origin.

Di dove sei?	**Where are you from?**
Io sono di Providence, ma abito a Boston.	**I am from Providence but I live in Boston.**

Comparisons

Di is used in expressions making comparisons.

Matteo è più piccolo di Marco.	**Matteo is smaller than Marco.**
Mio fratello suona la chitarra meglio di me.	**My brother plays the guitar better than me.**

The preposition *di* is also used after certain verbs when they are followed by an infinitive (verb + *di* + infinitive of verb).

Table 9-5
Verb + *di* + infinitive

Italian	English	Italian	English
accettare di	to accept	*finire di*	to finish
accorgersi di	to realize	*immaginare di*	to imagine
ammettere di	to admit	*lamentarsi di*	to complain about
avere bisogno di	to need to	*offrire di*	to offer
avere paura di	to be afraid of	*pensare di*	to think of
cercare di	to try to	*permettere di*	to allow
chiedere di	to ask to	*proibire di*	to forbid
consigliare di	to advise to	*rendersi conto di*	to realize, to become aware
decidere di	to decide to	*ricordarsi di*	to remember
essere in grado di	to be in a position to	*smettere di*	to stop
fingere di	to pretend to	*sperare di*	to hope to
tentare di	to attempt to	*trattare di*	to be about; deal with
vietare di	to forbid		

Repeat each sentence after the narrator to practice your pronunciation.

TRACK 54

Il bambino smette di piangere.	**The little boy stops crying.**
Pensate di andare al cinema venerdì sera?	**Are you thinking of going to the movies on Friday evening?**
Ti proibisco di prendere la macchina!	**I prohibit you from taking the car!**
Ho bisogno di parlare con te.	**I need to speak with you.**

FACT

What's that *si* doing in some of the infinitives listed in Table 9-5? No, it's not a typo. Those are reflexive verbs. A reflexive verb's subject and object are identical. For example, the subject and object are the same in the phrase "enjoy yourself." Reflexive verbs are covered in Chapter 10.

Other Uses

The preposition *di* is also used after some adjectives to link them to the infinitive form of a verb.

Non sono capace di capire il tuo discorso.

I am not capable of understanding your point.

Table 9-6

Italian Adjective	English Equivalent
contento di	happy to
desideroso di	eager to
felice di	happy to
incapace di	incapable of
sicuro di	sure of
soddisfatto di	satisfied to
spiacente di	sorry to
stanco di	tired of
triste di	sad to

The preposition *di* is used in certain phrases that refer to time.

Table 9-7

Time References

Italian	English	Italian	English
di sera	in the evening	*di solito*	usually
di mattina	in the morning	*di nuovo*	again
di notte	at night	*di rado*	rarely
d'inverno	in the winter		

The Partitive—Some or Any

L'articolo partitivo (partitive article) is used to indicate approximate quantities. It is used before singular nouns (*del miele, del caffè, del burro*) as well as before plural nouns of an unspecified amount (*dei libri, delle ragazze, degli studenti*). The partitive is expressed by the preposition *di* (of, from) combined with the definite article.

Ho degli amici.	**I have some friends.**
Prendiamo del vino rosso.	**We're having some red wine.**

Table 9-8

The Partitive Articles

	Singular	Plural	
Feminine	*della*	*delle*	
Feminine (before a vowel)	*dell'*	*delle*	
Masculine	*del*	*dei*	
Masculine (before a vowel)	*dell'*	*degli*	
Masculine (before the letters *z, x* +consonant, and *gn*)	*dello*	*degli*	

The partitive is not used with negative sentences. It is not correct to say *Non ho degli amici.* One would simply say *Non ho amici.*

FACT

With the seasons—*primavera* (spring), *estate* (summer), *autunno* (fall), and *inverno* (winter)—the Italian prepositions *in* and *di* are interchangeable: *d'estate/in estate* (in the summer), *di primavera/in primavera* (in the spring) are equally acceptable.

The Preposition *in*

The Italian preposition *in* can mean "in," "to," or "by." It is used to express a location or a destination, to describe means of transportation, and to express a date. The preposition *in* is used to express location or destination with countries, continents, regions, large islands, and addresses.

Vado in Italia.	**I am going to Italy.**
Vado nella Sicilia.	**I am going to Sicily.**
Roma è in Italia.	**Rome is in Italy.**
Mario abita in via Veneto, a Milano.	**Mario lives on Veneto Street in Milan.**

The preposition *in* is used to describe a means of transportation.

Table 9-9

Italian	English	Italian	English
in macchina	by car	*in barca*	by boat
in aereo	by plane	*in treno*	by train
in moto	by scooter	*in autobus*	by bus
in bicicletta	by bicycle	*in pullman*	by coach

The preposition *in* is used with common expressions that refer to rooms or places.

ESSENTIAL

With nouns that refer to rooms of the house, such as *salotto*, *cucina*, and *sala da pranzo*, an article is usually not used with the preposition *in*. For example: *Mangiano in sala da pranzo, non in cucina.* (They eat in the dining room, not in the kitchen.)

Table 9-10

Italian	English	Italian	English
in biblioteca	in the library	*in città*	in the city
in camera	in the bedroom	*in giardino*	in the garden
in campagna	in the countryside	*in montagna*	in the mountains
in centro	downtown, in the center of town	*in paese*	in town
in chiesa	in the church	*in salotto*	in the living room

The preposition *nel (in+il)* is used to express the year.

Matteo è nato nel 2007.	**Matteo was born in 2007.**
Elena è nata nel 1975.	**Elena was born in 1975.**

The Prepositions *per*, *su*, *con*, *tra*, and *fra*

The prepositions *per*, *su*, *con*, *tra*, and *fra* are a little more straightforward than their cousins *a*, *da*, *di*, and *in*.

The Preposition *per*

The preposition *per* means "for" or "through" in English. It is used to indicate movement through a place or space.

Sono passati per Boston.	**They passed through Boston.**

It is also used to express duration of time in the past.

Ho studiato per un'ora.	**I studied for an hour.**
Abbiamo guardato la televisione per dieci minuti.	**We watched television for ten minutes.**

The preposition *per* is also used to designate the recipient of an object.

Il regalo è per mio fratello.	**The gift is for my brother.**

The Preposition *su*

Another useful preposition to know is *su,* which means "on." The use of this preposition is very similar to its use in English. It is used in Italian to indicate location or a topic of discussion. *Su* is also used after a few verbs.

La penna è sulla scrivania.	**The pen is on the desk.**
È una conferenze su Dante.	**It is a conference on Dante.**

Table 9-11

Italian	English	Italian	English
contare su	to count on	*reflettere su*	to reflect on, to ponder
giurare su	to swear on	*scommettere su*	to bet on

The Preposition *con*

The Italian preposition *con* is very similar to the English word "with."

Eugenio parla con un accento italiano.	**Eugenio speaks with an Italian accent.**
Filippo è partito con la sua famiglia.	**Filippo left with his family.**
Marcello è con Luciano.	**Marcello is with Luciano.**

The Prepositions *tra* and *fra*

Finally, there are the prepositions *tra* and *fra*. They both mean "between" and can be used interchangeably in all cases. They can also be used to mean "within" when indicating a time in the future.

Il quaderno e tra i due libri.	**The notebook is between the two books.**
Arriveremo fra dieci minuti.	**We will arrive (with)in ten minutes.**

Exercise 9-4

Underline the prepositions in the following sentences.

Ho dato delle rose a mia moglia.	**I gave some roses to my wife.**
Partiamo da Boston.	**We are leaving from Boston.**
Pensano di fare un viaggio.	**They are thinking about taking a trip.**
Studio in biblioteca.	**I am studying in the library.**
Lascio un messaggio per mia moglie.	**I am leaving a message for my wife.**

Tutto/a/i/e, Ogni, Alcuni, and *Alcune*

When the adjective *tutto/a* is used in the singular, it means "the whole;" when it is used in the plural (*tutti/e*), it means "all" or "every." The adjective *tutto/a/i/e* is always followed by the definite article.

Io studio tutto il giorno.	**I study the whole day.**
Tutti gli studenti studiano molto.	**All of the students study a lot.**
Io mangio tutta la pizza.	**I eat the whole pizza.**
Tutte le professoresse insegnano tutti i giorni.	**All of the professors teach every day.**

Exercise 9-5

Read each sentence aloud to practice your pronunciation.

1. *Io studio tutta la sera.*	**I study all night.**
2. *Tutti i vini italiani sono buoni.*	**All Italian wines are good.**
3. *Ho letto tutti i racconti di Alberto Moravia.*	**I've read all of Alberto Moravia's short stories.**
4. *Mio fratello ha pulito tutta la casa.*	**My brother cleaned the entire house.**

Ogni

Ogni is an invariable adjective that means "each" or "every." It is always followed by a singular noun.

Ogni studente studia molto.	**Each student studies a lot.**

You will see that this construction carries the same meaning as the following:

Tutti gli studenti studiano molto.	**All the students study a lot.**

Alcuni and *Alcune*

Alcuni and *alcune* mean "some." They are both used before plural nouns. *Alcune* is used before a feminine plural noun; *alcuni* is used before a masculine plural noun.

Alcuni bambini giocano nel parco.	**Some children are playing in the park.**

Qualche

Qualche is also used to mean "some." It is invariable, and it is always followed by a singular noun in Italian even though its meaning is plural.

Stasera vedo qualche amico.	**I am seeing some friends tonight.**
Ho passato qualche ora nell'aeroporto.	**I spent a few hours in the airport.**

Un po' di

Un po' di means "a little," "a bit of," or "some." It is invariable, and it is used before measurable nouns in the singular.

Beviamo un po' di vino.	**We are drinking a little wine.**
Metto un po' di zucchero nel caffè.	**I put a bit of sugar in my coffee.**

Refined Uses of the Definite Article

In Italian, the definite article generally corresponds to its use in English. In other words, when you need one in English, you probably need one in the Italian equivalent.

Il libro è sullo scaffale.	**The book is on the shelf.**

There are, however, some noteworthy differences.

Before Geographical Names

The definite article is used before geographical names such as countries, cities, continents, rivers, islands, regions, mountains, and lakes.

La francia è bella.	**France is beautiful.**

The definite article is not used after *in* if the geographical term is feminine, singular, and unmodified.

La Lombardia è in Italia.	**Lombardy is in Italy.**
(feminine, singular, unmodified)	
La Lombardia è nell'Italia settentrionale.	**Lombardy is in northern Italy.**
(feminine, singular, modified)	

The definite article is used before a proper name preceded by a professional or respectful title when speaking about the person.

La signora Romeo è di Roma.	**Mrs. Romeo is from Rome.**

When talking directly to the person, the article is omitted.

Signora Romeo, è di Roma Lei?	**Mrs. Romeo, are you from Rome?**

Colloquially, it is often used before names of women.

Hai visto la Laura ieri sera?	**Did you see Laura last night?**

The definite article is used before the names of languages.

Studio l'italiano e il francese, ma non studio l'inglese.	**I study Italian and French, but I do not study English.**

The definite article is used before abstract or concrete nouns that are used to express a general sense.

Mi piacciono i vini italiani.	**I like Italian wines.**
Lo zucchero è dolce.	**Sugar is sweet.**

The definite article is used when referring to parts of the body or articles of clothing.

Mi lavo le mani.	**I wash my hands.**

The definite article is used after the verb *avere* when giving a physical description.

Marcello ha gli occhi azzurri.	**Marcello has blue eyes.**

CHAPTER 10

Pronouns, the Impersonal *si,* and Useful Verb Constructions

Now that you've been introduced to verbs in the present indicative tense, we will take a look at direct and indirect objects. Many (not all!) of the verbs that we have seen can take either a direct or indirect object. As with any noun, a pronoun can be substituted for it. This chapter will help to sharpen your understanding of these useful parts of speech.

Direct Objects and Direct Object Pronouns

A direct object answers the question "whom?" or "what?" in relation to the action of the verb. For example, take the sentence "John reads a book." The direct object in this sentence—a book—answers the question "What does John read?" In the sentence "I see John," the direct object—John—answers the question "Whom do I see?" It is important to bear in mind that not all verbs can take a direct object. Only a verb that can perform an action on someone or something can take a direct object. These verbs are commonly referred to as transitive verbs. Intransitive verbs, on the contrary, cannot be followed by a direct object.

Transitive and Intransitive Verbs

The following verbs are transitive, meaning they can take a direct object:

leggere (to read)	*restituire* (to give back)	*mangiare* (to eat)
bere (to drink)	*prendere* (to take)	*offrire* (to offer)

The following verbs are intransitive, meaning they cannot take a direct object:

andare (to go)	*venire (to come)*
partire (to depart)	*arrivare (to arrive)*

Exercise 10-1

Underline the direct objects in each sentence. Not all of the sentences will contain a direct object.

1. *Marco scrive una lettera.*
2. *Voglio mangiare la pizza.*
3. *Il treno parte alle otto.*
4. *Telefono all'agenzia di viaggi.*
5. *Mio figlio ha molti amici.*

To avoid repeating the same word over and over, we can use a direct object pronoun in the place of the direct object. The direct object pronouns in Italian are:

Table 10-1

Singular		Plural	
mi	me	*ci*	us
ti	you	*vi*	you
lo	him, it	*li*	them
la	her, it	*le*	them
La	you (formal)	*Li, Le*	you (formal)

FACT

In some cases, knowing which pronoun to use is a bit more complicated in Italian than it is in English. The equivalent of "it" can be either *lo* (used for a masculine singular direct object) or *la* (used for a feminine singular direct object); the pronouns *li* (masculine plural) and *le* (feminine plural) are used to mean "them."

In Italian, the direct object pronoun is always placed before the conjugated verb. When the sentence is negative (using the word *non*), the direct object pronoun is placed between the *non* and the conjugated verb.

| He doesn't eat it. | *Non **la** mangia.* |
| Why don't you invite them? | *Perché non **li** inviti?* |

Note that *mi, ti, lo,* and *la* change to *m', t',* and *l'* in front of a vowel or silent *h*.

Indirect Objects and Indirect Object Pronouns

An indirect object answers the question "to what or whom?" or "for what or whom?" in relation to the action of the verb. Take for example the sentence "John gives the book to me." We've already seen the direct object in this sentence—a book. The indirect object—me—answers the question "to whom?" in relation to the action of the verb.

Exercise 10-2

Underline the indirect object in each sentence.

1. *Do il libro al mio amico.*
2. *Puoi telefonare a mio padre stasera.*
3. *Non vuole chiedere soldi a suo padre.*
4. *Restituisco la penna a Lei.*
5. *Tommaso dice bugie a noi.*

Indirect object pronouns replace indirect object nouns. They are identical in form to direct object pronouns, except for the third person forms *gli*, *le*, and *loro*. Note that *mi* and *ti* change to *m'* and *t'* in front of a vowel or silent *h*.

Table 10-2

Singular		Plural	
mi	to/for me	*ci*	to/for us
ti	to/for you	*vi*	to/for you
gli	to/for him	*loro*	to/for them
le	to/for her	*Loro*	to/for you (formal)
Le	to/for you (formal)		

Like the direct object pronoun, the indirect object pronoun is always placed before the conjugated verb. The only exception is *loro/Loro*, which always follow the conjugated verb. When the sentence is negative (using the word *non*), the indirect object pronoun is placed between the *non* and the conjugated verb.

Gli parlo ogni giorno.	**I speak to him every day.**
Non le parlo mai.	**I never speak to her.**
Dico loro la verità.	**I am telling them the truth.**

The following verbs require an indirect object in order to specify the recipient of the action of the verb. Note that the English equivalents of these verbs do not all require an indirect object.

Table 10-3

Italian	English	Italian	English
assomigliare	to resemble	*offrire*	to offer
badare	to look after	*portare*	to bring
chiedere/domandare	to ask	*prestare*	to lend
consigliare	to advise	*regalare*	to give as a gift
dare	to give	*restituire*	to return (something to someone)
dire	to say, to tell	*rispondere*	to reply
disubbidire	to disobey	*scrivere*	to write
importare	to matter	*spedire*	to send
insegnare	to teach	*spiegare*	to explain
interessare	to interest	*telefonare*	to telephone
mandare	to send	*ubbidire*	to obey
mostrare	to show	*obbedire*	to obey

QUESTION

Should I use an indirect object pronoun or a direct object pronoun?
If the object is preceded by a preposition, that person/thing is an indirect object. If it is not preceded by a preposition, it is a direct object.

Reflexive Pronouns and Reflexive Verbs

Myself, herself, and themselves are all reflexive pronouns we use in English to indicate that the subject performing the action was also the object of that action. Reflexive verbs are very easy to recognize and conjugate.

Reflexive Pronouns

Reflexive pronouns are placed before the conjugated verb.

Table 10-4

Subject Pronoun	Reflexive Pronoun	Subject Pronoun	Reflexive Pronoun
io	mi	noi	ci
tu	ti	voi	vi
lui	si	loro	si
lei	si	Loro	si
Lei	si		

Just like direct object pronouns, reflexive pronouns are placed before a conjugated verb. *Mi, ti, si,* and *vi* may become *m', t', s',* and *v'* before a vowel or silent *h. Ci* may only become *c'* before an *i* or *e.*

Nonreflexive: *Io chiamo Giovanni.* **I call Giovanni.**
Reflexive: *Io mi chiamo Giovanni.* **I call myself Giovanni.**

Reflexive Verbs

Reflexive verbs are verbs whose action falls back on the subject. They can be found in the *–are, –ere,* and *–ire* categories. You can recognize a reflexive verb by the reflexive pronoun (*si*) attached to the end of the infinitive.

Exercise 10-3

Write whether each verb is reflexive or not.

1. *dormire* _____
2. *chiamarsi* _____
3. *mettere* _____
4. *parlare* _____
5. *vestirsi* _____

Conjugating reflexive verbs isn't all that tricky. The only difference between a reflexive and non-reflexive verb is the addition of the reflexive pronoun. The reflexive pronoun must correspond with the subject of the verb, and it is placed immediately before the conjugated verb.

Listen to and repeat the present-tense conjugations of the reflexive verb *annoiarsi* (to get bored).

Table 10-5

annoiarsi

mi annoio	si annoia	vi annoiate
ti annoi	ci annoiamno	si annoiano

TRACK 55

The following table contains some commonly used reflexive verbs.

Table 10-6

Italian	English	Italian	English
accorgersi (di)	to notice	*fermarsi*	to stop
addormentarsi	to fall asleep	*innamorarsi*	to fall in love
alzarsi	to get up	*laurearsi*	to graduate
annoiarsi	to get bored	*lavarsi*	to wash
arrabbiarsi	to get angry	*mettersi*	to put on
chiamarsi	to be called, to call oneself	*pettinarsi*	to comb one's hair
coprirsi	to cover oneself	*preoccuparsi*	to worry
divertirsi	to enjoy oneself	*prepararsi*	to prepare oneself
farsi la barba	to shave	*radersi*	to shave
riposarsi	to rest	*spogliarsi*	to undress
scusarsi	to apologize	*sposarsi*	to get married
sedersi	to set	*svegliarsi*	to wake up
sentirsi	to feel	*vestirsi*	to get dressed

Reciprocal Verbs

Reciprocal verbs are verbs that express a reciprocal action. By definition they must have a plural subject.

Noi ci vediamo ogni giorno.   **We see each other every day.**

The action of the verb in the sentence above is reciprocal: I see you every day, and you see me every day = We see each other every day. You may have noticed the expression *ci vediamo* could have two possible meanings: we see ourselves (reflexive) or we see each other (reciprocal). The context of the conversation will help to clear up any misunderstandings! The following table contains some useful reciprocal verbs:

Table 10-7

Italian	English	Italian	English
abbracciarsi	to embrace each other	*insultarsi*	to insult each other
aiutarsi	to help each other	*riconoscersi*	to recognize each other
amarsi	to love each other	*rispettarsi*	to respect each other
ammirarsi	to admire each other	*rivedersi*	to see each other again
baciarsi	to kiss each other	*salutarsi*	to greet each other
conoscersi	to know/meet each other	*scriversi*	to write to each other
consolarsi	to comfort each other	*sposarsi*	to get married
incontrarsi	to meet	*vedersi*	to see each other
innamorarsi	to fall in love	*visitarsi*	to visit each other

Exercise 10-4

In each of the following sentences, determine how each pronoun (underlined) is being used. Is it a direct object pronoun? Indirect object pronoun? Reflexive pronoun? Reciprocal pronoun?

1. *Ci vediamo stasera!* _____
2. *Il professore le ha spiegato il problema.* _____
3. *Gli hai detto di comprare dei fiori per sua madre?* _____
4. *Non ti vedo!* _____
5. *Mi sveglio presto ogni mattina.* _____

Double Verb Constructions with Object Pronouns

We have already seen some double verb constructions with the verbs *dovere*, *potere*, and *volere*. The sentence *Io voglio andare al cinema* (I want to go to the movies) is considered a double verb construction because two verbs are being used. The first verb (*voglio*, in this case) is conjugated, while the second verb is used in its infinitive form. When using the verbs *dovere, potere, volere,* and *sapere* in a double verb construction with either a direct object pronoun or an indirect object pronoun, the object pronoun can either come before the conjugated verb or attach to the end of the infinitive.

Noi vogliamo vederli stasera.	**We want to see them this evening.**
Non li possiamo vedere stasera.	**We can't see them this evening.**

Double Object Pronouns

Up to this point we have substituted a pronoun for either the direct or indirect object. As it is in English, it is possible to substitute for both pronouns in Italian. Let's revisit the sentence "I give the book to John." If we substitute both a direct object pronoun and an indirect object pronoun for the objects in this sentence, we end up with the statement "I gave it to him." When both pronouns are used in a sentence in Italian, the indirect object pronoun will always precede the direct object pronoun, except when the indirect object pronoun *loro/Loro* is used. The following is a table of the indirect/direct double object pronoun combinations. *Lo, la, li,* and *le* are direct object pronouns. *Mi, ti, gli/le, ci, vi,* and *loro* are indirect object pronouns.

Table 10-8

Reflexive Pronoun	Direct Object Pronoun			
	+lo	**+la**	**+li**	**+le**
mi	*me lo*	*me la*	*me li*	*me le*
ti	*te lo*	*te la*	*te li*	*te le*
gli/le	*glielo*	*gliela*	*glieli*	*gliele*
ci	*ce lo*	*ce la*	*ce li*	*ce le*
vi	*ve lo*	*ve la*	*ve li*	*ve le*
loro	*lo . . . loro*	*la . . . loro*	*li . . . loro*	*le . . . loro*

It is possible to use a direct object with a reflexive verb as well. Let's look at the sentence *Mi metto una cravatta.* This sentence is reflexive, since I am putting something on myself, and it also has a direct object—*una cravatta* (necktie). It is possible to use both a reflexive pronoun and a direct object pronoun in the same sentence. If we were to substitute a direct object pronoun for this sentence, we would have *Me la metto* (I put it on.) The following table shows the reflexive/direct double object pronoun combinations.

Table 10-9

Reflexive Pronoun	Direct Object Pronoun			
	+*lo*	+*la*	+*li*	+*le*
mi	*me lo*	*me la*	*me li*	*me le*
ti	*te lo*	*te la*	*te li*	*te le*
si	*se lo*	*se la*	*se li*	*se le*
ci	*ce lo*	*ce la*	*ce li*	*ce le*
vi	*ve lo*	*ve la*	*ve li*	*ve le*
si	*se lo*	*se la*	*se li*	*se le*

When using the verbs *dovere*, *potere*, *volere*, and *sapere* in a double verb construction with a double object pronoun, you have the choice of either putting the double object pronouns before the conjugated verb or attaching them to the end of the infinitive verb. The pronouns combine to form one word when they are attached to the end of the infinitive verb.

Te li do domani.	**I will give them to you tomorrow.**
Posso darteli domani.	**I can give them to you tomorrow.**

Disjunctive Pronouns

Disjunctive or stressed pronouns are used after prepositions and verbs to show emphasis. They are used after the preposition *di* when used with the following prepositions: *senza*, *dopo*, *sotto*, and *su*. When disjunctive pronouns are used, the adverbs *anche*, *proprio*, and *solamente* are often used.

Vengo con te.	**I'll come with you.**
Amo te, non lei.	**I love you, not her.**
Ho un regalo per te.	**I have a gift for you.**

Table 10-10
Disjunctive Pronouns

Italian	English	Italian	English
me	me, myself	*noi*	us, ourselves
te	you, yourself	*voi*	you, yourselves
Lei	you (formal)	*Loro*	you (formal)
lui, lei	him, her	*loro*	them
sé	yourself (formal), oneself, himself, herself	*sé*	yourselves (formal), themselves

Possessive Pronouns

Possessive pronouns take the place of possessive adjectives. Possessive pronouns are always preceded by the definite article, even when referring to a singular family member.

Table 10-11

Possessive Pronoun	English Equivalent
il mio/la mia/i miei/le mie	mine
il tuo/la tua/i tuoi/le tue	yours (singular, informal)
il suo/la sua/i suoi/le sue	his or hers
il Suo/la Sua/i Suoi/le Sue	yours (singular, formal)
il nostro/la nostra/i nostri/le nostre	ours
il vostro/la vostra/i vostri/le vostre	yours (plural, informal)
il loro/la loro/i loro/le loro	theirs
il Loro/la Loro/i Loro/le Loro	yours (plural, formal)

I miei amici sono simpatici. I tuoi non lo sono affatto.	**My friends are nice. Yours aren't at all.**
Restituisco i vostri libri, ma non i loro.	**I am returning your books, but not theirs.**

The Impersonal Si Construction

In Italian, impersonal statements are formed by using the pronoun *si* followed by the third-person singular form of the verb. This is similar to impersonal statements in English that are preceded by the subjects "one," "they," or "people." In Italian, the impersonal subject is implied because the sentence does not have a direct object.

Si mangia bene in quel ristorante.	**One eats well in that restaurant.**

If the sentence contains a singular direct object, Italian uses the pronoun *si* followed by the third-person singular form of the verb. When the sentence has a plural direct object, *si* is followed by the third person plural form of the verb. This construction implies the passive voice.

Si parlano italiano e francese in Svizzera.	**Italian and French are spoken in Switzerland.**

Exercise 10-5

Restate the sentences using the impersonal *si* construction.

1. *Se studi molto, impari molto.* _____.
2. *Parlate molte lingue straniere.* _____.
3. *Andiamo a teatro stasera?* _____.
4. *Dicono che Roma sia bella.* _____.
5. *Partiamo alle otto.* _____.

When the impersonal *si* construction is followed by an adjective, the adjective must have a masculine plural ending.

Quando si è stanchi, non si deve guidare.	**When you're tired, you shouldn't drive.**

TRACK 56

Repeat each expression to practice your pronunciation.

1. *Quando si è ricchi, non si è sempre felici.*
2. *Quando si è stanchi, non si lavora.*
3. *Quando si è simpatici, si fanno amicizie.*

Reflexive verbs can be used in both impersonal and passive constructions. When a reflexive verb is used in an impersonal or passive construction, it must be preded by *ci si*, as opposed to simply *si* for nonreflexive verbs.

Ci si sveglia presta.	**One wakes up early.**

Introduction to *Piacere*

Often translated to mean "to like," the Italian verb *piacere* really means "to be pleasing to." In English, we say "John likes coffee." In Italian, we say *A John piace il caffè*. A literal English translation is "Coffee is pleasing to John." The subject + verb + object structure of English is transformed into indirect object + verb + subject in Italian.

A Massimo piacciono le moto.	**Massimo like motorcycles. (Literally, "Motorcycles are pleasing to Massimo.")**

Other verbs that follow this construction are listed in the following table:

Table 10-12

Italian	English
bastare	to be sufficient, to suffice
dispiacere	to displease, to upset
mancare	to be lacking, to miss
occorrere	to require, to need
restare	to remain, to have left
servire	to serve, to be of use

TRACK 57

Mi bastano 100 euro.	**One hundred Euros is all I need.**
Ti dispiace se non vengo?	**Are you sorry that I can't come?**
Mi manca molto mio padre.	**I miss my father a lot.**
Che cosa mi occorre sapere?	**What do I need to know?**
Ci restano dieci minuti.	**We have ten minutes left.**
Mi serve un nuovo ombrello.	**I need a new umbrella.**

More Useful Expressions and Constructions: To Feel and to Stop

There are a few different ways to translate the verb "to feel" into Italian.

Table 10-13

Italian	English
sentire	to sense or feel something, to hear, to smell
sentirsi	to feel (physical or emotional state)

Sento la musica.	**I hear the music.**
Sento il profumo.	**I smell the perfume.**
Sento il dolore.	**I feel the pain.**
Mario si sente triste.	**Mario feels sad.**
Come ti senti?	**How do you feel?**

There are a few different ways to translate the verb "to stop" in Italian.

Table 10-14

Italian	English
fermare	to stop someone or something
fermarsi	to stop (oneself)
smettere di	to stop/quit doing something

Non riesco a fermare la macchina.	**I can't stop the car.**
Ci fermiamo al negozio.	**Let's stop at the store.**
Mio padre smette di fumare.	**My father is quitting smoking.**

CHAPTER 11

Past Tenses: The *Passato Prossimo*, the Imperfect, and the *Trapassato Prossimo*

The *passato prossimo* can have a few different meanings: *Io ho mangiato* could translate as "I have eaten," "I ate," or "I did eat," depending on the context. The imperfect tense is a simple tense, formed by a single word, that is used to express a habitual or ongoing action in the past—for example, I used to go swimming at the lake. The imperfect actions are clearly happening in the past. We know that it used to happen, or that it was happening, but we don't know when the actions were brought to an end.

The Passato Prossimo with *Avere* and *Essere*

The first component of the *passato prossimo* is the auxiliary verb (*avere* or *essere*). Can you recall their present indicative tense conjugations?

Exercise 11-1: Present Tense of *Avere* and *Essere*

Conjugate *avere* and *essere* in the present tense for each subject provided below.

1. *io* _____   *io* _____
2. *tu* _____   *tu* _____
3. *lui/lei/Lei* _____   *lui/lei/Le*i _____
4. *noi* _____   *noi* _____
5. *voi* _____   *voi* _____
6. *loro/Loro* _____   *loro/Loro* _____

The second component of the *passato prossimo* conjugations is the past participle. In Italian the past participle is formed by replacing the *–are*, *–ere*, or *–ire* of the infinitive with *–ato*, *–uto*, or *–ito*, respectively.

Table 11-1
Past Participles

Infinitve	Past Participle
mangiare	mangiato
vedere	veduto
partire	partito

Avere or *Essere*?

For most Italian verbs—and for all transitive verbs (verbs that can take a direct object)—the passato prossimo is formed with the present tense of the auxiliary verb *avere* plus the past participle of the main verb. For example, "I have eaten" is *Ho mangiato*; "We have slept" is *Abbiamo dormito*. The present tense of the auxiliary verb *essere* is used with most intransitive verbs, usually verbs of motion and verbs that cannot take a direct object. When the auxiliary verb *essere* is used, the last letter of the past participle must agree in number and in gender with the subject of the verb. For example, "We have gone" is *Siamo andati*; "Marie has arrived" is *Maria è arrivata*.The following is a list of common verbs conjugated with *essere* in the past tense. Note that most of them are verbs that express coming or going.

Table 11-2

Italian	English	Italian	English
andare	to go	partire	to leave
arrivare	to arrive	restare	to remain
cadere	to fall	ritornare	to return
diventare	to become	salire	to go up/to climb
entrare	to enter	scendere	to come down/to descend
essere	to be	stare	to be/to stay
morire	to die	uscire	to go out
nascere	to be born	venire	to come

The examples below illustrate the *passato prossimo* with the auxiliary verbs *avere* and *essere*.

Noi abbiamo letto il libro.	**We read the book.**
Loro sono andati al supermercato.	**They went to the supermarket.**
Maria ha guardato il film.	**Maria watched the movie.**
Laura e Anna sono arrivate in ritardo.	**Laura and Anna arrived late.**

Table 11-3
From Present to Past

Present Tense	Past Tense
Maria va a casa.	*Maria è andata a casa.*
Bevo il caffè.	*Ho bevuto il caffè.*
Loro dicono la verità.	*Loro hanno detto la verità.*
Lei legge molti libri.	*Lei ha letto molti libri.*
Maria e Marco partono alle otto.	*Maria e Marco sono partiti alle otto.*

There are many irregular past participles, especially with second-conjugation (*–ere*) verbs.

Table 11-4

Infinitive	Irregular Past Participle	Infinitive	Irregular Past Participle
accendere	acceso	nascere	nato
aprire	aperto	offrire	offerto
bere	bevuto	perdere	perduto or perso
chiedere	chiesto	prendere	preso
chiudere	chiuso	rendere	reso
conoscere	conosciuto	rispondere	risposto
cuocere	cotto	scegliere	scelto
dire	detto	scendere	sceso
essere	stato	scrivere	scritto
fare	fatto	spendere	speso
leggere	letto	vedere	veduto or visto
mettere	messo	vincere	vinto
morire	morto		

Exercise 11-2

Provide the past participle of the infinitive.

Infinitive	Past Participle
prendere	
mangiare	
andare	
scendere	
dire	

The *passato prossimo* + *per* is used to indicate the duration of an action that was started and completed in the past. *Ho studiato per due ore* = I studied for two hours.

Common Adverbial Expressions of Time in the Past

The following expressions of time will prove very useful when talking about events in the past.

Table 11-5

Adverbial Expressions

Italian	English	Italian	English
ieri	yesterday	*la notte scorsa*	last night
ieri pomeriggio	yesterday afternoon	*la settimana scorsa*	last week
ieri sera	last night	*martedì scorso*	last Tuesday
il mese scorso	last month	*non . . . ancora*	not yet
l'altro giorno	the other day	*non . . . mai*	never
l'altro ieri	the day before yesterday		

Negative Statements in the Past

The negative word *non* is placed immediately before the conjugated verb and its pronoun to make a sentence negative.

Table 11-6

Negative Sentences

Affirmative	Negative
Matteo ed Elena sono andati in Italia l'anno scorso.	*Matteo ed Elena non sono andati in Italia l'anno scorso.*
Gli ho partato.	*Non gli ho mai parlato.*

When used in an affirmative question, the adverb *mai* means "ever." *Hai mai mangiato il fegato?* means "Have you ever eaten liver?" *No, non l'ho mai mangiato.* translates to "No, I have never eaten it."

The *Passato Prossimo* and Special Constructions

Now that you know the basics of the *passato prossimo*, it's time to move forward and focus on using it with other constructions.

Reflexive and Reciprocal Verbs

All reflexive and reciprocal verbs are conjugated with the auxiliary verb *essere* in the *passato prossimo*. Since they are conjugated with *essere*, the last letter of the past participle must agree in number and gender with the subject of the sentence. The reflexive and reciprocal pronouns should precede the auxiliary verb *essere*.

Present

Maria si sveglia alle otto.	**Maria wakes up at 8:00.**

Past

Maria si è svegliata alle otto.	**Maria woke up at 8:00.**

Repeat each track to practice your pronunciation.

TRACK 58

Noi ci siamo svegliati molto presto.	**We woke up very early.**
Luisella si è arrabbiata ieri sera.	**Luisella got angry last night.**
Eugenio e Davide si sono conosciuti alla festa.	**Eugenio and Davide met at the party.**
Le bambine si sono lavate le mani.	**The little girls washed their hands.**
Elena e Caterina si sono viste ieri sera.	**Elena and Carterina saw each other last night.**

Double Verb Constructions

You have already been introduced to the modal verbs *dovere*, *potere*, and *volere*. These verbs are often followed by an infinitive, forming a double verb construction. When forming the *passato prossimo* of a double verb construction, the modal verbs can be preceded by *avere* or *essere*, depending on whether the main verb is transitive or intransitive.

Transitive Verbs That Take *Avere*

Ieri non hai potuto studiare.	**You couldn't study yesterday.**
Elena e Maria hanno voluto guardare il film.	**Elena and Maria wanted to watch the movie.**
Paolo ha dovuto lavorare molto.	**Paolo had to work.**

Intransitive Verbs That Take *Essere*

Ieri non sono potuto andare a teatro.	**I couldn't go to the theater yesterday.**
Loro sono voluti tornare a casa tardi.	**They wanted to return home late.**
Caterina si è dovuta alzare presto.	**Caterina had to get up early.**

The *Passato Prossimo* with Direct Object Pronouns

When using a direct object pronoun with the *passato prossimo*, remember that the direct object pronouns precede the conjugated auxiliary verb *avere*. In addition, the past participle of the verb conjugated with *avere* must agree in number and gender with the direct object pronouns *lo, la, La, li, le, Li,* and *Le.* Agreement of the past participle is optional with the direct object pronouns *mi, ti, ci,* and *vi.*

Table 11-7

Present	Past	
Io ho letto il libro.	*Io l'ho letto.*	
Noi abbiamo mangiato la pizza.	*Noi l'abbiamo mangiata.*	
Ho visto te e Marianna.	*Vi ho visto* OR *Vi ho visti.*	
Maria ha conosciuto noi.	*Maria ci ha conosciuto* OR *Maria ci ha conosciuti.*	

Exercise 11-3: From Present to Past

Rewrite the sentences, substituting the direct object pronouns for the direct objects.

1. *Io ho letto i libri.*_____.
2. *Noi abbiamo mangiato la pasta.*_____
   _____.
3. *Gli studenti hanno fatto gli esercizi.*_____
   _____.
4. *Maria ha visto me e Mario.*_____.
5. *Cerchiamo te e tua sorella.*_____.

FACT

Unlike their English equivalents, the verbs *ascoltare* (to listen), *aspettare* (to listen), *cercare* (to look for), and *guardare* (to look at/to watch) are not followed by a preposition. These verbs all take direct objects: *Io ascolto la musica* (I listen to music), *Tu aspetti il treno* (You wait for the train).

The *Passato Prossimo* with Indirect Object Pronouns

When using an indirect object pronoun with the *passato prossimo*, remember that the indirect object pronouns precede the conjugated auxiliary verb *avere*. Note that the past participle of the verb conjugated with *avere* never agrees in number or gender with the indirect object pronouns.

Table 11-8

Present	Past
Ho risposto a Pietro.	*Gli ho risposto.*
Ho telefonato a Maria.	*Le ho telefonato.*

The *Passato Prossimo* with Double Object Pronouns

When using a double object pronoun with the *passato prossimo*, the past participle must agree with the number and gender of the direct object pronoun.

Table 11-9

Present	Past
Le ho prestato la macchina.	*Gliel'ho prestata.*
Ti ho dato i libri ieri.	*Te li ho dati ieri.*

Exercise 11-4: Double Object Pronouns in the Past Tense

Rewrite the sentences, substituting double object pronouns for the direct and indirect objects, and changing from present to past tense.

1. *Portiamo la torta a lei.*_____
2. *Restituisci il libro a lui.*_____

3. *Do la macchina a Paolo.*_____
4. *Mandate i regali ai noi.*_____
5. *Mio padre porta i documenti a voi.*_____

The Imperfect

The past imperfect tense is a simple tense, formed by a single word, that is used to express a habitual or ongoing action in the past. Here are some examples of the imperfect tense in English:

I was listening to the radio.
My brother was watching television.
I used to play baseball when I was a child.
The weather was beautiful, the sun was shining, and the birds were singing.
Every Sunday they went to the supermarket.
Every morning she would wait for her brother to call.

In all of these instances, the actions are clearly happening in the past. However, the actions are incomplete (or imperfect). We know that it used to happen, or that it was happening, but we don't know when the actions were brought to an end. The following table shows the conjugations of –*are*, –*ere*, and –*ire* verbs in the imperfect tense.

Table 11-10

	parlare	scrivere	dormire	
io	*parlavo*	*scrivevo*	*dormivo*	
tu	*parlavi*	*scrivevi*	*dormivi*	
lui/lei/Lei	*parlava*	*scriveva*	*dormiva*	
noi	*parlavamo*	*scrivevamo*	*dormivamo*	
voi	*parlavate*	*scrivevate*	*dormivate*	
loro/Loro	*parlavano*	*scrivevano*	*dormivano*	

The imperfect tense is used to describe habitual actions in the past.

Giocavo a baseball il sabato pomeriggio.   **I used to play baseball on Saturday afternoons.**

Mio padre mi leggeva favole tutte le sere.	**My father used to read me fables every night.**

The imperfect tense is used to describe environment, time, weather, physical and mental states, and other past states.

Erano le due.	**It was two o'clock.**
Il sole splendeva e faceva caldo.	**The sun was shining and it was hot out.**
Mi sentivo in forma.	**I was feeling fine.**
Avevo diciotto anni.	**I was eighteen years old.**

The imperfect is also used to express an action in progress while another action was taking place or when another action was completed.

Both actions take place at the same time

Paolo leggeva mentre io suonavo la chitarra.	**Paolo was reading while I was playing the guitar.**

One action precedes the other

Il telefono squillava quando sono entrato in camera.	**The phone was ringing when I walked into the room.**

The word *mentre* (while) is often a good indicator that the imperfect will be used. For example: *Mentre camminavo, ho visto Paolo.* (While I was walking, I saw Paolo.)

Adverbial Expressions

The following adverbs and adverbial expressions are often used with the imperfect tense. Note that the time frames to which they refer are vague or denote a habitual action.

Table 11-11

Adverbs

Italian	English	Italian	English
a volte	at times	*ogni settimana*	every, each week
continuamente	continuously	*sempre*	always
giorno dopo giorno	day after day	*spesso*	often
ogni tanto	once in a while	*tutti i giorni*	every day
ogni giorno	every, each day		

A volte la vita era dura.   **Life was hard at times.**

Ogni tanto andavo al cinema.   **I used to go to the movies every once in a while.**

Spesso faceva freddo.   **It was often cold outside.**

ALERT

Take a look at the phrases *ogni mese* (each month) and *ogni settimana* (each week). Though *mese* is a masculine noun and *settimana* is a feminine noun, the word *ogni* does not change its ending. In addition, it does not exist in the plural; "each" is always a singular modifier.

Irregular Verbs

The following verbs have irregular conjugations in the imperfect tense.

Table 11-12

Irregular Verbs in the Imperfect Tense

	fare	dire	bere	porre	tradurre
io	*facevo*	*dicevo*	*bevevo*	*ponevo*	*traducevo*
tu	*facevi*	*dicevi*	*bevevi*	*ponevi*	*traducevi*
lui/lei/Lei	*faceva*	*diceva*	*beveva*	*poneva*	*traduceva*
noi	*facevamo*	*dicevamo*	*bevevamo*	*ponevamo*	*traducevamo*
voi	*facevate*	*dicevate*	*bevevate*	*ponevate*	*traducevate*
loro/Loro	*facevano*	*dicevano*	*bevevano*	*ponevano*	*traducevano*

The following table contains other verbs that are conjugated like *porre* (to put):

Table 11-13

Italian	English	Italian	English
comporre	to compose	*posporre*	to place or put after
disporre	to arrange, to set out	*proporre*	to propose, to put
esporre	to exhibit, to display	*riporre*	to put back, to replace
imporre	to impose	*supporre*	to suppose
opporre	to oppose		

The following table contains other verbs that are conjugated like *tradurre* (to translate):

Table 11-14

Italian	English
condurre	to take, to lead
indurre	to inspire, to infuse
introdurre	to introduce, to show
produrre	to produce, to yield
ridurre	to reduce, to curtail

Io bevevo l'acqua.	**I was drinking some water.**
Marco traduceva il documento.	**Marco was translating the document.**
Noi ponevamo le domande e loro cercavano di rispondere.	**We were asking the questions and they were trying to respond.**
Voi facevate attenzione mentre io parlavo.	**You were paying attention while I was speaking.**
Gli studenti dicevano bugie.	**The students were telling lies.**

The Imperfect + *da* + Expression of Time

The imperfect can be used with *da* + an expression of time to express an action that started in the past and was still in progress when another action occurred, or to express the equivalent of the English pluperfect (I had slept for . . .).

Dormivo da otto ore.	**I had been sleeping for eight hours.**
Il professore parlava da dieci	**The professor had been speaking for**
minuti quando io sono arrivato.	**ten minutes when I arrived.**

Exercise 11-5: The Imperfect

Give the correct form of the imperfect of the verbs listed below. Each of the following verbs will be used only once:

- *aspettare*
- *guardare*
- *rispondere*
- *fare*
- *giocare*

1. *Io _____ la televisione.*
2. *Noi _____ attenzione.*
3. *Tutti i ragazzi _____ a calcio.*
4. *Voi _____ l'autobus.*
5. *Marco non _____ alle mie domande.*

Comparison of *Passato Prossimo* and Imperfect

Non-native English speakers often have trouble differentiating between the *passato prossimo* and the imperfect. The *passato prossimo* is used to express an action that has taken place in the past. The imperfect, on the other hand, represents the vagueness of time with respect to an action that has taken place in the past.

Table 11-15
Contrast between the *Passato Prossimo* and the Imperfect

Passato prossimo	Imperfect
An action that occurs as a single event.	An action that was customary in the past.
An action limited in the times it is performed.	An action that may be ongoing indefinitely.
An action that is defined within a specific time period.	An action that is defined within a broad time period.

FACT

> A good strategy that you can use to help you to understand the difference between the *passato prossimo* and the imperfect is to ask yourself if the action happened once (*passato prossimo*) or if it took place over a period of time (imperfect).

The following examples should help you differentiate between the imperfect and the preterite. Notice how the time references can help you understand whether the action happened once or if it is a habitual action.

Passato prossimo

Mia madre mi ha telefonato ieri sera.	**My mother called me last night.**
Io ho giaocato a baseball sabato scorso.	**I played baseball last Saturday.**
Tutti i ragazzi sono andati al cinema ieri sera.	**All the kids went to the movies last night.**
Mia moglie ha fatto delle spesei ieri pomeriggio.	**My wife did some shopping yesterday afternoon.**
Ho guardato la TV ieri sera.	**I watched TV last night.**

Imperfect

Mia madre mi telefonava tutte le sere.	**My mother called me every night.**
Io giocavo a baseball il sabato.	**I played baseball on Saturdays.**
Tutti i ragazzi andavano al cinema il venerdì sera.	**All the kids went to the movies on Friday evenings.**
Mia moglie faceva le spese nel pomeriggio.	**My wife used to go shopping in the afternoon.**
Guardavo la TV ogni sera.	**I watched TV every night.**

Five Verbs: *Passato Prossimo* and Imperfect

The five verbs *dovere*, *potere*, *volere*, *sapere*, and *conoscere* have different meanings depending on whether they are used in the *passato prossimo* or the imperfect. Generally speaking, the *passato prossimo* describes an action, while the imperfect describes a circumstance or a state of being.

dovere

Dovevo partire alle otto, ma non mi sono svegliato in tempo.	**I was supposed to leave at eight o'clock, but I didn't wake up in time.**
Noi siamo dovuti partire alle otto perché il negozio chiudeva alle otto e trenta.	**We had to leave at eight o'clock because the store closed at eight-thirty.**

potere

Potevo finire i miei compiti, ma non ne avevo voglia.	**I could have finished my homework but I didn't feel like it.**
Ho potuto finire i miei compiti in un'ora.	**I was able to finish my homework in an hour.**

volere

Voleva accompagnarci al ristorante, ma ha dovuto lavorare.	**He wanted to accompany us to the restaurant but he had to work.**
Mio fratello ha voluto vedere il film con noi.	**My brother wanted to see the movie with us.**

sapere

Sapevo che lui era simpatico.	**We knew that he was a nice guy.**
Abbiamo saputo che lui ha comprato una nuova macchina.	**We found out that he bought a new car.**

conoscere

Conoscevamo i tuoi fratelli.	**We knew your brothers.**
Abbiamo conosciuto i tuoi fratelli alla conferenza.	**We met your brothers at the conference.**

The *Trapassato Prossimo*

The *trapassato prossimo* is equivalent to the past perfect in English. It is used to express an action in the past that took place before another past action expressed by the *passato prossimo* or the imperfect.

Non sono andato al cinema venerdì sera perché avevo già visto il film.	**I did not go to the movies on Friday night because I had already seen the movie.**

It is clear that the second action of this sentence took place before the first. In Italian, the *trapassato prossimo* is formed with the imperfect tense of the auxiliary verbs *avere* or *essere*, plus the past participle of the main verb. The imperfect forms of *avere* and *essere* are as follows:

Table 11-16

	avere	essere
io	avevo	ero
tu	avevi	eri
lui/lei/Lei	aveva	era
noi	avevamo	eravamo
voi	avevate	eravate
loro/Loro	avevano	erano

Exercise 11-6

Transform the sentence from the *imperfetto* to the *trapassato prossimo* in the space provided.

1. *Vedevo il mio amico.* _____
2. *Andavamo a teatro.* _____
3. *Ci conoscevamo anni fa.* _____
4. *Il signor Gori comprava una Moto Guzzi.* _____
5. *Tu sapevi la verità.* _____

Exercise 11-7

Transform the following sentences from the *passato prossimo* to the *trapassato prossimo*.

1. *Non ha visto il film.* _____
2. *Mi sono alzato tardi.* _____
3. *Hai già letto quel libro.* _____
4. *Abbiamo ascoltato la musica.* _____
5. *Si sono innamorati.* _____

CHAPTER 12

Negative Expressions, Relative Pronouns, *Ci* and *Ne*, *Da quanto tempo?*, and the Gerund

This chapter introduces you to some useful expressions and adverbs that can be used to negate sentences. Just as in English, there are plenty of expressions that can be used, some of which can be tricky. We will also take a close look at the particles *ci* and *ne*, the very useful and tricky construction of *Da quanto tempo* (since when?), and the gerund. Though some of these are pretty straightforward, others are a little more difficult to master. Nothing that lots of practice can't take care of!

Niente and *Nulla*

The pronouns *niente* and *nulla* (nothing, not anything) are invariable (they only have one form) and are only used in the singular. They can be used to begin a sentence, or they may come after *non* + verb. They can be used interchangeably.

Niente è facile.	**Nothing is easy.**
Niente è pronto.	**Nothing is ready.**
Che cosa vuoi? Non voglio nulla, grazie.	**What do you want? Nothing, thanks.**
Non dico niente.	**I'm not saying anything.**

Niente takes *di* when it immediately precedes an adjective and *da* when it immediately precedes an infinitive.

Non ho letto niente di interessante.	**I didn't read anything interesting.**
Non faccio niente di nuovo.	**I'm not doing anything new.**
Non c'è niente da mangiare.	**There's nothing to eat.**
Non c'è niente da fare.	**There's nothing to do.**

ALERT

In English, double negatives are forbidden. Not so in Italian. You will come across numerous double negatives in Italian. Intuitively you may think that two negatives make a positive. In Italian two negatives make a negative!

Non . . . niente can be used as an invariable adjective before a singular noun to express no or not . . . any with singular nouns.

Non ha niente pazienza.	**He has no patience.**

Note that one can use a negative verb with a noun to express the same idea.

Non ha pazienza.	**He doesn't have patience.**

Nessuno

As an adjective, *nessuno* always precedes the noun, agreeing with the noun's gender. It is only used in the singular. It has the same endings as the adjective *buono*.

Table 12-1

un buo**n** ragazzo	nessu**n** ragazzo
un buo**no** studente	nessu**no** studente
una buo**n**'amica	nessu**n**'amica
una buo**na** studentessa	nessu**na** studentessa

When used as an adjective, *nessuno* may begin a sentence or come after *non* + verb.

Nessuna lingua è facile.	**No language is easy.**
Non ho nessun CD di Zucchero.	**I don't have any CDs by Zucchero.**
Non voglio nessun libro.	**I don't want any books.**

When *nessuno* is used as a pronoun to mean "no one" or "nobody," there are only two forms: *nessuno* or *nessuna*.

Nessuno vuole parlare.	**Nobody wants to talk.**
Nessuno mi capisce!	**No one understands me!**
Nessuna studentessa parla il tedesco.	**None of the girls speaks German.**

Nessun and *nessuna* are used in the expressions *in nessun luogo* and *da nessuna parte* to mean "nowhere" or "not anywhere."

Né . . . né

Né . . . né is a conjunction in Italian that corresponds to the correlative conjunctions "neither . . . nor" and "either . . . or" in English. *Né . . . né* means "neither . . . nor" when placed before the verb.

Né Elena né Caterina vogliono assistere alla conferenza.	**Neither Elena nor Caterina want to attend the conference.**
Né Marco né Davide vengono alla festa.	**Neither Marco nor David is coming to the party.**

FACT

When using *né . . . né* with the subject of a sentence (*Né Marco né Davide vengono alla festa*, for example), Italian uses a plural form of the verb, whereas English uses a singular form of the verb.

"*Non* + verb + *né . . . né*" also means "neither . . . nor" or "either . . . or:"

Non mangia né carne né pesce.	**He eats neither meat nor fish. OR He doesn't eat either meat or fish.**
Non so né sciare né nuotare.	**I know neither how to ski nor how to swim.**

Other Negative Adverbs and Expressions

Non . . . is used with many adverbs to form commonly used negative expressions. The formula is usually *non* + verb + adverb.

Table 12-2
Negative Expressions

Italian	English
non . . . affatto	not at all
non . . . ancora	not yet
non . . . mai (adverb)	never, not ever
non . . . neanche (adverb)	not even, neither
non . . . nemmeno (adverb)	not even, neither
non . . . neppure (adverb)	not even, neither
non . . . più	not anymore, no longer

Some of the words listed above are compound words. *Neanche, nemmeno, neppure, nessuno,* and *niente,* for example, begin with the Latin prefix *ne–* (*ne* = not).

- *ne + anche* (also, even) = *neanche* (not even, neither)
- *ne + meno* (less) = *nemmeno* (not even, neither)
- *ne + pure* (also, even) = *neppure* (not even, neither)
- *ne + uno* (one) = *nessuno* (nobody, no one, none)
- *ne + ente* (antiquated form of entity or thing) = *niente* (nothing)

Relative Pronouns

Relative pronouns connect a dependent clause and a main clause together. In English this is often expressed using the words that, who, whom, which, and whose. In the following example, two ideas are combined with the relative pronoun who.

The boy is playing in the park. + *The boy is my nephew.* = **The boy who is playing in the park is my nephew.**

FACT

In colloquial English, it is common to omit the relative pronoun: "The book I read is on the desk." This is not the case in Italian. The relative pronoun is always stated in Italian. We would say *Il libro che ho letto è sulla scrivania,* not *Il libro ho letto . . .*

The most common relative pronouns in Italian are *che* (who, whom, that, which); *cui* (whom, which); *il quale, la quale, i quali, le quali* (used in place of *cui* or *che*); *quello che, quel che* or *ciò che* (that, which, or what); and *chi* (the ones who, he who, those who).

Che (who, whom, that, which) is invariable and can be used either as a subject or a direct object. It can never be omitted, and it must not be used after a preposition.

Che as Subject

Il ragazzino che gioca nel parco è mio nipote.

Che as Direct Object

Il libro che ho letto è sulla scrivania.

The Italian relative pronoun *cui* (whom, which) is also invariable and is used in place of *che* after a preposition.

Il professore di cui ti ho parlato è simpatico.	**The professor I spoke to you about (about whom I spoke) is nice.**
La persona a cui scrivo è mio fratello.	**The person I'm writing to (to whom I am writing) is my brother.**

Cui is sometimes used in place of *a cui*.

Il ragazzo cui (a cui) parlo è mio cugino.	**The boy to whom I am speaking is my cousin.**

In cui and *che* translate as "when" in expressions of time.

il giorno in cui è morto	**the day (when) he died**
il giorno che ti ho visto	**the day (that) I saw you**

In cui translates as "where" or "in which" when referring to a place. When referring to place, it can be replaced by the word *dove*.

È la città in cui sono nato.	**It is the city in which I was born.**
È la città dove sono nato.	**It is the city in which I was born.**

La ragione per cui is a commonly used construction that is used to express the reason why.

la ragione per cui ti chiamo	**the reason (why) I am calling you**

Il modo (la maniera) in cui is a commonly used construction that is used to express the way in which.

il modo in cui tu reagisci	**the way (in which) you react**

Cui preceded by the definite article (*il cui, la cui, i cui, le cui*) translates as "whose" or "of which." The article must agree with the object that follows *cui*.

Ecco il ragazzo la cui sorella studia all'università.	**Here's the guy whose sister studies at the university.**

Il quale (masculine singular), *la quale* (feminine singular), *i quali* (masculine plural), and *le quali* (feminine plural) can be used in place of *cui* or *che* to avoid ambiguity or repetition.

Ho visto il fratello di Maria che lavora alla Fiat.

In this example, it is unclear whether Maria or her brother works at Fiat. This ambiguity can be cleared up with the use of *il quale*:

Ho visto il fratello di Maria, il quale lavora alla Fiat.	**I saw Maria's brother, who works for Fiat.**

Since the relative pronoun *il quale* is masculine (and singular), it must be referring to *il fratello* (masculine singular) and not *Maria* (feminine singular).

FACT

Here's a quick set of rules to help you keep all the relative pronouns straight: *che* is invariable and never used with a preposition; *cui* is invariable but is always used with a preposition. *Il quale* (and its variations) can be used with articles or articles and prepositions. They are mostly used in formal speech and for clarity.

The forms *il quale, la quale, i quali,* and *le quali* can replace *cui*. In these cases, the article is contracted when the preposition is *a, da, di, in,* or *su*.

il giorno nel quale è morto	**the day on which he died**
la città nella quale sono nato	**the city in which I was born**
la ragione per la quale ti chiamo	**the reason why I called you**

Quello che, *quel che*, *ciò che*, and *quanto* all mean "that," "which," or "what." They are all invariable, they can function as subject or object, and they can be used in place of things or ideas.

Hai fatto quello che (quel che,	**You did what you could.**
ciò che, quanto) hai potuto.	

As a relative pronoun, *chi* is followed by the third person singular of the verb. It does not have an antecedent and therefore it refers to indefinite persons. It is often found as the subject of proverbs and sayings. It is never used as a relative pronoun referring to a defined person.

Chi cerca, trova.	**He who seeks, finds.**
Chi studia, impara.	**He who studies, learns.**

Chi cannot be used when speaking about a specific person. The statement *Giovanni è il ragazzo chi cantava* is incorrect because the relative pronoun refers to the (defined) person Giovanni. In Italian, one would say *Giovanni è il ragazzo che cantava* to convey that Giovanni was the boy who sang.

FACT

An antecedent is the noun or pronoun that the relative pronoun refers back to. The relative pronouns in English are that, what, which, whom, and whose. In the phrase *the book that I read*, the book is the antecedent.

Exercise 12-1

Provide the correct relative pronoun in the spaces below.

1. *È il film di _____ ti ho parlato.*
2. *Il libro _____ ho letto è molto interessante.*

3. _____ *studia, impara.*
4. *La persona a* _____ *scrivo è mio fratello.*
5. *La città* _____ *sono nato è molto bella.*

The Particles *Ci* and *Ne*

Listen closely to native speakers of Italian and you will hear two little words being used frequently. *Ci* and *ne* can be difficult to learn as they seem to be used in so many different contexts and constructions. Don't be discouraged by these intimidating little words—lots of practice will help unlock their mystery!

FACT

A particle refers to a word that lacks a strict definition. It has a grammatical function, but the word does not belong to a specific part of speech. Some examples in the English language include "to," "well," "not," and "oh."

Ci

Ci (or *vi*) is used as a pronoun to replace a prepositional phrase that states location or direction, often indicated by the pronouns *a*, *in*, *per*, etc. It most commonly translates as "there" in English. *Ci* is used more often than *vi* in spoken and written Italian.

Sono andato in Scozia l'anno scorso.	**I went to Scotland last year.**
Ci sono andato ieri sera.	**I went there last night.**
Sono stato a Parigi e non ci voglio ritornare.	**I've been to Paris and I don't want to return (there).**
Vieni alla festa? Sì, ci vengo.	**Are you coming to the party? Yes, I'm coming (to the party).**
Vado in montagna e ci rimango una settimana.	**I'm going to the mountains and I'm staying (there) for a week.**

Ci can also be used to mean "in that," "on that," or "about that."

Credi all'astrologia? Sì, ci credo.	**Do you believe in astrology? Yes, I believe in it.**
Ci devi pensare!	**You have to think about it!**
Ci rifletto da un po'.	**I've been reflecting on that for a while.**

Ci is also used to replace the impersonal *si* in a reflexive construction to avoid the doubling up of two *si's*. See Chapter 10 for more on the impersonal construction.

Marco si lava la faccia.	**Marco washes his face.**
Ci si lava la faccia.	**One washes one's face.**

The particle *ci* is also used after a few commonly used verbs:

Table 12-3

Verbs + *ci*

Italian	English	Italian	English
capirci	to understand	*rimanerci male*	to feel badly/to be disappointed
entrarci	to have to do with something	*sentirci*	to be able to hear
metterci	to take time	*volerci*	to take time

The Particle *Ne*

Ne is often used in the partitive sense (a part of a whole), when referring to quantity. In this sense it translates as "of it" or "of them."

Quante pagine leggi in un'ora? Ne leggo settanta.	**How many pages do you read in an hour? I can read seventy (of them).**
La pizza è buona. Ne vuoi un po'?	**The pizza is delicious. Do you want some (of it)?**
Quanti errori hai fatto? Ne ho fatti molti.	**How many mistakes did you make? I made many (of them).**
Hai mangiato tutti i biscotti? No, ne ho mangiati due.	**Did you eat all of the cookies? No, I ate two (of them).**

Ne can be used to substitute for words or phrases that are introduced by the preposition *di*.

Hai parlato di tuo padre? Sì, ne ho parlato.	**Did you talk about your father? Yes, I spoke about him.**
Discutete di politica? Sì, ne discutiamo.	**Are you discussing politics? Yes, we are discussing it.**
Hai paura del tuo capo? No, non ne ho paura.	**Are you afraid of your boss? No, I am not afraid of him.**
Che cosa pensi di questo problema? Che cosa ne pensi?	**What do you think about this problem? What do you think of it?**
Ti intendi di musica jazz? Te ne intendi?	**Do you know jazz music? Do you know it?**
Ti sei ricordato di farlo? Te ne sei ricordato?	**Did you remember to do it? Did you remember (it)?**

When using *ne* with the *passato prossimo,* the last letter of the past participle must agree with the number and gender of the direct object that *ne* is referring to.

Quante mele hai mangiato? Ne ho mangiate tre.	**How many apples did you eat? I ate three (of them).**

This agreement does not take place when *ne* refers to a prepositional phrase.

Hai parlato dell'esame con il tuo professore? Sì, ne ho parlato.	**Did you talk about the exam with your professor? Yes, I talked about it.**

Exercise 12-2

Translate the sentences into Italian. When do you need to use *ci* or *ne*?

1. I live in Boston._____
2. I live there._____
3. I have some apples._____
4. I have some (of them)._____

5. I have five brothers._____

6. I have five (of them)._____

FACT

Ne is not used with *tutto* to express a quantity. Instead the direct object pronouns *lo, la, li,* and *le* are used. For example, you would say, *Quanta pasta vuoi? La voglio tutta,* not *Ne voglio tutta. Ne* is used with other adjectives: *Ne voglio poca* or *Ne voglio molta.*

Idiomatic Uses of Ci and Ne

Translating idiomatic expressions literally from one language to another is almost always impossible. The use of *ci* and *ne* in the following expressions doesn't follow the rules. Be patient in learning these expressions. It might take a little while to develop an ear for them.

Hai per caso un fazzoletto? Mi dispiace ma non ce l'ho.	**Do you have a handkerchief? I'm sorry, I don't have one.**
Sei stanco di correre? Sì, non ne posso più.	**Are you tired of running? Yes, I can't take it any more.**
Ce l'hai con me?	**Are you mad at me?**
Non ce la faccio.	**I can't do it.**
Me ne vado.	**I'm leaving.**

Repeat each sentence after it is read by the narrator.

TRACK 59

Quante pagine leggi in un'ora? Ne leggo settanta.	**How many pages can you read in an hour? I can read seventy (of them).**
Quanti errori hai fatto? Ne ho fatti molti.	**How many mistakes did you make? I made many (of them).**
Hai parlato di tuo padre? Sì, ne ho parlato.	**Did you talk about your father? Yes, I talked about him.**
Che cosa ne pensi?	**What do you think about it?**
Te ne sei ricordato?	**Did you remember it?**

Da quanto tempo? and Da quando?

Da quanto tempo? and *Da quando?* are expressions used to indicate actions that began in the past and continue into the present. In English we say, "I have been reading since six o'clock" or "I have been living here since 1994." Italian uses the present tense of the verb + *da* + the time expression to convey these same ideas.

Io suono la chitarra da nove anni.	**I have been playing the guitar for nine years.**
Noi studiamo l'italiano da un anno.	**We have been studying Italian for a year.**

Da quanto tempo . . . ? (How long have you been . . . ?) and *Da quando . . . ?* (Since when . . . ?) can be used to introduce a question.

Da quanto tempo giochi a tennis?	**How long have you been playing tennis?**
Da quando tu abiti in questa città?	**Since when have you been living in this city?**

Exercise 12-3

Write an answer to the question in the space provided.

1. *Da quando studi l'italiano?*_____
2. *Da quanto tempo hai la patente di guida?*_____
3. *Da quanti anni lavori?*_____
4. *Da quanti giorni sei in vacanza?*_____
5. *Da quanti minuti guardi il telegiornale?*_____

The Gerund

Though the English gerund and the Italian *gerundio* possess similar characteristics, there are some key differences between the two that we need to consider. Generally speaking, the *gerundio* in Italian corresponds to the –ing verb in English: running, jumping, eating, drinking, etc. Forming the *gerundio* in Italian is actually quite easy: add –*ando* to the stem of –*are* verbs and –*endo* to the stem of –*ere* and –*ire* verbs.

Parlando con i suoi colleghi, ha capito qual'era il problema.	**He understood what the problem was while speaking to his colleagues.**

In Italian there is also a compound or past *gerundio* (*il gerundio composto*). It is formed with the gerund form of the auxiliary verbs *avere* or *essere*, and the past participle of the main verb: *avendo capito* (having understood); *essendo partito* (having left).

Avendo capito il problema, mio padre non disse più nulla.	**Having understood the problem, my father said nothing more.**

Table 12-4
Forming *Il gerundio*

Il gerundio	*Il gerundio composto*
andando	*essendo andato*
correndo	*avendo corso*
dormendo	*avendo dormito*

FACT

The imperfect stems are used to form the gerunds of irregular verbs such as *dire* (*dicendo*), *fare* (*facendo*), *porre* (*ponendo*), and *tradurre* (*traducendo*). The reflexive verbs attach the reflexive pronoun to the end of the word: *svegliandosi, mettendosi, arrabbiandosi.*

The *gerundio* may be used alone or in a subordinate clause to express the conditions (manner, cause, means) that relate to the main action. In this case it corresponds to the English gerund that is preceded by the words "while," "by," "on," "in," or "upon." *Il gerundio* must have the same subject as the verb in the main clause. Repeat each sentence after it is read by the narrator to practice your pronunciation.

TRACK 60

Cantando, ha ingoiato una mosca.	**He swallowed a fly while singing.**
Entrando la stanza ha capito il perché.	**Upon entering the room he understood why.**
Studiando, si impara.	**One learns by studying.**

Ti ho visto camminando in via Roma.	**I saw you while (I was) walking on Via Roma.**
Ti ho visto mentre camminavi in via Roma.	**I saw you while you were walking on Via Roma.**

ESSENTIAL

In English, the gerund is often used as the subject of a sentence or as a direct object: "Smoking is forbidden" or "He doesn't like eating after 10 P.M." In Italian, this is not the case—the infinitive is used instead: *È vietato fumare* or *Non gli piace mangiare dopo le dieci.*

The Progressive Forms

The verb *stare + il gerundio* can be used to express an action that is in progress in the present, was in progress in the past, or will be in progress in the future. The present progressive is formed with the present tense of the verb *stare + il gerundio*:

Sto cantando.	**I'm singing.**
Sta ballando.	**He's dancing.**
Ci stiamo divertendo.	**We're having a good time.**

The present progressive is used to describe an action that is currently in progress. In Italian the sentence *Io mangio gli spaghetti* could translate as "I eat spaghetti" (in general); "I am eating spaghetti" (right now); or "I do eat spaghetti." The present progressive *Sto mangiando gli spaghetti* clears up any ambiguity and makes it clear that the action is in progress.

Che cosa stai facendo?	**What are you (in the process of) doing?**

The past progressive is formed with the imperfect tense of the verb *stare + il gerundio*:

Table 12-5
Past Progressive Verbs

	cantare	divertirsi
io	stavo cantando	mi stavo divertendo
tu	stavi cantando	ti stavi divertendo
lui/lei/Lei	stava cantando	si stava divertendo
noi	stavamo cantando	ci stavamo divertendo
voi	stavate cantando	vi stavate divertendo
loro/Loro	stavano cantando	si stavano divertendo

Io stavo cantando.	**I was singing.**
Lui stava ballando.	**He was dancing.**
Ci stavamo divertendo.	**We were having a good time.**

The future progressive is formed with the future tense (for more on the future tense, see Chapter 13) of the verb *stare* + *il gerundio*. Note that this form in Italian is less common than its equivalent in English.

Table 12-6
Future Progressive Verbs

	cantare	divertirsi
io	starò cantando	mi starò divertendo
tu	starai cantando	ti starai divertendo
lui/lei/Lei	starà cantando	si starà divertendo
noi	staremo cantando	ci staremo divertendo
voi	starete cantando	vi starete divertendo
loro/Loro	staranno cantando	si staranno divertendo

Starò cantando.	**I will be singing.**
Starà ballando.	**He will be dancing.**
Ci staremo divertendo.	**We will be having a good time.**

Exercise 12-4

Write the present progressive form of the verb given.

1. *io dormo* _____
2. *tu mangi* _____
3. *Marco parte* _____
4. *noi leggiamo* _____
5. *voi andate* _____
6. *loro cantano* _____

FACT

Il gerundio functions as an adverb, such as "slowly," "lately," or "now." In Italian, gerunds are invariable in form and do not agree in gender or number with the subject of the verb. *Maria sta arrivando?* (Is Maria on her way?) *No, è già arrivata!* (No, she's already arrived!)

Exercise 12-5

Answer the following questions.

1. *Che cosa stai leggendo?* _____
2. *Che cosa stai guardando alla TV?* _____
3. *Stavi dormendo?* _____
4. *Ti stai divertendo?* _____

CHAPTER 13

The Future Tense, the Imperative Mood, and Exclamations

This chapter will introduce the future indicative, a simple tense that is used to express events that will take place in the future. We will also take a look at the imperative mood, which, as its name implies, is used to give a command. The imperative can be tricky because many of its conjugations may look similar to present indicative forms. Remember, what sets the imperative apart from the present indicative is the presence of an exclamation point. Finally, we will take a look at some common and useful exclamations.

The Future Tense

The future tense is used to express an action that will take place in the future. It corresponds to "will + verb" in the English, "I will go" or "He will see."

Future Tense of Regular Verbs

With regular verbs, the future tense is formed by adding the future tense endings to –*are*, –*ere*, and –*ire* verbs.

Table 13-1

	parlare (to speak)	rispondere (to repond)	dormire (to sleep)
io	*parlerò*	*risponderò*	*dormirò*
tu	*parlerai*	*risponderai*	*dormirai*
lui/lei/Lei	*parlerà*	*reisponderà*	*dormirà*
noi	*parleremo*	*risponderemo*	*dormiremo*
voi	*parlerete*	*risponderete*	*dormirete*
loro/Loro	*parleranno*	*risponderanno*	*dormiranno*

Though we can use the present tense to express an action that will take place in the future—I am going to Italy next summer—the future tense is more precise.

The Future Tense of Irregular Verbs

In the future tense, the verbs *dare*, *stare*, and *fare* simply drop the final –*e* of their infinitives and form the stems *dar–*, *star–*, and *far–*, respectively; the stem of *essere* is *sar–*. These stems are then combined with the regular future tense endings.

There are two other irregular constructions you should be aware of: verbs with infinitives that end in –*ciare* and –*giare* and those that end in –*care* and –*gare*. Verbs with infinitives ending in –*ciare* and –*giare* drop the *i* before adding the future endings to the root: *tu comincerai, noi viaggeremo*. Verbs with infinitives ending in –*care* and –*gare* add an *h* to the root for the future to preserve the hard sound of the *c* or *g* of the infinitive: *io cercherò, loro pagheranno*.

The following table shows some irregular verbs in the future tense.

Table 13-2
Future Tense of Irregular Verbs *Dare, Stare, Fare,* and *Essere*

	dare	stare	fare	essere
io	darò	starò	farò	sarò
tu	darai	starai	farai	sarai
lui/lei/Lei	darà	starà	farà	sarà
noi	daremo	staremo	faremo	saremo
voi	darete	starete	farete	sarete
loro/Loro	daranno	staranno	faranno	saranno

Table 13-3
Future Tense of Irregular Verbs Ending in *–care, –gare,* and *–ciare*

	giocare	pagare	incominciare
io	giocherò	pagherò	incomincerò
tu	giocherai	pagherai	incomincerai
lui/lei/Lei	giocherà	pagherà	incomincerà
noi	giocheremo	pagheremo	incominceremo
voi	giocherete	pagherete	incomincerete
loro/Loro	giocheranno	pagheranno	incominceranno

When the verb ends in *–ciare* or *–giare,* the *–iare* is dropped and the future ending is added. When the verb ends in *–iare* without the *–c* or *–g* (*svegliare,* for example), the *i* is not dropped.

L'estate prossima io andrò in Italia e vedrò i miei cugini.
Next summer I will go to Italy and I will see my cousins.

Table 13-4
Other Irregular Verbs in the Future Tense

	bere	andare	avere	dovere
io	berrò	andrò	avrò	dovrò
tu	berrai	andrai	avrai	dovrai
lui/lei/Lei	berrà	andrà	avrà	dovrà
noi	berremo	andremo	avremo	dovremo
voi	berrete	andrete	avrete	dovrete
loro/Loro	berranno	andranno	avranno	dovranno

	potere	vedere	venire	volere
io	potrò	vedrò	verrò	vorrò
tu	potrai	vedrai	verrai	vorrai
lui/lei/Lei	potrà	vedrà	verrà	vorrà
noi	potremo	vedremo	verremo	vorremo
voi	potrete	vedrete	verrete	vorrete
loro/Loro	potranno	vedranno	verranno	vorranno

Exercise 13-1

TRACK 61

Can you recognize the future tense when it is spoken? Listen to each conjugation and underline the one that is in the future tense.

1. *loro dormivano, noi dormiamo, tu dormirai*
2. *lui vuole, io vorrò, noi volevamo*
3. *noi siamo, loro saranno, io ero*
4. *lui pagherà, voi pagavate, tu paghi*
5. *loro facevano, io faccio, voi farete*

Exercise 13-2: From Present to Future

Rewrite each sentence, changing the verb from the present to the future tense.

1. *Tu impari l'italiano.*_____
2. *Domani sera io sto a casa.*_____
3. *Mio figlio è famoso.*_____
4. *Non veniamo a casa tua.*_____
5. *Balliamo tutta la sera.*_____

The Future Tense in Action

There are many different ways to use the future tense in Italian.

Future Tense and Probability

The future tense may be used to express probability or the notion that something is probably true. In English, we express probability with the construction "must be."

Che ore sono?	**What time is it?**
Sono le otto.	**It's eight o'clock. (certainty)**
Saranno le otto.	**It must be eight o'clock. (uncertainty)**

Future Tense and Time

The future tense is often used after conjunctions like *quando*, *appena*, *non appena*, *finchè*, and *se* to express an action that will take place in the future.

Quando avrò vent'anni, andrò in Italia.	**When I am twenty, I will go to Italy.**
Appena saprà la risposta, chiamerà i suoi genitori.	**As soon as he knows the answer, he will call his parents.**

FACT

When a conjunction is used, both of the verbs must be in the same tense: *Appena saprà la risposta, chiamerà i suoi genitori*. This might not sound correct when you translate the sentence into English, but it's an important rule in Italian!

Future Tense and Pronouns

Using pronouns with the future tense is very straightforward. You already know that pronouns (direct object, indirect object, and reflexive) precede the conjugated verb or are attached to an infinitive that might follow the conjugated verb. The same rule is true when using the future tense.

Table 13-5
Pronouns and the Future Tense

Present	*Future*
Io lo chiamo stasera.	*Io lo chiamerò stasera.*
Tu non lo vuoi.	*Tu non lo vorrai.*
Giovanni gli telefona quando è pronto.	*Giovanni gli telefonerà quando sarà pronto.*
Ci svegliamo alle otto.	*Ci sveglieremo alle otto.*
Vi divertite alla festa.	*Vi divertirete alla festa.*
I ragazzi si salutano.	*I ragazzi si saluteranno.*

Table 13-6
Pronouns and the Future Tense with Double Verb Constructions

Present	*Future*
Io lo devo chiamare stasera.	*Io lo dovrò chiamare stasera.*
Tu non lo vuoi vedere.	*Tu non lo vorrai vedere.*
Giovanni gli può telefonare quando è pronto.	*Giovanni gli potrà telefonare quando sarà pronto.*
Ci dobbiamo svegliare alle otto.	*Ci dovremo svegliare alle otto.*
Vi potete divertire alla festa.	*Vi potrete divertire alla festa.*
I ragazzi si devono salutare.	*I ragazzi si dovranno salutare.*

The Future Perfect Tense

The future perfect is a compound tense used to express an event that will have happened before something else happens. It can also be used to express probability—something that must have already happened. It is formed by pairing the future tense of the verbs *avere* or *essere* with the past participle of the main verb. Let's review the future tense of the verbs *avere* and *essere*.

Table 13-7

	avere	*essere*
io	*avrò*	*sarò*
tu	*avrai*	*sarai*
lui/lei/Lei	*avrà*	*sarà*
noi	*avremo*	*saremo*
voi	*avrete*	*sarete*
loro/Loro	*avranno*	*saranno*

Tu sarai già partito quando io arriverò.	**You will have already left when I arrive.**
Loro avranno mangiato.	**They must have eaten.**

Exercise 13-3

Transform the sentences from the present tense to the future tense.

1. *Sono le otto di sera.*_____
2. *Giovanni è stanco.* _____
3. *Mangia appena è pronta la pastasciutta.* _____
   _____
4. *Appena finisce di mangiare, va a letto.* _____
   _____
5. *Domani mattina si alza presto.* _____
   _____
6. *Si fa la doccia, fa colazione, e parte per la stazione.* _____
   _____
7. *Prende il treno delle otto e venti, e arriva in ufficio per le nove.*_____
   _____

The Imperative Mood

The imperative is often called the command mood, but it is also used to make requests. When you request, ask, or demand something, you are using the imperative. The imperative verb forms are used to give orders or advice, to urge strongly, and to exhort. It is a simple tense and has only one form, the present.

The conjugations of the imperative mood are fairly easy to master. Simply provide the appropriate endings and place an exclamation mark at the end for emphasis. Note that there are only five forms of the imperative: *tu*, *Lei*, *noi*, *voi*, and *Loro*, because you must address someone other than yourself. The tricky thing is that some affirmative commands (do!) are different than negative commands (don't!).

Tu in the Imperative

The *tu* form (informal, singular) is perhaps the most widely used form of the command; you are more likely to use the imperative with somebody you know well. As the *tu* subject suggests, it is used to give a command to one person you know quite well and whom you would normally address informally.

Table 13-8
Affirmative *tu* Commands

–are verb	*–ere* verb	*–ire* verb	
Mangia! Eat!	*Rispondi!* Answer!	*Parti!* Leave!	

Table 13-9
Negative *tu* Commands

are verb	*–ere* verb	*–ire* verb	
Non mangiare! Don't eat!	*Non rispondere!* Don't answer!	*Non partire!* Don't leave!	

Note that the affirmative *tu* command endings of *–are* verbs are the same as the third person singular (*lui/lei/Le*) endings of the present tense *–are* verbs, and the affirmative *tu* command endings of *–ere* and *–ire* verbs are the same as the second person singular (*tu*) endings of the present tense *–ere* and *–ire* verbs.

ESSENTIAL

Remember that there are three moods in Italian: indicative (statements, what you might think of as the "regular" verb tenses), imperative (the command mood), and the subjunctive (a hypothetical mood, which you will look at in Chapter 15).

Whereas the affirmative *tu* commands actually have a conjugated form, the negative *tu* commands use the construction *non* + infinitive.

There are several verbs that have irregular conjugations—that is, they don't follow the rules outlined previously.

Table 13-10

Irregular *tu* Commands

Verb	English	Affirmative *tu* Command	Negative *tu* Command
andare	to go	*Va'!* or *Vai!*	*Non andare!*
avere	to have	*Abbi!*	*Non avere!*
dare	to give	*Da'!* or *Dai!*	*Non dare!*
dire	to say, to tell	*Di'!*	*Non dire!*
essere	to be	*Sii!*	*Non essere!*
fare	to make, to do	*Fa'!* or *Fai!*	*Non fare!*
stare	to be, to stay	*Sta'* or *Stai!*	*Non stare!*
tenere	to keep	*Tieni!*	*Non tenere!*
venire	to come	*Vieni!*	*Non venire!*

Exercise 13-4

Give the affirmative *tu* commands of the verb provided.

1. (*Mangiare*) _____ *la frutta!*
2. *Non* (*fare*) _____ *così!*
3. (*Prendere*) _____ *le chiavi!*
4. *Non* (*bere*) _____ *quel vino!*
5. (*Dire*) _____ *la verità!*
6. *Non* (*aprire*) _____ *la finestra!*

FACT

The pattern for the commands of *–ire/–isc* verbs (see Chapter 7) is as follows: *(Tu) Finisci!, (Lei) Finisca!, (Noi) Finiamo!, (Voi) Finite!, (Loro) Finiscano!*

Voi Commands

The *voi* command is used to address two or more people, or a group. As the subject suggests, it is an informal command. The *voi* command of *–are*, *–ere*, and *–ire* verbs are identical to the corresponding forms of the present tense.

Table 13-11

Affirmative *voi* Commands

–*are* verb	–*ere* verb	–*ire* verb	
Mangiate! Eat!	*Rispondete!* Answer!	*Partite!* Leave!	

Table 13-12

Negative *voi* Commands

–*are* verb	–*ere* verb	–*ire* verb
Non mangiate! Don't eat!	*Non rispondete* Don't answer!	*Non partite!* Don't leave!

Table 13-13

Irregular *voi* Commands

Verb	English	voi Command
avere	to have	*Abbiate!* (*Non abbiate!*)
essere	to be	*Siate!* (*Non siate!*)

TRACK 62

Repeat each command after it is read by the narrator to practice your pronunciation.

Andate via!	**Go away!**
Non parlate!	**Don't talk!**
Bevete l'acqua!	**Drink the water!**
Non scrivete!	**Don't write!**
Servite le lasagne!	**Serve the lasagna!**
Non offrite il caffè!	**Don't offer the coffee!**

FACT

Though there is a difference in the forms of the affirmative and negative *tu* commands, there is no difference in the spelling of the affirmative and negative forms of the *voi* command. Simply add the word *non* to the affirmative command to make it negative.

Lei and *Loro* Commands

The *Lei* (singular) and *Loro* (plural) commands are used in formal situations—with people you don't know, your elders, and in business situations. They are considered very polite; they're not so much commands as polite requests. The spelling does not change from affirmative to negative.

Table 13-14

Affirmative (and Negative) *Lei* Commands

–*are* verbs	–*ere* verbs	–*ire* verbs
Ascolti! (*Non ascolti!*)	Prenda! (*Non prenda!*)	Segua! (*Non segua!*)

Table 13-15

Affirmative (and Negative) Loro Commands

–*are* verbs	–*ere* verbs	–*ire* verbs
Ascoltino! (*Non ascoltino!*)	Prendano! (*Non prendano*)	Seguano! (*Non seguano!*)

Table 13-16

Verb	English	*Lei* Command	*Loro* Command
andare	to go	Vada!	Vadano!
avere	to have	Abbia!	Abbiano!
dare	to give	Dia!	Diano!
dire	to say, to tell	Dica!	Dicano!
essere	to be	Sia!	Siano!
fare	to make, to do	Faccia!	Facciano!
stare	to be, to stay	Stia!	Stiano!
tenere	to keep	Tenga!	Tengano!
venire	to come	Venga!	Vengano!

Abbi pazienza!	**Be patient!**
Entrino!	**Come in!**
Non stia qui!	**Don't stay here!**
Dia il libro a Giovanni!	**Give the book to Giovanni!**
Servano gli spaghetti!	**Serve the spaghetti!**
Offra aiuto al ragazzino!	**Offer help to the little boy!**

Noi Commands

In the *noi* form, the commands take on the meaning of the English "Let's . . . " *Andiamo!* means "Let's go!"; *Non parliamo!* means "Let's not talk!" The spelling of the *noi* commands—both affirmative and negative—is the same as the spelling of their corresponding present tense forms.

Table 13-17
***Noi* Commands**

–are verbs	*–ere* verbs	*–ire* verbs	
Andiamo!	*Prendiamo!*	*Dormiamo!*	

TRACK 63

Repeat each sentence after it is read by the narrator to practice your pronunciation.

Guardiamo un bel film!	**Let's watch a nice movie!**
Non andiamo in macchina, andiamo in treno!	**Let's not go by car, let's go by train!**
Scriviamo una lettera ai nonni!	**Let's write a letter to our grandparents!**
Offriamo un caffè al signore!	**Let's offer a coffee for the gentleman!**

ALERT

Please note that the *Lei*, *noi*, and *Loro* imperative forms look identical to the conjugations of the present tense of the subjunctive mood. For more on the subjunctive, see Chapter 15.

Object and Reflexive Pronouns with Commands

As you learned, object pronouns generally precede the verb:

Non ti capisco.	**I don't understand you.**
Vi abbiamo visti a teatro.	**We saw you at the theater.**
I ragazzi si svegliano tardi.	**The kids wake up late.**
Non la mangio.	**I'm not eating it.**

The rules governing the placement of object and reflexive pronouns with the imperative forms in Italian are a bit more complicated. In Italian, all object pronouns attach to the end of the *tu*, *noi*, and *voi* imperative forms and precede the *Lei* and *Loro* forms. The only exceptions are the indirect object pronouns *loro* and *Loro*, which always follow the verb.

Mangialo!	**Eat it!**
Leggetela!	**Read it!**
Svegliati!	**Wake up!**
Lo chiami! (you, singular, formal)	**Call him!**
Le mangino! (you, plural, formal)	**Eat them!**

When a command is used that only has one syllable (*Da'!, Di'!, Fa'!*), the first consonant of the object or reflexive pronoun is doubled (except when *gli* is used).

Dammi un po' di vino!	**Give me some wine!**
Fatti un caffè!	**Make yourself a coffee!**
Digli la verità!	**Tell him the truth!**

When using the negative *tu*, *noi*, and *voi* commands, object and reflexive pronouns may be placed either before or after the command.

Non lo fare! OR *Non farlo!*
Non le parliamo! OR *Non parliamole!*
Non vi alzate! OR *Non alzatevi!*

Exercise 13-5

Rewrite the commands substituting a pronoun (direct object or indirect object) for the object.

1. *Mangia il pane!*_____
2. *Leggete la rivista!*_____
3. *Da un po' di vino a me!*_____
4. *Di' la verità a tuo padre!*_____

5. *Non fare il compito!* _____

6. *Non parliamo a Maria!* _____

Exclamations

The dictionary defines an exclamation as an outcry, an emphatic utterance or saying, or a sudden expression of sound or words indicative of emotion. Exclamations don't necessarily have to be commands, but like commands, they are emphatic.

Table 13-18

Italian	English	Italian	English
Ma sei pazzo?	Are you crazy?	*Buon divertimento!*	Have a good time!
Stai zitto!	Be quiet!	*Buon Natale!*	Merry Christmas!
Auguri!	Best wishes!	*Che fortuna!*	How lucky!
Salute!	Cheers!	*Magari!*	I wish!
Complimenti!	Congratulations!	*Grazie mille!*	Thanks a million!
Figurati!	Don't mention it!	*Per carita!*	No way!
Non dire sciocchezze!	Don't talk nonsense!	*Basta!*	Enough!
In bocca al lupo!	Good luck!	*Bravo!/Brava!*	Well done!
Che casino!	What a mess!		

The words *che*, *come*, and *quanto* are often used in exclamations. The exclamation "What . . . !" is expressed in Italian with the help of the word *che*.

FACT

The expression *Che casino!*, though widely used, is considered vulgar. The word *casino* means whorehouse in Italian (not to be confused with the Italian word *casinò*, which is the equivalent to the English word casino). The expression means "What a whorehouse!" To put it more mildly, use the expression *Che macello!* or *Che pasticcio!* (both mean "What a mess!").

Table 13-19

Che	
Che bei fiori!	What beautiful flowers!
Che belle ragazze!	What beautiful girls!
Che buon'idea!	What a good idea!
Che partita!	What a game!
Che rumore!	What a noise!
Come and **Quanto**	
Come sei bello!	How handsome you are!
Come sei brava!	You're so good!
Quanto mangi!	You're eating so much!
Quanto dormono!	How much they sleep!
Quanto vino!	How much wine!
Quanta roba!	How much stuff!

The following examples contain some very useful expressions and exclamations:

Mamma mia! **My goodness!**

Italians use *Mamma mia!* to express surprise, impatience, happiness, sorrow, or any strong emotion.

Che bello! **How nice!**

Che bello! is used when you're enthusiastic about something.

Uffa! **Aargh!**

Uffa! is a clear way to show that you're annoyed, bored, angry, or fed up.

Che ne so! **How should I know?**

When Italians want to say that they have no idea, they shrug their shoulders and say *Che ne so!*

| *Magari!* | **If only!** |

Magari! is just one word, but it expresses a lot. It indicates a strong wish or hope. It's a good answer if, for instance, somebody asks you if you'd like to win the lottery.

| *Che macello!* | **What a mess!** |

Figuring out the derivation of *Che macello!* isn't difficult. The literal translation is "What a slaughterhouse!"

| *Mi raccomando!* | **Please, I beg you!** |

With *Mi raccomando!*, you express a special emphasis in asking for something. An example is *Mi raccomando, non dimeticare di telefonarmi!* (Please don't forget to call me!) Repeat each expression after it is read by the narrator to practice your pronunciation.

TRACK 64

Che bei fiori!	*Quanta roba!*
Che belle ragazze!	*Mamma mia!*
Che partita!	*Uffa!*
Come sei bello!	*Che ne so!*
Come sei brava!	*Magari!*
Quanto mangi!	*Che macello!*
Quanto dormono!	*Mi raccomando!*

CHAPTER 14

The Conditional Mode and Causative Constructions

This chapter delves deeper into Italian grammar by introducing the conditional mode and causative constructions. The conditional mode is used to express a hypothetical situation or an event that is contingent upon another set of circumstances. Both the conditional and causative constructions can be useful tools in developing your ability to speak and understand Italian. After we discuss these two points, we will move on to a discussion of some of the refined uses of verbs of perception (to hear, to see, etc.). Finally, we will discuss comparitives and superlatives.

The Present Conditional

The present conditional is used to express something that "would" happen. It corresponds to the English "would + verb," as in "I would go" or "They would come." The present conditional, like the simple future tense, is one word (verb stem + conditional ending). Verbs that have an irregular stem in the simple future tense have the same irregular stem in the present conditional.

Table 14-1

–are Verbs

	parlare (to speak)	*studiare* (to study)	*rispondere* (to respond)	
io	parlerei	studierei	risponderei	
tu	parleresti	studieresti	risponderesti	
lui/lei/Lei	parlerebbe	studierebbe	risponderebbe	
noi	parleremmo	studieremmo	risponderemmo	
voi	parlereste	studiereste	rispondereste	
loro/Loro	parlerebbero	studierebbero	risponderebbero	

Exercise 14-1

Conjugate the verb *leggere* (to read) in the present conditional.

1. *io* _____
2. *tu* _____
3. *lui* _____
4. *noi* _____
5. *voi* _____
6. *loro* _____

Table 14-2

–ire Verbs dormire (to sleep)

io dormirei	noi dormiremmo
tu dormiresti	voi dormireste
lui/lei/Lei dormirebbe	loro/Loro dormirebbero

Exercise 14-2

Conjugate the verb *partire* (to leave) in the present conditional.

1. *io* _____
2. *tu* _____
3. *lui* _____
4. *noi* _____
5. *voi* _____
6. *loro* _____

Verbs that have an irregular stem in the simple future tense have the same irregular stem in the present conditional.

Table 14-3
Irregular Verbs

	giocare	pagare	incominciare	bere	dare	fare
io	giocherei	pagherei	incomincerei	berrei	darei	farei
tu	giocheresti	pagheresti	incominceresti	berresti	daresti	faresti
lui, lei, Lei	giocherebbe	pagherebbe	incomincerebbe	berrebbe	darebbe	farebbe
noi	giocheremmo	pagheremmo	incominceremmo	berremmo	daremmo	faremmo
voi	giochereste	paghereste	incomincereste	berreste	dareste	fareste
loro, Loro	giocherebbero	pagherebbero	incomincerebbero	berrebbero	darebbero	farebbero
	stare	andare	dovere	volere	volere	
io	starei	andrei	dovrei	vorrei	vorrei	
tu	staresti	andresti	dovresti	vorresti	vorresti	
lui, lei, Lei	starebbe	andrebbe	dovrebbe	vorrebbe	vorrebbe	
noi	staremmo	andremmo	dovremmo	vorremmo	vorremmo	
voi	stareste	andreste	dovreste	vorreste	vorreste	
loro, Loro	starebbero	andrebbero	dovrebbero	vorrebbero	vorrebbero	

Berresti del vino?	**Would you drink some wine?**
Saremmo contenti poi!	**Then we'd be happy!**
Lui verrebbe con noi.	**He would come with us.**
Non avrei niente da fare.	**I wouldn't have anything to do.**
Faresti meglio a deciderti presto.	**You'd be better off deciding soon.**

Exercise 14-3

Conjugate the following irregular verbs into the present conditional.

	potere	*vedere*
io	_____	_____
tu	_____	_____
lui, lei, Lei	_____	_____
noi	_____	_____
voi	_____	_____
loro, Loro	_____	_____

The present conditional is used to express the potential for something to happen based on the condition of something else taking place. Repeat each sentence after it is read by the narrator to practice your pronunciation.

TRACK 65

Parlerei con il mio capo.	**I would speak to my boss (if he were in the office today).**
Andrei in Italia.	**I would go to Italy (if I had the money).**
Loro verrebbero stasera, ma non hanno trovato un babysitter.	**They would come tonight, but they didn't find a babysitter.**
Io mangerei del gelato, ma non c'è ne più.	**I would eat some ice cream, but there isn't any more.**

The Conditional Perfect

The conditional perfect is used to describe an action that would have taken place but did not. The conditional perfect is a compound tense that is formed by pairing the present conditional of the verbs *avere* or *essere* with the past participle of the main verb.

Table 14-4
Present Conditional of *Avere* and *Essere*

	avere	*essere*
io	avrei	sarei
tu	avresti	saresti
lui/lei/Lei	avrebbe	sarebbe
noi	avremmo	saremmo
voi	avreste	sareste
loro/Loro	avrebbero	sarebbero

TRACK 66

Loro sarebbero andati in Italia, ma non avevano i soldi.	**They would have gone to Italy, but they didn't have money.**
Io avrei mangiato il gelato, ma non ce n'era più.	**I would have eaten ice cream, but there wasn't any.**

The Conditional with Pronouns

The placement of the direct, indirect, and reflexive object pronouns is the same with the conditional as it is with all other verbs. The pronoun precedes the conjugated form of the verb. When a conjugated verb is followed by an infinitive, the pronoun can attach to the end of the infinitive.

Non mi capiresti.	**You wouldn't understand me.**
Si divertirebbe parecchio.	**He would enjoy himself a lot.**
Le parlerei volentieri.	**I would gladly speak to her.**
Non vorrei vederla.	**I wouldn't want to see her.**

In the conditional perfect, when the direct object pronouns *lo*, *la*, *li*, and *le* are used, the last letter of the past participle must agree in number and gender with those of the direct object pronoun. Agreement with the remaining direct object pronouns is optional.

Li avrei letti.	**I would have read them.**
Non l'avrebbero mangiata.	**They wouldn't have eaten it.**
Non vi avrei visti (or visto).	**I wouldn't have seen you.**

Different Uses of the Conditional and the Conditional Perfect

The present conditional corresponds to the English "would + verb." The conditional perfect corresponds to the English "would have + verb." It is important to be aware of exactly how you're using the word "would" because it is often used to relate an imperfect or past action.

Ogni sabato io andavo (habitual action = imperfect) *al cinema con mio fratello.*

Every Saturday I would go to the movies with my brother.

ESSENTIAL

The conditional tense also appears in if/then constructions that are posed in the past tense. For instance, in English you would say, "If I had the money, I would take a trip to Italy." In Italian, you would use the conditional for the "then" clause: *Se avessi i soldi, farei un viaggio in Italia.*

The conditional is also used to express a future action when it is introduced by verbs of saying, telling, promising, informing, and knowing (i.e., *dire, promettere, sapere*).

Davide ha promesso che avrebbe telefonato alle dieci.

Davide promised that he would call at ten.

Avete detto che ci avreste pensato voi.

You said that you'd take care of it.

The conditional can also be used to express a hypothesis or a rumor, often on television news or in newspapers:

Il presidente sarebbe in ospedale dal 18 del mese.

The president has supposedly been in the hospital since the 18th of this month.

The idiomatic expression *faresti meglio a* + verb translates as "you had better." For example, *faresti meglio a smettere di fumare* means "you had better quit smoking."

Dovere, *Potere*, and *Volere* in the Conditional

The present conditional of the three modal verbs (*dovere*, *potere*, and *volere*) is often used in polite conversation.

Table 14-5

Present		Conditional	
Puoi aiutarmi?	Can you help me?	*Potresti aiutarmi?*	Could you help me?
Voglio una bistecca.	I want a steak.	*Vorrei una bistecca.*	I would like a steak.
Devi venire.	You have to come.	*Dovresti venire.*	You should come.

ALERT

Be polite! When ordering food in a restaurant, it is considered polite to use the conditional when telling the waiter what you would like: *Vorrei gli spaghetti alla carbonara.* Using the present tense in this situation (*Voglio gli spaghetti alla carbonara*) may come across as impolite.

Exercise 14-4

Underline the verb conjugation that is in the present conditional.

1. *noi beviamo, loro berranno, io berrei*
2. *loro farebbero, lui farà, loro fanno*
3. *noi saremo, noi saremmo, io ero*
4. *tu dirai, lei diceva, io direi*
5. *loro puliscono, tu puliresti, voi pulirete*

Exercise 14-5

Fill in the blanks with the correct form of the verb in the present conditional.

1. *Marco* _____ *la mancia al cameriere, ma è al verde.* (to give)
2. *Che cosa* _____ *tuo padre?* (to think)
3. *Noi* _____ *un arrosto di vitello.* (to want)
4. *Loro* _____ *alle otto, se avessero i biglietti.* (to leave)
5. *Mio figlio* _____ *presto.* (to wake up)

Exercise 14-6

Rewrite each sentence, changing the verb from the present tense to the conditional perfect.

1. *Voi non dovete mangiare prima delle otto.* _____
   _____
2. *Anna e Carlo aiutano il figlio.* _____
   _____
3. *Mi vesto in fretta.* _____
4. *Gaetano mangia gli spaghetti.* _____
5. *Tu e Marcello tornate presto.* _____

ALERT

There's a subtle spelling difference between the first person plural (*noi*) forms of the future and conditional tenses. *Noi andremo in Italia* is the future tense. *Noi andremmo in Italia* is the conditional. Be careful—the spelling and pronunciation is slightly different!

Causative Constructions

As its name suggests, in a causative construction something causes something else to happen. In a non-causative statement, the subject performs the action. In a causative statement, the subject has someone or something else perform the action.

Non-Causative Statement

> *Gianni ripara la macchina.*   **Gianni fixes the car.**

Causative Statement

> *Gianni fa riparare la macchina.*   **Gianni has the car repaired.**

In a causative construction the verb *fare* is followed by an infinitive. In addition to expressing the idea of causing something to happen, the causative construction can also be used to express the idea of making someone do or make something. When there is one object in a causative construction, that object is a direct object.

> *Faccio leggere gli studenti.*   **I make the students read.**
> *Il capo fa lavorare gli impiegati.* **The boss makes the employees work.**
> *Non fate entrare il cane!*   **Don't let the dog in!**
> *Abbiamo fatto fare quella sedia.*   **We had that chair made.**

FACT

When written in their non-conjugated forms (*fare* + infinitive), the final *e* of the verb *fare* is omitted for pronunciation purposes. One would say *far lavare,* instead of *fare lavare.*

With causative constructions, word order can be tricky. When the object is a noun, it must follow the infinitive form of the verb.

> *Marco fa lavare la macchina.*   **Marco is having his car washed.**

However, when the object is a pronoun, the pronoun must precede the conjugated verb *fare.*

> *Marco la fa lavare.*   **NOT** *Marco fa lavarla.*   **Marco is having it washed.**
>
> *Marco l'ha fatta lavare.* **NOT** *Marco ha fatto lavarla.* **Marco had it washed.**

Non lo fate entrare!	**NOT** *Non fate entrarlo.*	**Don't let him in!**
Il capo li fa lavorare.	**NOT** *Il capo fa lavorarli.*	**The boss makes them work.**
Vi ho fatto partire in ritardo.	**NOT** *Ho fatto partirvi in ritardo.*	**I made you leave late.**

When the infinitive, gerund, past participle, or the second-person imperative of *fare* is used, the object pronoun is attached to that form.

Ha sbagliato a farvi partire in ritardo.	**He made a mistake in making you leave late.**
Facendovi partire in ritardo, si è sentito male.	**He felt bad, having made you leave late.**

It is possible for a causative construction to have two objects. In these cases, the person being made to do something becomes the indirect object of the verb and is introduced by the preposition *a*. The object upon which the action of the verb is being performed is the direct object.

Table 14-6

One Object	Two Objects
Marco fa lavare la macchina.	*Marco fa lavare la macchina a suo figlio.*
Faccio leggere gli studenti.	*Faccio leggere l'articolo agli studenti.*
Elena ha fatto aprire la porta.	*Elena ha fatto aprire la porta a Caterina.*

When either or both of the objects is stated as a pronoun, the object pronoun precedes the conjugated form of the verb *fare*. In causative constructions, if the indirect object pronoun is *loro* or *Loro*, the pronoun must follow the infinitive. *Faccio leggere loro i compiti* (I make them read the assignments.). Sometimes the exact meaning of the indirect object introduced by the preposition *a* can be ambiguous. To avoid this ambiguity, the preposition *da* can be used in place of *a* to introduce the indirect object.

Hai fatto restituire le chiavi a Mario.	**I had the keys returned to Mario. OR I had Mario return the keys.**

This ambiguity can be cleared up with the preposition *da*.

Hai fatto restituire le chiavi da Mario.　**I had Mario return the keys.**

FACT

Though it may appear awkward, the expression *far fare* is acceptable and grammatically correct. It can be used to express the action of having something made or done. *Faccio fare i compiti ai ragazzi* means "I'm having the kids do the homework."

Common Causative Expressions

The following list highlights some commonly used causative expressions.

Table 14-7

far arrabbiare	to make someone angry	*far pagare*	to charge
far aspettare	to make someone wait	*far saltare*	to blow up something
far capire	to make someone understand	*far sapere*	to inform
far crescere	to grow something	*far uscire*	to let out
far entrare	to let in	*far vedere*	to show
far fare	to make someone do something	*farsi vedere*	to show one's face
far impazzire	to make someone crazy		

Reflexive Verbs in Causative Constructions

The reflexive verb *farsi* can be used in causative constructions when the subject of the sentence is having something done or made to or for himself or herself. When *farsi* is used in a causative construction, the following word order is used:

farsi + infinitive of verb + noun object + da (someone)

Ti fai tagliare i capelli dal barbiere.　**You are having your hair cut by the barber.**

Mio zio si fa costruire una nuova casa al mare.	**My uncle is having a new house built (for himself) at the beach.**
Le signore si faranno fare tre gonne.	**The women are having three skirts made for themselves.**

With *farsi*, the direct object pronoun always follows the reflexive pronoun, and the spelling rules of the double object pronouns apply.

Te li fai tagliare dal barbiere.	**You are having them cut by the barber.**
Mio zio se la fa costruire al mare.	**My uncle is having it built at the beach.**
Le signore se ne faranno fare tre.	**The women are having three of them made for themselves.**

Farsi is also used to express the idea of making or getting oneself something. For example, "I made myself understood" or "You get yourself invited to the party."

Mi faccio capire?	**Am I making myself understood?**
Perché non ti fai sentire ogni tanto?	**Why don't you get in touch (literally, make yourself heard) every now and then?**

FACT

In Italian the verb *costruire* means "to build." The verb *far costruire* means to have something built. Unless you're a general contractor, the latter will probably be more useful!

When the reflexive verb *farsi* is used in a compound tense (*passato prossimo*, past conditional, *futuro anteriore*, for example), the auxiliary verb *essere* is used.

Table 14-8

Simple Tense	Compound Tense
Mi faccio tagliare i capelli dal barbiere.	Mi sono fatto tagliare i capelli dal barbiere.
Mio zio si farà costruire una nuova casa al mare.	Mio zio si sarà fatto costruire una nuova casa al mare.
Le signore si farebbero fare tre nuove gonne.	Le signore si sarebbero fatte fare tre nuove gonne.

We've seen that the reflexive verb *farsi* can be used to express the idea of having something done for oneself by someone else. But what happens when the infinitive verb that follows the conjugated form of the verb *fare* is also reflexive? In cases where the infinitive is reflexive, the reflexive pronoun is omitted. Have a look at the following examples:

Table 14-9

Non-Causative Construction	Causative Construction
I bambini si svegliano presto.	Faccio svegliare i bambini presto. (NOT *Faccio svegliarsi i bambini presto.*)
Carlo si arrabbia facilmente.	Faccio arrabbiare Carlo facilmente. (NOT *Faccio arrabbiarsi Carlo facilmente.*)

Allowing and Perceiving

Two constructions are very similar to causative constructions. One—*lasciare* + verb infinitive—expresses that the subject allowed something to happen rather than explicitly causing it to occur. The other—verb of perception + verb infinitive—expresses the sensations your five senses experience.

Lasciare + Infinitive

Lasciare (to allow, to let, to permit) followed by an infinitive is used to express the English "let + verb," as in "The professor let me leave early." Note that the structure of the causative constructions (*fare* + infinitive) is similar. The difference is that *fare* + infinitive carries the meaning of making someone do something, whereas *lasciare* + infinitive carries the meaning of allowing someone to do something.

Table 14-10

Fare + infinitive	Lasciare + infinitive
Il professore mi ha fatto partire presto. (The professor made me leave early.)	Il professore mi ha lasciato partire presto. (The professor let me leave early.)

As with the causative *fare* + infinitive, a noun object must follow the infinitive, but a pronoun (direct object, indirect object, or reflexive) must precede the conjugated form of *lasciare*. When the infinitive, gerund, past participle, or second-person imperative of *lasciare* is used, the object pronoun is attached to that form.

Ha sbagliato a lasciarvi partire in ritardo.	**He made a mistake in letting you leave late.**
Lasciandovi partire in ritardo, si è sentito male.	**He felt bad, having let you leave late.**

As with *fare* + infinitive, if the verb following *lasciare* is reflexive, the reflexive pronoun is omitted.

Non ti lascio alzare perché stai male.	**I won't let you get up because you're not feeling well.**

It is possible for the *lasciare* + infinitive construction to have two objects. In these cases, the person being allowed to do something becomes the indirect object of the verb, and is introduced by the preposition *a*. The object upon which the action of the verb is being performed is the direct object.

Table 14-11

One Object	Two Objects
Marco lascia lavare la macchina.	Marca lascia lavare la macchina a suo figlio.
Lascio leggere gli studenti.	Lascio leggere l'articolo agli studenti.
Elena ha lasciato aprire la porta.	Elena ha lasciato aprire la porta a Caterina.

When either one or both of the objects is stated as a pronoun, the object pronoun precedes the conjugated form of the verb *lasciare*.

Table 14-12

Marco lascia lavare la macchina a suo figlio.	*Marco la lascia lavare a suo figlio.*	*Marco gli lascia lavare la macchina.*
Lascio leggere l'articolo agli studenti.	*Lo lascio leggere agli studenti.*	*Gli lascio leggere l'articolo.*
Elena ha lasciato aprire la porta a Caterina.	*Elena l'ha lasciata aprire a Caterina.*	*Elena le ha lasciato aprire la porta.*

Verbs of Perception + Infinitive

I saw him studying in the library. He saw her crying. I hear the children playing. To express these ideas in Italian, the verb of perception is followed directly by an infinitive.

L'ho visto studiare in biblioteca.	**I saw him studying in the library.**
L'ha vista piangere.	**He saw her crying.**
Sento i bambini giocare.	**I hear the children playing.**

Object placement is similar to that of *fare* + infinitive and *lasciare* + infinitive. Noun objects must follow the infinitive.

Ho visto partire la nave.	**I saw the ship leaving.**
Ho sentito dire.	**I've heard it said.**

FACT

The Italian verb *sentire* means "to hear." The expression *sentir dire* has a slightly different meaning. It means "to hear a rumor" or "to hear a report."

If the infinitive has it's own object, then the word order changes slightly.

Ho sentito Lorenzo suonare il pianoforte.	**I heard Lorenzo playing the piano.**
Ho guardato il pollo attraversare la strada.	**I watched the chicken cross the road.**

Comparisons

Bigger than. Wider than. Better than. These are just a few terms we use in English to compare something to something else. In Italian, we have to consider comparisons of inequality or comparisons of equality. The comparisons of inequality (more than, less than, –er than) are expressed with the following terms:

più . . . di (more than) or *più . . . che* (more than)
meno . . . di (less than) or *meno . . . che* (less than)

Both *più . . . di* (more than) and *meno . . . di* (less than) are used when two persons or things are compared in terms of one quality or level of ability.

Giovanni ha più amici di Stefano.	**Giovanni has more friends than Stefano.**
Giovanni è più simpatico di Stefano.	**Giovanni is nicer than Stefano.**
Giovanni è meno felice di Stefano.	**Giovanni is less happy than Stefano.**
L'Australia è più grande dell'Italia.	**Australia is bigger than Italy.**

Più . . . di (more than) and *meno . . . di* (less than) are also used before numbers.

Ho meno di quaranta dollari.	**I have less than forty dollars.**
Hai fatto più di dieci errori.	**You made more than ten mistakes.**

Both *più . . . che* (more than) and *meno . . . che* (less than) are used when two adjectives, adverbs, or verbs are compared in relation to the same subject.

Giovanni è più bello che intelligente.	**Giovanni is more handsome than intelligent.**
Mi piace più nuotare che sciare.	**I like swimming more than skiing.**
Caterina mangia più verdure che carne.	**Caterina eats more vegetables than meat.**

Irregular Comparatives

The adjectives *buono*, *cattivo*, *grande*, and *piccolo* have both regular and irregular comparative forms.

Table 14-13

Adjective	Regular Comparative	Irregular Comparative
buono	più buono	migliore
cattivo	più cattivo	peggiore
grande	più grande	maggiore
piccolo	più piccolo	minore

The regular and irregular forms of the comparative are interchange-able in some contexts, but not in others. As a general rule, the regular forms are used to describe size and character traits, whereas the irregular forms are used to express opinions about less tangible qualities, such as skill or ability.

Mio fratello più piccolo si chiama Marco.	**My smaller brother's name is Marco.**
Mio fratello minore si chiama Marco.	**My younger brother's name is Marco.**

The adverbs *bene*, *male*, *molto*, and *poco* have irregular comparative forms.

Table 14-14

Adverb	Irregular Comparative
bene	meglio
male	peggio
molto	più, di più
poco	meno, di meno

Marco canta meglio di Luigi.	**Marco sings better than Luigi.**
Marisa dorme più che studia.	**Marisa sleeps more than she studies.**

Comparisons of Equality

The comparisons of equality are used to express the same quality when comparing two nouns, adjectives, or adverbs. Comparisons of equality (as . . . as) are expressed with *così . . . come* and *tanto . . . quanto*. *Così* and *tanto* are placed before the adjective or adverb, and *come* and *quanto* are placed after the adjective or adverb.

Marco è così intelligente come Angela.	**Marco is as intelligent as Angela.**
Nuotare è tanto difficile quanto sciare.	**Swimming is as difficult as skiing.**

Italians commonly omit *così* and *tanto* when comparing two nouns.

Davide studia quanto Filippo.	**Davide studies as much as Filippo.**
Elena è bella come un fiore.	**Elena is as beautiful as a flower.**

Tanto + noun + *quanto* is used to express the English "as much + noun + as" or "as many + noun + as." Since *tanto* is being used as an adjective, it must agree in number and gender with the noun that follows.

Ho tanta pazienza quanto te.	**I have as much patience as you.**
Voi avete tanti amici quanto loro.	**You have as many friends as them.**

Exercise 14-7

Underline the correct comparative term.

1. *Marco canta (meglio di/quanto di) Luigi.*
2. *Marco è così intelligente (tanto/come) Angela.*
3. *Nuotare è tanto difficile (così/quanto) sciare.*
4. *Elena è bella (come/meglio) un fiore.*
5. *Ho tanta pazienza (quanto/tanta) te.*

Superlatives

Superlatives are adjectives and adverbs used to describe something to an extreme or unsurpassable extent. The tallest building and the greatest singer are examples of superlatives in English. In Italian, there are two types of superlatives: relative superlatives and absolute superlatives.

Relative Superlatives

The relative superlative (the . . . –est, the most . . . , the least . . .) is formed in the following manner: definite article + noun + *più* (or *meno*) + adjective or adverb.

il ragazzo più simpatico	**the nicest guy**
gli studenti meno pigri	**the least lazy students**

In English the superlative is often followed by a qualifying prepositional phrase introduced by "in." In Italian, the preposition *di* is used.

Marcello è lo studente più intelligente della classe.	**Marcello is the most intelligent student in the class.**

When using the qualifying prepositional phrase introduced by *di*, the noun is understood and is therefore often omitted from the construction.

Elena è la più bella di tutte le sorelle.	**Elena is the most beautiful of all the sisters.**
Il Chianti è il più conosciuto dei vini toscani.	**Chianti is the most known of the Tuscan wines.**

When using the superlative in front of an adverb, the definite article is often omitted, unless the qualifying word *possibile* follows the adverb.

Marcello studia più diligentemente di tutti.	**Marcello studies more diligently than everyone.**
Il ragazzo studia il più diligentemente possibile.	**The boy studies as diligently as possible.**

Irregular Superlatives

The adjectives *buono*, *cattivo*, *grande*, and *piccolo* have both regular and irregular comparative forms.

Table 14-15

Adjective	Regular Superlative	Irregular Superlative
buono	*il più buono*	*il migliore*
cattivo	*il più cattivo*	*il peggiore*
grande	*il più grande*	*il maggiore*
piccolo	*il più piccolo*	*il minore*

In the table, the masculine singular definite article (*il*) is given. *La*, *le*, and *i* are also used, depending on the number and gender of the noun being modified. The irregular comparatives *migliore* and *peggiore* may drop the final *e* before words beginning with a vowel or a consonant (except s + consonant, or z).

FACT

As with the regular and irregular forms of the comparative, the regular and irregular superlatives are interchangeable in some contexts. As a general rule, the regular forms are used to describe size and character traits, whereas the irregular forms are used to express opinions about less tangible qualities, such as skill or ability.

Elena è la mia miglior amica.	**Elena is my best friend.**
Matteo è il più piccolo dei tre fratelli.	**Matteo is the smallest of the three brothers.**

The Absolute Superlative

The absolute superlative expresses an extreme degree of something without comparison. In English this is indicated by placing words such as very and extremely before an adjective.

The pizza is very good!   It is exceptionally cold outside!

In Italian, there are three ways of forming the absolute superlative. The first and perhaps most common is to add a modifier—*molto, troppo,* or *assai*—before an adjective or adverb.

È arrivato molto tardi.	**He arrived very late.**
Giovanni e Marco sono molto simpatici.	**Giovanni and Marco are very nice.**
Il signor Gates è assai ricco!	**Mr. Gates is very rich!**

The second is formed by dropping the last vowel of the adjective and adding *–issimo, –issima, –issimi,* or *–issime,* or by dropping the final vowel of an adverb and adding *–issimo.*

La pizza è buonissima!	**The pizza is very good!**
La moto andava velocissimo!	**The motorcycle was going very fast!**

FACT

Adjectives that end in *–co/–ca* or *–go/–ga* add an *h* before the *–issimo/a* ending to maintain the hard consonant sound. Adjectives with an unstressed second-to-last syllable like *vecchio* drop the final vowel before adding the *–issimo/a/i/e* endings.

The adjectives *buono* and *cattivo* have both regular and irregular absolute superlatives.

Table 14-16

Adjective	Regular Absolute Superlative	Irregular Absolute Superlative
buono	*molto buono/buonissimo*	*ottimo*
cattivo	*molto cattivo/cattivissimo*	*pessimo*

The irregular forms *ottimo* and *pessimo* are used most often to describe skills and qualities of individuals and the material qualities of objects.

Giovanni è un ottimo falegname,   **Giovanni is a very good carpenter,**
ma usa materiali di pessima qualità.   **but he uses materials of the**
     poorest quality.

The last way to form the absolute superlative is to do so by repeating the adjective or adverb.

Lei parla piano piano.   **She speaks very softly.**
È un ragazzo buono buono.   **He's a very good boy.**

Exercise 14-8: Superlatives

Provide the Italian form of the term in parentheses.

1. *È arrivato* _____. (very late)
2. *Elena è la mia* _____. (best friend)
3. *Matteo è* _____ *dei tre fratelli.* (the smallest)
4. *Giovanni e Marco sono* _____. (very nice)
5. *Il signor Gates è* _____! (very rich)
6. *La pizza è* _____! (very good)
7. *La moto andava* _____! (very fast)
8. *Giovanni è un* _____ *falegname, ma usa materiali di* _____ *qualità.* (very good, very bad)
9. *Lei parla* _____. (very slow)
10. *È un ragazzo* _____. (very good)

CHAPTER 15

The *Passato Remoto* and the Subjunctive

The remote past tense (*il passato remoto*) is used mainly in literature to describe historical events that are distant from the present. This trend seems to be slowly fading, as younger Italians tend to prefer the *passato prossimo* in spoken Italian. The subjunctive is used much more liberally in Italian than in English. In English, we say, "If I were rich, I would buy a Ferrari." The "If I were . . . " is the subjunctive. In Italian, the subjunctive is used to express personal feelings, possibility, or doubt.

The *Passato Remoto*

Il passato remoto (the remote past) is used in writing, especially in Italian literature. It is used to describe events that happened in the past and is often used with the imperfect just as the *passato prossimo* is. Although you can get away without using it in spoken Italian, you certainly need to be able to recognize it and understand it since you're bound to come across it at some point.

Formation

The *passato remoto* is a simple tense and is formed by one word. For *–are* verbs, drop the infinitive ending and add one of these personal endings to the root.

Table 15-1

–are Verb Endings for the *Passato Remoto*

Subject	Ending
io	–ai
tu	–asti
lui/lei/Lei	–ò
noi	–ammo
voi	–aste
loro/Loro	–arono

Table 15-2

The Verb *parlare* in the *Passato Remoto*

io parlai	noi parlammo
tu parlasti	voi parlaste
lui parlò	loro, Loro parlarono

For *–ere* verbs, drop the infinitive ending and add these personal endings to the root.

Table 15-3

–ere Verb Endings for the *Passato Remoto*

Subject	Ending	Subject	Ending
io	–ei	noi	–emmo
tu	–esti	voi	–este
lui/lei/Lei	–é	loro/Loro	–erono

FACT

Many regular –*ere* verbs have an alternative form in the first-person singular (*io*), third-person singular (*lui/lei/Lei*), and third-person plural forms (*loro/Loro*) of the *passato remoto* tense.

Table 15-4
Alternative –*ere* Conjugations

Subject	Regular	Irregular
io	*ricevei*	*ricevetti*
tu	*ricevesti*	
lui/lei/Lei	*ricevé*	*ricevette*
noi	*ricevemmo*	
voi	*riceveste*	
loro/Loro	*riceverono*	*ricevettero*

Table 15-5

TRACK 67

io ricevei	*lui ricevé*	*loro riceverono*
io ricevetti	*lui ricevette*	*loro ricevettero*

For –*ire* verbs, drop the infinitive ending and add these personal endings to the root.

Table 15-6
–*ire* Verb Endings for the *Passato Remoto*

Subject	Ending
io	–*ii*
tu	–*isti*
lui/lei/Lei	-*ì*
noi	–*immo*
voi	–*iste*
loro, Loro	–*irono*

Exercise 15-1

Conjugate the verb *capire* in the *passato remoto*.

1. *io* _____   4. *noi* _____
2. *tu* _____   5. *voi* _____
3. *lui* _____   6 *loro* _____

The *Passato Remoto* Tense of Irregular Verbs

Bere, *dare*, *dire*, *fare*, and *stare* are five common verbs that have irregular conjugations in the *passato remoto* tense.

Table 15-7

	bere	dare	dire	fare	stare
io	bevvi	diedi	dissi	feci	stetti
tu	bevesti	desti	dicesti	facesti	stesti
lui/lei/Lei	bevve	diede	disse	fece	stette
noi	bevemmo	demmo	dicemmo	facemmo	stemmo
voi	beveste	deste	diceste	faceste	steste
loro/Loro	bevvero	diedero	dissero	fecero	stettero

The following verbs are irregular only in the *io*, *lei*, and *loro* forms in the *passato remoto* tense. To conjugate these verbs, add –*i*, –*e*, or –*ero* to the irregular stems for the *io*, *lei*, and *loro* forms. The irregular stems are given.

Table 15-8

Verb	Irregular stem	Verb	Irregular stem
chiedere	chies–	rispondere	rispos–
chiudere	chius–	rompere	rupp–
conoscere	conobbi–	sapere	sepp–
decidere	decis–	scrivere	scriss–
leggere	less–	vedere	vid–
mettere	mis–	venire	venn–
nascere	nacqu–	vivere	viss–
prendere	pres–	volere	voll–

Exercise 15-2

Conjugate the verb *leggere* in the *passato remoto*.

1. *io* _____   4. *noi* _____
2. *tu* _____   5. *voi* _____
3. *lui* _____   6. *loro* _____

Here are a few examples of how the *passato remoto* tense is used in Italian:

Il mio nonno partí per l' America nel 1919.	**My grandfather left for America in 1919.**
Cristoforo Colombo scoprí il nuovo mondo nel 1492.	**Christopher Columbus discovered the New World in 1492.**
Michelangelo nacque nel 1475.	**Michelangelo was born in 1475.**

The *Trapassato Remoto*

Also used in literature, *il trapassato remoto* (known in English as the preterite perfect) is a compound tense formed with the *passato remoto* of the auxiliary verb *avere* or *essere* and the past participle of the verb. *Avere* and *essere* are both irregular in the *passato remoto* tense.

TRACK 68

Table 15-9

Avere* and *Essere* in the *Passato Remoto

	avere	essere
io	ebbi	fui
tu	avesti	fosti
lui/lei/Lei	ebbe	fu
noi	avemmo	fummo
voi	aveste	foste
loro/Loro	ebbero	furono

The *trapassato remoto* is only used in subordinate clauses that are introduced by expressions of time like *appena* (as soon as), *dopo che* (after), *finché non* (until), *come* (as), or *quando* (when) and only when the verb in the main clause is in the *passato remoto*.

Lucia risposi alla lettera che ebbe ricevuto qualche mese prima.	**Lucia responded to the letter that she received a few months earlier.**
Partirono dopo che Maria fu arrivata.	**They left after Maria arrived.**
Elena andò in Italia quando ebbe ricevuto la notizia.	**Elena went to Italy when she heard the news.**

FACT

A *scioglilingua* is a tongue twister. Can you master this one? Can you find the verbs in the *passato remoto* tense? *Apelle figlio d'Apollo fece una palla di pelle di pollo; tutti i pesci vennero a galla per vedere la palla di pelle di pollo, fatta da Apelle, figlio d'Apollo.*

Passato Remoto or Imperfetto?

Knowing when to use the *passato prossimo* or the *imperfetto* can be tricky. The *passato remoto*, like the *passato prossimo*, can be used in combination with the *imperfetto* to express an action that was completed (*passato remoto*) when another action was taking place (*imperfetto*). You may see certain adverbs of time, which are a good indicator that the *passato remoto* or the *passato prossimo* should be used, such as the following:

Table 15-10
Adverbs of Time

ieri	yesterday	*un anno fa*	a year ago
ieri sera	yesterday evening	*lunedì, martedì, ecc.*	Monday, Tuesday, etc.
la settimana scorsa	last week	*l'anno scorso*	last year
due mesi fa	two months ago		

As we know, the *passato remoto* is used mainly for actions that happened in the distant past or in literature. So instead of *ieri* (yesterday), you may see the expression *cinquant'anni fa* (fifty years ago).

The *imperfetto* is used to describe a habitual or ongoing action in the past. It is also used to describe physical and emotional states in the past. It is likely that you will see the following vague indicators of time being used with the *imperfetto* tense.

Table 15-11
Indicators of Time

molti anni fa	many years ago
di solito	usually
sempre	always
una volta	some time ago, once
il lunedì, il martedì, ecc.	Mondays, Tuesdays, etc.

Giovanni andava al supermercato il sabato.	**Giovanni used to go to the supermarket on Saturdays.**
Giovanni è andato al supermercato sabato scorso.	**Giovanni went to the supermarket last Saturday.**
Nel 1975 andammo a Roma. Mio padre non venne con noi perché si sentiva male.	**We went to Rome in 1975. My father didn't come with us because he wasn't feeling well.**
Gli diedi la mano mentre usciva.	**I shook hands with him while I was walking out.**
Telefonarono ai genitori perché avevano bisogno di aiuto.	**They called their parents because they needed help.**

This is a *scioglilingua* (tounge-twister). It will be difficult, but listen to the track and give it a try!

Apelle figlio d'Apollo fece una palla di pelle di pollo; tutti i pesci vennero a galla per vedere la palla di pelle di pollo, fatta da Apelle, figlio d'Apollo.

TRACK 69

Apelle, son of Apollo, made a ball of the skin of a chicken; all of the fish came to the surface to see the ball made of the skin of a chicken, made by Apelle, son of Apollo.

The Subjunctive

The subjunctive can be elusive. It is difficult to tell when and where it is required. It is used to express "what might be" or "what ought to be." This mood is different from the indicative mood (used to express fact) in that it allows expression of doubt, desire, emotion, impersonal opinion, and uncertainty. Native speakers of Italian employ the subjunctive naturally. For many students of Italian, mastering the subjunctive is often the final piece in gaining full proficiency in the language.

Subjunctive Tenses

The subjunctive mood in Italian has four tenses: *presente* (present), *imperfetto* (imperfect), *passato* (perfect past), and *trapassato* (pluperfect past). The *presente* and the *imperfect* tenses are simple tenses (one word), and the *passato* and *trapassato* tenses are compound tenses (auxiliary verb + past participle).

When to Use the Subjunctive

Correct use of the subjunctive is not left as a free choice. It has to be used when the sentence expresses one of the following situations:

Uncertainty, doubt, or possibility
- I'm not sure he can come. (He will come or he will not.)
- We doubt it is true. (It may be true or false.)
- It's possible she is telling the truth. (She may or may not be telling the truth.)

Personal Opinion, Judgment, Comments, Remarks, or Denial
- I think he is studying French. (I think, but it may or may not be true.)
- It is better that you don't know. (This is an opinion.)
- They say it's a good idea. (This is an opinion.)
- It is unfair that they blame you for this. (This is an opinion.)
- They deny that it is true. (This is a denial.)

Wishes, Hopes, or Desires
- I want them to come. (It is my wish.)
- We hope you can stay. (It is our wish.)

Orders or Demands
- I demand that you leave.
- He wants you to return.

Joy, Sorrow, Surprise, Fear, or Anger
- I am happy you showed up.
- They fear he won't show up.
- I'm surprised she arrived early.

The subjunctive mood is needed for the verbs in the subordinate clauses, which are most often introduced by a conjunction (that, if, what, whether, despite, provided that, etc.). In each of the previous examples, the verb does not indicate something that has happened or that is in progress. Instead, it indicates a desire or a wish, or to a supposition or opinion. Each action, despite the speaker's expectations or desires, may still not take place.

Whenever there is a possibility that a statement may or may not be true, the subjunctive mood is required. This is the fundamental difference between the indicative (used to express fact) and the subjunctive (used to express feelings, volition, uncertainty, etc.) moods.

Present Indicative

Giovanni sta ascoltando la musica.   **Giovanni is listening to music.**

Present Subjunctive

Credo che Giovanni stia ascoltando la musica.   **I believe he is listening to music (but he might not be).**

The Present Subjunctive: Regular Verbs

The present subjunctive of regular verbs is formed by dropping the verb endings and adding the subjunctive endings.

Table 15-12

	–are	–ere	–ire
io	–i	–a	–a
tu	–i	–a	–a
lui, lei, Lei	–i	–a	–a
noi	–iamo	–iamo	–iamo
voi	–iate	–iate	–iate
loro, Loro	–ino	–ano	–ano

Exercise 15-3

Let's see if you can remember the present subjunctive conjugations. Complete the following verb table with the present subjunctive of the verbs indicated.

Subjuntive Mood

	parlare	*leggere*	*partire*
io			
tu			
lui, lei, Lei			
noi			
voi			
loro, Loro			

Repeat each sentence after it is read by the narrator to practice your pronunciation.

TRACK 70

The present subjunctive of the verb *parlare*

Lui crede che io parli bene l'italiano. — **He believes that I speak Italian well.**

Loro pensano che tu parli bene l'italiano. — **They think that you speak Italian well.**

The present subjunctive of the verb *parlare*—continued

Credo che Marco parli bene l'italiano.	I believe that Marco speaks Italian well.
È importante che noi parliamo bene l'italiano.	It's important that we speak Italian well.

The present subjunctive of the verb *parlare*

È necessario che voi parliate bene l'italiano.	It is necessary that you speak Italian well.
Pare che loro parlino bene l'italiano.	It seems that they speak Italian well.

The present subjunctive of the verb *leggere*

Il professore è contento che io legga l'articolo.	The professor is happy that I am reading the article.
Davide vuole che tu legga l'articolo.	Davide wants that you read the article.
È importante che Maria legga l'articolo.	It is important that Maria reads the article.
Bisogna che leggiamo l'articolo.	It is necessary that we read the article.
È probabile che voi leggiate l'articolo.	It is probable that you are reading the article.
Mi piace che loro leggano l'articolo.	I like that you are reading the article.

The present subjunctive of the verb *partire*

È necessario che io parta presto.	It is necessary that I leave early.
Non vogliamo che tu parta presto.	We want you to leave early.
Io penso che lui parta presto.	I think that he is leaving early.
Sei felice che noi partiamo presto.	You are happy that we are leaving early.
Temo che voi partiate presto.	I fear that you are leaving early.
È bene che loro partano presto.	It is good that they are leaving early.

The following verbs and expressions usually require the subjunctive in the dependent clause. Notice that the infinitive is used in impersonal expressions when no subject is expressed: for example, *È necessario lavorare.*

Table 15-13

volere che	to want	*è necessario che*	it is necessary
desiderare che	to want/wish	*è improbabile che*	it is improbable
preferire che	to prefer	*è impossibile che*	it is impossible
sperare che	to hope	*è bene che*	it is good
credere che	to believe	*è meglio che*	it is better
pensare che	to think	*è importante che*	it is important
dubitare che	to doubt	*è ora che*	it is time
non essere sicuro che	to not be sure	*pare che*	it seems
avere paura che	to be afraid	*sembra che*	it seems
essere contento che	to be happy	*può darsi che*	it is possible
dispiacere che	to be sorry	*è un peccato che*	it is a shame
bisogna che	it is necessary		

È un peccato che piova oggi.	**It's a shame that it is raining today.**
Pare che lui lavori presso la Fiat.	**It seems that he works for Fiat.**
È necessario che cominci in orario.	**It is necessary that you begin on time.**

In the previous examples, the subjunctive is used in the dependent clauses that are introduced by the conjunction *che*. Note that the subjects of the main clause are different than those of the dependent clause. If the subject is the same, the infinitive is used. Compare these two sentences:

È necessario che cominci in orario.	**It is necessary that you begin on time.**
È necessario cominciare in orario.	**It is necessary to begin on time.**

The Present Subjunctive: Irregular Verbs

Conjugating verbs in Italian just wouldn't be the same without irregular verbs. The following table contains the present tense of the usual suspects—*avere* and *essere*—and other common verbs.

Table 15-14

	avere	essere	andare	bere	dare	dire
io	abbia	sia	vada	beva	dia	dica
tu	abbia	sia	vada	beva	dia	dica
lui, lei, Lei	abbia	sia	vada	beva	dia	dica
noi	abbiamo	siamo	andiamo	beviamo	diamo	diciamo
voi	abbiate	siate	andiate	beviate	diate	diciate
loro, Loro	abbiano	siano	vadano	bevano	diano	dicano

	dovere	fare	potere	sapere
io	debba	faccia	possa	sappia
tu	debba	faccia	possa	sappia
lui, lei, Lei	debba	faccia	possa	sappia
noi	dobbiamo	facciamo	possiamo	sappiamo
voi	dobbiate	facciate	possiate	sappiate
loro, Loro	debbano	facciano	possano	sappiano

	stare	uscire	venire	volere
io	stia	esca	venga	voglia
tu	stia	esca	venga	voglia
lui, lei, Lei	stia	esca	venga	voglia
noi	stiamo	usciamo	veniamo	vogliamo
voi	stiate	usciate	veniate	vogliate
loro, Loro	stiano	escano	vengano	vogliano

Exercise 15-4

Provide the present subjunctive of the verb in parentheses.

1. *Credo che Maria* _____ *oggi. (venire)*
2. *È necessario che tu* _____ *l'articolo. (leggere)*

3. *Pare che lui* _____ *stasera.* (*partire*)
4. *È un peccato che Marco* _____ *triste.* (*essere*)

The Past Subjunctive

The past subjunctive is a compound tense, comprised of the present subjunctive of either *avere* or *essere*, together with the past participle of the verb.

Table 15-15

	avere	essere
io	abbia	sia
tu	abbia	sia
lui, lei, Lei	abbia	sia
noi	abbiamo	siamo
voi	abbiate	siate
loro, Loro	abbiano	siano

È un peccato che piova oggi.	It's a shame it is raining today.
È un peccato che abbia piovuto ieri.	It's a shame it rained yesterday.
Sono contento che Marco venga alla festa.	I am happy that Marco is coming to the party.
Sono contento che Marco sia venuto alla festa.	I am happy that Marco came to the party.
Penso che Davide lavori alla Fiat.	I think that Davide works for Fiat.
Penso che Davide abbia lavorato alla Fiat.	I think Davide worked for Fiat.

FACT

A *scioglilingua* is a tongue twister. Can you master this one? Can you find the verbs in the *passato remoto* tense? *Apelle figlio d'Apollo fece una palla di pelle di pollo; tutti i pesci vennero a galla per vedere la palla di pelle di pollo, fatta da Apelle, figlio d'Apollo.*

Imperfect Subjunctive

The imperfect subjunctive (*congiuntivo imperfetto*) is used when the verb in the dependent clause is in a past tense (*passato prossimo, imperfetto, trapassato prossimo*) or in the conditional.

Table 15-16
Imperfect Subjunctive Verb Conjugations

	cantare	sapere	finire
io	cantassi	sapessi	finissi
tu	cantassi	sapessi	finissi
lui, lei, Lei	cantasse	sapesse	finisse
noi	cantassimo	sapessimo	finissimo
voi	cantaste	sapeste	finiste
loro, Loro	cantassero	sapessero	finissero

Credevo che avessi ragione.	**I thought that you were right.**
Lui desiderava che suo figlio diventasse musicista.	**He wanted that his son become a musician.**
Ho pensato che lui ci fosse.	**I thought he was there.**
Sarebbe impossibile che lui venisse.	**It would be impossible for him to come.**

Imperfect Subjunctive Irregular Verbs

The verbs *essere*, *dire*, *bere*, *fare*, and *dare* all have irregular foms in the imperfect subjunctive conjugations.

Table 15-17

	essere	dire	bere	fare	stare	dare
io	fossi	dicessi	bevessi	facessi	stessi	dessi
tu	fossi	dicessi	bevessi	facessi	stessi	dessi
lui, lei, Lei	fosse	dicesse	bevesse	facesse	stesse	desse
noi	fossimo	dicessimo	bevessimo	facessimo	stessimo	dessimo
voi	foste	diceste	beveste	faceste	steste	deste
loro, Loro	fossero	dicessero	bevessero	facessero	stessero	dessero

The Pluperfect Subjunctive

The pluperfect subjunctive is a compound tense, comprised of the imperfect subjunctive of either *avere* or *essere*, together with the past participle of the verb.

Table 15-18

	avere	essere
io	avessi	fossi
tu	avessi	fossi
lui, lei, Lei	avesse	fosse
noi	avessimo	fossimo
voi	aveste	foste
loro, Loro	avessero	fossero

Imperfect

Speravo che tu telefonassi.	**I was hoping that you called.**

Pluperfect

Speravo che le avessi già telefonato.	**I was hoping you had already called her.**
Non sapevo che Mario avesse preso la patente.	**I didn't know Mario had gotten his license.**
Ero contento che Marco fosse venuto alla festa.	**I was happy Marco had come to the party.**
Pensavo che Davide avesse lavorato alla Fiat.	**I thought Davide had worked for Fiat.**

Exercise 15-5

Provide the imperfect subjunctive of the verb in parentheses.

1. *Speravamo che tu _____ in orario. (arrivare)*
2. *Speravo che Marco _____. (venire)*
3. *Non sapevo che loro _____ alla conferenza. (partecipare)*

4. *Ero contento che tu* _____ *la spesa.* (*fare*)
5. *Pensava che io* _____ *il caffè.* (*prendere*)

The Subjunctive after Compound Conjunctions

The subjunctive is used mainly in dependent clauses introduced by *che* (that), or by a compound conjunction, ending with *–ché* (*benché*, *affinché*, *purché*, etc.). Besides these compounds, some others require subjunctive tenses. Each of them introduces a subordinate clause.

Table 15-19

affinché	so that	*ammesso che*	on condition that, provided that
benché	although, despite	*sempre che*	provided that
sebbene	although	*a patto che*	provided that
nonostante	despite, notwithstanding	*a meno che*	unless
affinché	in order to, so that	*prima che*	before
perché	in order to, in order for, so that	*qualora*	if, in the case, should
in modo che	in order to, in order for, so that	*nel caso che*	in the case that, if
purché	provided that	*per quanto*	however + adverb or adjective
a condizione che	on condition that, provided that		

Scrivo il suo nome affinché me lo ricordi.
I am writing his name so that I will remember it.

Vado a un concerto di musica classica benché non me ne intenda.
I am going to a classical music concert even though I don't know too much about it.

Volevano tornare a casa prima che piovesse.
They wanted to return home before it rained.

Il concerto avrà luogo, a meno che non piova.
The concert will take place unless it rains.

If/Then Statements

The conjunction *se* (if, whether) is often followed by the subjunctive (either imperfect or *trapassato*) when the sentence contains a conditional clause:

Se fossi ricco, comprerei una Ferrari.	**If I were rich, I would buy a Ferrari.**
Se avessi studiato medicina, sarei diventato medico.	**If I had studied medicine, I would have become a doctor.**
Si sarebbero divertiti se fossero venuti alla festa.	**They would have had fun if they had come to the party.**

When the *se* (if) statement is not followed by conditional, the indicative mood is used.

Indicative

Se partiamo ora, non arriviamo tardi.	**If we leave now, we won't arrive late.**

Subjunctive

Se partiamo ora, non arriviamo tardi.	**If we left now, we wouldn't arrive late.**
Scrivo il suo nome affinché me lo ricordi.	**I am writing his name so I remember it.**
Vado a un concerto di musica classica benché non me ne intenda.	**I'm going to a classical music concert even though I don't know much about it.**
Il concerto avrà luogo, a meno che non piova.	**The concert will take place unless it rains.**

The Subjunctive after Adverbs Ending in –unque

The subjunctive is required with adverbs that end in *–unque*.

Table 15-20

chiunque	whoever, anybody
comunque	however, in any case
ovunque or dovunque	wherever, everywhere
qualunque or qualsiasi	whatever, any
quantunque	although, despite

Chiunque telefoni, digli che non ci sono.	**Whoever calls, tell them I'm not here.**
Dovunque vada, si diverte.	**Wherever he goes, he has fun.**
Qualunque gusto tu scelga, ne sarai soddisfatto.	**You will be satisfied with whichever flavor you choose.**

Now that you've developed your knowledge of Italian grammar, try to make every effort to use the language as much as possible! The more you know about the language, the more you can understand about Italy's rich past, and *vice versa!*

CHAPTER 16

Survival Phrases: Don't Leave Home Without Them

You've conjugated verbs, learned to pronounce double consonants, and know the difference between *passato prossimo* and *passato remoto*. Now you want to practice your Italian in Italy! Make sure you commit to memory the following Italian phrases, essential for visitors who would like to ingratiate themselves with native Italians. If you try to communicate in Italian, it's likely Italian-speakers will return your thoughtfulness with goodwill and graciousness. *Buon viaggio!*

Common Greetings and Expressions

Here are some of the basic expressions that can help you navigate a basic conversation. Try to use them wherever and whenever possible!

Everyday Words

Italian	English	Italian	English
A domani!	See you tomorrow.	*Come va?*	How're you doing?
A presto!	See you soon.	*Ci sentiamo bene.*	We're feeling fine.
Arrivederci!	Good-bye!	*Ciao!*	Hi!/Bye!
Buon giorno!	Good morning!	*Come si chiama?*	What is your name?
Buon pomeriggio!	Good afternoon!	*Di dove sei? / Di dove è?*	Where are you from?
Buona sera!	Good evening!	*Piacere di conoscerla.*	Pleased to meet you.
Buona notte!	Good night!	*Siamo qui da una settimana.*	We've been here for a week.
Come sta?	How are you?		

Everyday Expressions

English	Italian
I don't speak much Italian.	*Non parlo bene l'italiano.*
Repeat, please.	*Ripeta, per favore.*
Can you speak more slowly?	*Può parlare più piano?*
I don't understand.	*Non capisco.*
Do you speak English? (informal)	*Parli inglese?*
Do you speak English? (formal)	*Parla inglese?*
What does . . . mean?	*Che cosa vuol dire . . . ?*
How do you say . . . in Italian?	*Come si dice . . . in italiano?*

Common Idiomatic Expressions

The following expressions apply to a great variety of situations and are commonly used and understood throughout the Italian peninsula. Most can be used in both formal and informal situations.

Common Idiomatic Expressions

A chi lo dici!	You don't say!	*Fatti gli affari tuoi*	Mind your business
A tutti i costi	At any cost; no matter what	*Fra l'altro . . .*	Among other things . . .
Affare fatto.	It's a deal.	*In ogni modo . . .*	Anyway . . . ; at any cost . . .
Alla buon'ora!	It's about time!	*In poche parole . . .*	In a few words . . .
Altro che!	Of course; you can bet your life!	*Lascia perdere.*	Forget it.
Bell'affare!	That's really good! (ironic)	*Lascia stare.*	Forget it.
Bella roba!	Very nice! (ironic)	*Lasciami stare.*	Leave me alone.
Beato te!	Lucky you!	*Ma va.*	I don't believe you. That's impossible.
Che barba!	How boring!	*Manco per sogno!*	Not even in your dreams!
Che macello!	What a mess!	*Meglio così.*	It's better this way.
Che noia!	How boring!	*Meglio di niente.*	Better than nothing.
Che roba!	I can't believe it!	*Meno male!*	Luckily!
Che schifo!	How disgusting!	*Non ne posso più.*	I can't take it anymore.
Che ti passa per la testa?	What's the matter with you?	*oggi come oggi*	nowadays
Ci mancherebbe altro!	God forbid!	*Per carità!*	God forbid!
Ci vuole altro!	It takes much more than that!	*Per farla breve . . .*	To keep it short . . .
D'altro canto . . .	On the other hand . . .	*Porca miseria!*	Damn it!
da morire	a lot	*Roba da matti.*	That's crazy.
Davvero?	Really?	*Sei sicuro/a?*	Are you sure?
Fa presente che . . .	Bear in mind . . .	*Senz'altro . . .*	Certainly . . .
Siamo alle solite . . .	Here we go again . . .	*Tanto peggio.*	So much the worse.
Sul serio?	Really?	*Tieni presente . . .*	Keep in mind . . .
Tanto meglio.	So much the better.	*Tutt'altro . . .*	On the contrary . . .
Vale la pena.	It's worth it.		

What Your Teacher Never Taught You!

By no means exhaustive nor rife with vulgarities, the following list contains some colorful expressions to be used in a variety of situations.

accidenti	a mild expletive, like darn or heck
alito puzzolente	bad breath
amore a prima vista	love at first sight
arrapare	to become sexually excited
bel niente	nothing, nada, zip
bischero (Tuscany)	a stupid person
casino	a lot or a mess
Mi è piaciuto un casino.	I liked it a lot.
Io ci sono stato un casino di volte.	I've been there many a time.
Che casino!	What a mess!
chiudere il becco	to shut up, to shut one's trap
fannullone	a lazy bum
fregare	to cheat or swindle somebody (mildly offensive)
Non me ne frega niente.	I don't give a damn.
Mi ha fregato!	He screwed me!
fuori di testa	to be out of one's mind
leccaculo or *leccapiedi*	ass licker or brownnoser
mollare qualcuno	to dump someone
morire dalla noia	to die of boredom
parolaccia	dirty word
pigrone/a	a lazy bum
portare male gli anni	to age badly
roba da matti	crazy stuff
preso in giro	to be made fun of, made a fool of
scemo/a	a stupid person, a jerk
schifo	disgust, grossness
Che schifo!	Ew! Gross!
Mi fa schifo.	It grosses me out.
scocciare	to irritate or annoy
valere la pena	to be worth the trouble

Travel to Italy

Before your first taste of authentic *crostini misti* and a glass of *Chianti*, you'll have some paperwork to do. Check to see that your passport is current, and remember that returning to the United States with an expired passport is illegal.

ESSENTIAL

If you hear an expression that you don't understand, make sure you ask for clarification or write it down so you can look it up later. Italian is a very colorful language—so don't miss out!

Visas are generally required for citizens of the United States only if they stay in Italy for longer than three months. If that's the case, you'll need an application form, a detailed itinerary, proof of adequate medical insurance, a valid return airline ticket, and proof of accommodations. Also carry two or more forms of identification on your person, including at least one photo ID. Many banks require several IDs in order to cash traveler's checks.

Customs

Going through *la dogana* (customs) shouldn't be much of a bother as long as you have all the right identification. In addition, if you've purchased goods and gifts at a duty-free shop, you'll have to pay a duty if the value of those articles exceeds the allowance established by the Italian customs service.

"Duty-free" simply means that you don't have to pay a tax in the country of purchase. Be sure to keep receipts for major purchases while in Italy— non–EU citizens can claim a refund for the value added tax (VAT or IVA).

Airport and Flight Vocabulary

The hustle and bustle of the airport can be stressful. The following terms and expressions will hopefully help to alleviate some of that stress!

People, Places, and Things

airplane	*un aereo*	ea	
airport	*un aeroporto*	late	
baggage	*i bagagli*	baggage chec	
boarding pass	*la carta d'imbarco*	passenger	*il p*
carry-on luggage	*i bagagli a mano*	passport	*il passap*
checked luggage	*i bagagli da stiva*	pilot	*il pilota*
cart	*un carello*	security check	*il controllo di sicure*
check-in desk	*il banco di check-in*	shuttle	*lo shuttle*
departures	*partenze*	visa	*il visto*
steward/stewardess	*l'assistente di bordo*		

FACT

Freedom of movement isn't just for those wearing stretch pants. If you're an EU citizen, you can take the specially designated lane at the airport and breeze right through customs. It's all part of the efforts to ease border-patrol regulations and ease travel between participating countries.

Ticket Information

airline	*la compagnia aerea*	one-way ticket	*un biglietto solo andata*
first class	*la prima classe*	round-trip ticket	*un biglietto andata e ritorno*
flight	*il volo*	terminal	*il terminal*
gate	*l'uscita*		

Travel Verbs

to board	*imbarcare*
to buy a ticket	*fare il biglietto*
to check bags	*consegnare i bagagli*
to make a reservation	*fare una prenotazione*
to sit down	*sedersi* or *accomodarsi*
to take off	*decollare*
to land	*atterrare*

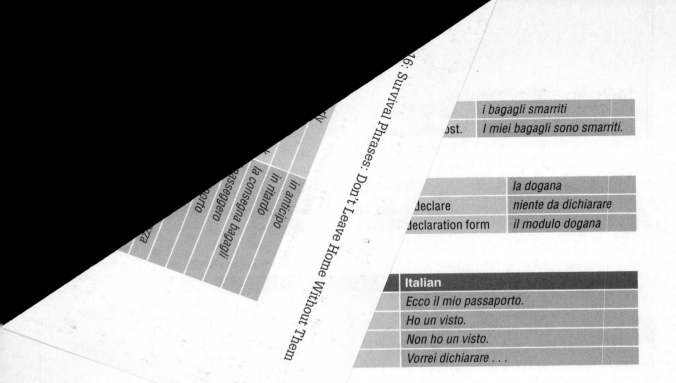

	i bagagli smarriti
...ost.	*I miei bagagli sono smarriti.*

	la dogana
...declare	*niente da dichiarare*
...declaration form	*il modulo dogana*

Italian
Ecco il mio passaporto.
Ho un visto.
Non ho un visto.
Vorrei dichiarare . . .

in anticipo
in ritardo
la consegna bagagli
...ssegero
...orto

Where to Tu... ...Need Assistance

Sometimes it happ... s no matter what you do to prevent it. You thought your wallet was safe in your pocket but you misplaced it. Your passport fell out of your pocket on that rough ride from Naples to Capri. If you lose your passport, immediately notify the local police and the nearest embassy or consulate. There are consulates in most major Italian cities, including Florence, Milan, Naples, Palermo, and Venice. They answer the phone around the clock and also have lists of English-speaking doctors and lawyers.

FACT

You will notice that English is often used for terms related to international travel. *La hostess* can be used to mean stewardess, *il duty free* is a duty free shop, *economy* and *coach* are widely used to refer to travel class options, many Italians will check in at *il check-in,* and *un volo con stopover* is a flight with a stopover.

Making a Telephone Call

At some point you'll want to speak on the telephone, either to make hotel reservations, purchase tickets to a show, or arrange for a taxi to pick you up. The *alfabeti telefonici* (phonetic alphabet) is useful when spelling out words over the telephone, for example, or when speaking to officials.

ESSENTIAL

The U.S. Embassy is at Via V. Veneto, 119a, 00187 Rome. There are U.S. Consulates in Florence, Milan, and Naples (*www.usembassy.it*). They all issue new passports the same day but are closed on U.S. and Italian holidays.

Italians tend to use the names of Italian cities (when there is a corresponding town) rather than proper nouns to spell out words. For example, while you might say "M as in Michael," an Italian is more likely to say *M come Milano* (M as in Milan). The following list will give you examples for all other letters, including those five foreign letters that sometimes appear in Italian.

Italian Letter	Italian Word	Italian Letter	Italian Word
A	*Ancona*	N	*Napoli*
B	*Bologna*	O	*Otranto*
C	*Como*	P	*Padova*
D	*Domodossola*	Q	*quarto*
E	*Empoli*	R	*Roma*
F	*Firenze*	S	*Savona*
G	*Genova*	T	*Torino*
H	*hotel*	U	*Udine*
I	*Imola*	V	*Venezia*
J	*Jérusalem*	W	*Washington*
K	*kilogramma*	X	*Xeres*
L	*Livorno*	Y	*York*
M	*Milano*	Z	*Zara*

Telephones aren't the only way to communicate in Italy. New Internet cafés, Internet bars, and even Internet laundromats are popping up everywhere, so you can access e-mail providers and even surf the web while in Italy.

The Italian Government

The Italian government isn't known for its efficiency. After all, there have been close to sixty governments since the country formed a democratic republic in 1946 following World War II, and political scandals seem to be the norm rather than the exception. On the other hand, it may be that term limits are simply a theoretical concept, and politicians and their parties mutate as the economy, geopolitics, and social programs demand.

FACT

Wondering where all the Machiavellian intrigue takes place? In Rome there's the *Palazzo Montecitorio*, where the Chamber of Deputies is located. *Palazzo Madama* is the Senate seat, and the president of Italy lives in the *Palazzo del Quirinale*, a splendid former papal palace. *Palazzo Chigi* is the center of the Italian government.

Much like many democratic governments today, the Italian government is divided into three branches. The executive branch has two members: the *presidente*, who is elected by an electoral college, and the *primo ministero*, who is generally the leader of the party that has the largest representation in the Chamber of Deputies. The prime minister is also sometimes called *il Presidente del Consiglio dei Ministri*. The legislative branch consists of a *bicameral Parlamento*, which includes the *Senato della Repubblica* and the *Camera dei Deputati* (Chamber of Deputies). The *Corte Costituzionale* (Constitutional Court) rounds out the government. For a more in-depth look at Italian government, visit the official Italian government website at *www. governo.it*.

APPENDIX A

Italian-to-English Glossary

a
at, in, to

a volte
sometimes

abbastanza
enough, rather

l'abitante
inhabitant

abitare
to live

l'abitudine
habit, practice

accendere
to light

l'acciuga
anchovy

accogliere
to welcome

accompagnare
to accompany

accorgersi
to notice

l'acqua
water

addormentarsi
to fall asleep

adesso
now

l'aeroplano
airplane

l'aeroporto
airport

affittare
to rent

africano
African

l'agenzia di viaggi
travel agency

l'agenzia
agency

l'aggettivo
adjective

l'aglio
garlic

agosto
August

agressivo
aggressive

aiutare
to help

l'aiuto
help

l'albergo
hotel

l'albero
tree

alto
tall

altro
other

alzarsi
to get up

americano
American

l'amica
female friend

l'amico
male friend

l'amore
love

ancora
again, still

andare
to go

l'anniversario
anniversary

l'anno
year

annoiarsi
to get bored

annoiato
bored

antipatico
unpleasant

appartenere
to belong

appena
as soon as

l'appuntamento
appointment

aprile
April

aprire
to open

l'aranciate
aranciata

argomento
subject

l'aria
air

arrabbiarsi
to get angry

arrivare
to arrive

l'arrosto
roast

asciugare
to dry

l'asciugatrice
clothes dryer

ascoltare
to listen (to)

aspettare
to wait (for)

assistere
to attend

assomigliare
to resemble

l'astrologia
astrology

l'atteggiamento
attitude

attendere
to wait

attentamente
attentively

attento
attentive

l'attenzione
attention

l'attore
actor

attualmente
currently

l'aula
classroom

australiano
Australian

l'autobus
bus

l'automobile
car

l'autore
author

l'autorità
authority

l'autostrada
highway

l'autunno
fall, autumn

avaro
stingy

avere
to have

avere bisogno (di)
to need, have need (of)

avere caldo
to be hot

avere fame
to be hungry

avere freddo
to be cold

avere fretta
to be in a hurry

avere paura (di)
to be afraid (of)

avere ragione
to be right, correct

avere sete
to be thirsty

avere sonno
to be tired, sleepy

avere torto
to be wrong, incorrect

avere voglia di
to feel like

aversela a male
to feel bad

l'avvocato
lawyer

azzurro
blue

il bagaglio
luggage

ballare
to dance

la bambina
female child

i bambini
children

il bambino
male child

il bar
bar

la base
base

basso
short

la bellezza
beauty

bello
beautiful

bene
well

benedire
to bless

bere
to drink

bianco
white

la biblioteca
library

la bicicletta
bicycle

il biglietto
ticket

biondo
blonde

la birra
beer

il biscotto
cookie

bisognare
to need

blu
blue

la bottiglia
bottle

brasiliano
Brazilian

bravo
good, capable

brutto
ugly

la bugia
lie

la bugia di convenienza
white lie

il buio
dark

buono
good

il burro
butter

cadere
to fall

il caffè
coffee

il calcio
soccer

caldo
warm

il calendario
calendar

cambiare
to change

la camera
room

la cameriera
waitress

il cameriere
waiter

camminare
to walk

la campagna
country, countryside

canadese
Canadian

il cane
dog

il cantante
singer

cantare
to sing

la canzone
song

i capelli
hair

capire
to understand

il capo
boss

il capoufficio
office manager

la cappella
chapel

il cappello
hat

la carne
meat

caro
dear, expensive

il carro
cart

la carta
paper

la carta di credito
credit card

la casa
house

il casinò
casino

la cassa
safe, case, cashier

castagno
chestnut, brunette

cattivo
bad

il cavallo
horse

il CD
compact disc

celebrare
to celebrate

la cena
dinner

cenare
to have dinner

cento
one hundred

cercare
to look for, search

Che (cosa)?
What?

Chi?
Who?, Whom?

chiaccherare
to chatter

chiamare
to call

chiamarsi
to call oneself, be called

chiaro
clear

chiasso
noise

la chiave
key

chiedere
to ask

la chiesa
church

la chitarra
guitar

chiudere
to close

il cinema
cinema, movie theater

cinese
Chinese

il cioccolato
chocolate

la città
city

la civiltà
civilization

la classe
class

classico
classic

il cliente
customer

il clima
climate

il cocomero
watermelon

cogliere
to pick

la colazione
breakfast

il/la collega
colleague

il collegio
boarding school

il colore
color

come
how, what, like

Come?
How?, What?

cominciare
to begin

la commedia
play

la compagna
friend, companion

**la compagna di
stanza**
roommate

la compagnia
company,
companionship

il compagno
friend, companion

**il compagno di
stanza**
roommate

comparire
to appear

compiere
to complete

il compito
homework

il compleanno
birthday

comporre
to compose

comprare
to buy

il computer
computer

con
with

il concerto
concert

il condominio
condominium

condurre
to lead

la conferenza
conference,
lecture

conoscere
to know, meet

consigliare
to advise

il consiglio
advice

contento
happy

il conto
check, bill

contraddire
to contradict

la conversazione
conversation

coprirsi
to cover oneself

correre
to run

corretto
correct

il corso
course

così
so

costare
to cost

costruire
to build

la cravatta
necktie

la creazione
creation

credere
to believe

il crepuscolo
dusk

crudo
raw, uncooked

cucinare
to cook

la cugina
female cousin

il cugino
male cousin

cuocere
to cook

la cura
cure

da
from

dare
to give

dare del Lei
to address some-
one formally

dare del tu
to address some-
one informally

la data
date

davanti a
in front of

decidere
to decide

desiderare
to want

di
about, from, of

di solito
usually

la diagnosi
diagnosis

il diario
diary

dicembre
December

difficile
difficult

difficilmente
difficultly

diligente
diligent

diligentemente
diligently

dire
to say, tell

il disco
record album

il discorso
speech, address

discutere
to discuss

disdire
to retract

disperatamente
desperately

disperato
desperate

dispiacere
to displease

disporre
to arrange

la ditta
company, firm

diventare
to become

divertente
fun, enjoyable

divertirsi
to have fun, enjoy
oneself

il dizionario
dictionary

il dolce
dessert

il dollaro
dollar

dolorosamente
painfully

doloroso
painful

la domanda
question

domandare
to ask a question

domani
tomorrow

domenica
Sunday

dopo
after, later

dormire
to sleep

il dormitorio
dormitory

il dottore
doctor

la dottoressa
female doctor

dove
where

dovere
to have to, must

dubitare
to doubt

durante
during

eccellente
excellent

Ecco!
Here it is!, Here
they are!

economicamente
economically

economico
economical

l'edicola
newsstand

l'edificio
building

educato
polite

egiziano
Egyptian

elegante
elegant

elettronico
electronic

l'elezione
election

l'email
e-mail

l'energia
energy

l'eroe
hero

l'esame
exam

l'esercizio
exercise

esporre
to exhibit

essere
to be

essere al verde
to be broke

essere in gioco
to be at stake

**essere nelle
nuvole**
to daydream

essere sazio
to be full

l'estate
summer

europeo
European

la fabbrica
factory

la faccia
face

facile
easy

facilmente
easily

falso
false

la famiglia
family

famoso
famous

fare
to do, make

fare attenzione
to pay attention

fare un bagno
to take a bath

fare caldo
to be hot
(weather)

fare colazione
to have breakfast

fare freddo
to be cold
(weather)

fare la doccia
to take a shower

fare la guerra
to wage war

fare la spesa
to go food
shopping

fare le spese
to go shopping

fare un errore
to make a mistake

fare un giro
to go for a ride

fare un regalo
to give a gift

fare un viaggio
to take a trip

**fare una
domanda**
to ask a question

fare una foto
to take a picture

fare una gita
to take a short trip

**fare una
passeggiata**
to take a walk

fare una pausa
to take a break

**fare una
telefonata**
to make a tele-
phone call

la farina
flour

la farmacia
pharmacy

farsi la barba
to shave

la fata
fairy

favolosamente
fabulously

favoloso
fabulous

il favore
favor

febbraio
February

felice
happy

la feria
holiday, vacation

fermare
to stop

fermarsi
to stop (oneself)

la festa
party

festeggiare
to celebrate

la fetta
slice

la fidanzata
fiancee

il fidanzato
fiance

fidarsi
to trust

la figlia
daughter

il figlio
son

la fila
row

il film
movie, film

la filosofia
philosophy

finale
final

la finestra
window

fingere
to pretend

finire
to finish

fino a
until

il fiore
flower

la foglia
leaf

il fondo
bottom

il formaggio
cheese

il forno
oven

la foschia
mist

la foto
photograph

fra
between

il francese
French

il fratellino
little brother

il fratello
brother

freddo
cold

frequentare
to attend

fresco
cool

la frutta
fruit

fumare
to smoke

il fungo
mushroom

il fuoco
fire

fuori
out, outside

furbo
shrewd

il futuro
future

la galleria
gallery

il garage
garage

il gatto
cat

il gelato
ice cream

il gelo
frost

generoso
generous

il genio
genius

i genitori
parents

gennaio
January

gettare
to throw, toss

il ghetto
ghetto

il ghiaccio
ice

già
already

la giacca
jacket

giacere
to lie down

giallo
yellow

il giapponese
Japanese

il giardino
garden

giocare a
to play (a sport or game)

il giocatolo
toy

il gioco
game

il giornale
newspaper

la giornata
day

il giorno
day

giovane
young

giovedì
Thursday

la gioventù
youth

giugno
June

gonfiare
to inflate

grande
big, large

la grandine
hail

grasso
fat

il greco
Greek

grigio
grey

grosso
big

guadagnare
to earn

guardare
to look at, watch

la guerra
war

la guida
guide

guidare
to drive

il guscio
shell

l'hotel
hotel

l'idea
idea

ieri
yesterday

immaginare
to imagine

imparare
to learn

impazzire
to go crazy

imporre
to impose

importante
important

impossibile
impossible

improbabile
improbable

in
at, in, to

in anticipo
early

in centro
downtown

in ritardo
late

incominciare
to begin

incontrare
to meet

incoraggiare
to encourage

incorretto
incorrect

indiano
Indian

l'indipendenza
independence

indire
to declare

indurre
to inspire

l'informazione
information

l'inglese
English

innamorarsi
to fall in love

l'insalata
salad

insegnare
to teach

intelligente
intelligent

intelligentemente
intelligently

interdire
to prohibit

interessante
interesting

introdurre
to introduce

inventare
to invent

l'inverno
winter

invitare
to invite

io
I

irlandese
Irish

l'isola
island

là
there

il lago
lake

lamentarsi
to complain

il lampo
lightning

le lasagne
lasagna

lasciare
to leave

il latte
milk

laurearsi
to graduate

lavare
to wash

lavarsi
to wash up

lavorare
to work

legare
to tie, bind

leggere
to read

leggero
light

lei
she

Lei
you (singular, formal)

lento
slow

il leone
lion

la lettera
letter

il letto
bed

la lezione
lesson

lì
there

liberamente
freely

libero
free

la libreria
bookstore

il libro
book

la lingua
tongue, language

il locale
place

loro
they

Loro
you (plural, formal)

luglio
July

lui
he

lunedì
Monday

lungo
long

il luogo
place

lussuoso
luxurious

la macchina
car, machine

la madre
mother

il maestro
teacher

la maga
witch

maggio
May

la maglietta
t-shirt

il maglione
sweater

magnificamente
magnificently

magnifico
magnificent

magro
thin

mai
never

male
bad, badly

maledire
to curse

mancare
to miss, lack

la mancia
tip

mandare
to send

mangiare
to eat

la mano
hand

mantenere
to maintain

il mare
ocean

il marito
husband

marocchino
Morrocan

marrone
brown

martedì
Tuesday

marzo
March

la mattina
morning

il meccanico
mechanic

il medico
doctor, medic

medio
middle

meglio
better

la mela
apple

mentre
while

mercoledì
Wednesday

il mese
month

la messa
mass

il messaggio
message

messicano
Mexican

mettere
to put, place

mettersi
to put on (oneself)

mezzanotte
midnight

mezzogiorno
noon

migliore
best

mille
one thousand

la minestra
soup

la moglie
wife

molto
many, much, a lot

la montagna
mountain

il monumento
monument

morire
to die

mostrare
to show

la moto
motorcycle

il museo
museum

la musica
music

napoletano
Neapolitan

nascere
to be born

la nascita
birth

il naso
nose

Natale
Christmas

la nebbia
fog

necessario
necessary

il negozio
store

neozelandese
New Zealander

nero
black

nessuno
no one

la neve
snow

nevicare
to snow

niente
nothing

la nipote
granddaughter, niece

il nipote
grandson, nephew

noi
we

noioso
boring

noleggiare
to rent (a car)

il nome
name, noun

la nonna
grandmother

i nonni
grandparents

il nonno
grandfather

normale
normal

la nostalgia
nostalgia

la notizia
news

la notte
night

notturno
nocturnal

novembre
November

nubile
single woman

il numero
number

il numero di telefono
telephone number

nuocere
to harm

nuotare
to swim

nuovo
new

la nuvola
cloud

nuvoloso
cloudy

l'occhio
eye

l'odore
odor

offrire
to offer

l'oggetto
object

oggi
today

ogni
each, every

ogni volta
each time

ognuno
everyone

olandese
Dutch

l'olio
oil

oltre
beyond

onesto
honest

opporre
to oppose

l'ora
hour, time

l'orologio
wristwatch

ortodosso
orthodox

l'ospedale
hospital

l'osteria
tavern, public house

ottenere
to obtain

ottobre
October

il pacco
package, parcel

il padre
father

pagare
to pay

la pagina
page

il paio
pair

il panino
sandwich

la panna
cream

il papa
pope

il papà
dad, daddy

la pappa
country soup, baby food

parcheggiare
to park

il parcheggio
parking lot

il parco
the park

parecchio
a lot

parere
to seem

parlare
to speak

la parola
word

partecipare
to participate

particolare
particular

particolarmente
particularly

partire
to leave

la partita
game, match

la patente di guida
driver's license

la paura
fear

la pazienza
patience

il peccato
sin

la pena
punishment

la penna
pen

pensare
to think

pensare a
to think about (someone or something)

pensare di
to think about (doing something)

per
for

il percento
percent, percentage

perché
why, because

perdere
to lose

perdersi
to get lost

la persona
person

pesante
heavy

il pesce
fish

il peso
weight

pessimo
worst

pettinarsi
to comb one's hair

il pezzo
piece

piacere
to be pleasing, please

piano
plan, floor

piano
slowly, softly

il piatto
plate, dish

la piazza
plaza, central square

piccante
spicy

piccolo
small

il piede
foot

pigro
lazy

la pioggia
rain

piovere
to rain

la piscina
swimming pool

più
most

più
no longer

la pizza
pizza

il pizzaiolo
pizza maker

poco
few, very little

il podestà
governor, chief magistrate

poi
then

polacco
Polish

la politica
politics

il politico
politician

la polizia
police

il pomeriggio
afternoon

il pomodoro
tomato

porre
to place

porre
to put

la porta
door

portare
to carry, bring, wear

portoghese
Portuguese

posporre
to put after

possibile
possible

il posto
place

potere
to be able, can

povero
poor

pranzare
to have lunch

il pranzo
lunch

preferire
to prefer

prendere
to take

preoccuparsi
to worry

la preoccupazione
worry, concern

preparare
to prepare

prepararsi
to prepare oneself

il presidente
president

prestare
to lend

presto
soon, early

prevedere
to foresee

prima
before

la primavera
springtime

il primo
first

probabile
probable

probabilmente
probably

produrre
to produce

il professore
professor (m.)

la professoressa
professor (f.)

promuovere
to promote

il pronome
pronoun

proporre
to propose

il prosciutto
prosciutto

prossimo
next

provare
to try

la psicologia
psychology

pubblico
public

pulire
to clean

il punto
point, period

puntuale
punctual

qua
here

il quaderno
notebook

qualcosa
something

Quale?
Which?

Quando?
When?

quanto
how much, how many

quello
that

questo
this

qui
here

raccogliere
to gather

raccontare
to tell, recount

il racconto
short story

radersi
to shave

la ragazza
girl, girlfriend

il ragazzo
boy, boyfriend

ragionare
to reason

la ragione
reason

ragionevole
reasonable

rapidamente
quickly

rapido
fast

il rappresentante
representative

raramente
rarely

raro
rare

recarsi
to go

recente
recent

recentemente
recently

regalare
to give a gift

il regalo
gift, present

la regola
rule

rendere
to give back, restore

restare
to stay, remain

restituire
to give back

ricco
rich

ricevere
to receive

ridurre
to reduce

riferire
to report, relate

rimanere
to remain

ripetere
to repeat

riporre
to put back

riposarsi
to rest

rispettare
to respect

rispondere
to respond, answer

la risposta
answer

il ristorante
restaurant

ritenere
to detain

ritornare
to return

la riunione
meeting

riuscire
to succeed

la rivista
magazine

il romanzo
novel

rosso
red

il rumore
noise

il russo
Russian

sabato
Saturday

il salame
salami

salire
to climb

il salotto
living room

salutarsi
to greet (one another)

la salute
health

salve
hello

salvo
safe, unharmed

sano
healthy

sapere
to know a fact, know how do something

il sassofono
saxophone

sbadigliare
to yawn

sbagliarsi
to be wrong

sbagliato
wrong, incorrect

lo scaffale
shelf

le scale
stairs

la scarpa
shoe

scegliere
to choose

la scelta
choice

la scena
scene

scendere
to descend, climb off

la scheda
card, file

lo schema
scheme, pattern

lo scherzo
joke

schiacciare
to crush, squish

lo schiavo
slave

schiuma
foam, froth

lo scialle
shawl

sciare
to ski

la sciarpa
scarf

scientifico
scientific

la scienza
science

lo scienziato
scientist

la scimmia
monkey

scintillare
to shine, sparkle

sciocco
foolish

sciogliersi
to loosen, melt

lo sciopero
strike

sciupare
to spoil, to reduce, to lose weight

scogliere
to undo

sconsigiare
to dissuade

scoprire
to discover

scorso
last, past

scozzese
Scottish

la scrivania
desk

scrivere
to write

lo scultore
sculptor

la scuola
school

la scusa
excuse

scusarsi
to apologize

lo sdegno
disdain

sdraiato
stretched out, lying down

il secolo
century

secondo
second

sedersi
to sit

seguente
following

seguire
to follow

sembrare
to seem

il semestre
semester

sempre
always

sensibile
sensible

sentire
to hear

sentirsi
to feel

senza
without

i senzatetto
the homeless

la sera
evening

sereno
serene, nice

servire
to serve

settembre
September

la settimana
week

sfidare
to challenge

sfilata
parade, show

sfortuna
misfortune

sgarbato
rude

sgretolarsi
to crumble to pieces

sicuramente
certainly

sicuro
certain, safe

la sigaretta
cigarette

il sigaro
cigar

la signora
madam, lady

il signore
gentleman, mister

la signorina
miss

simpatico
nice, agreeable

la sinagoga
synagogue

sincero
sincere

il sindaco
mayor

la situazione
situation

slegare
to untie

slogarsi
to dislocate

lo smalto
fingernail polish

smettere
to quit

snello
thin

snodare
to untie

sognare
to dream

il sogno
dream

i soldi
money

il sole
sun

la sorella
sister

la sorellina
little sister

sorridere
to smile

il sorriso
smile

sostenere
to support

sotto
under, beneath

i sottotitoli
subtitles

lo spagnolo
Spanish

lo spago
string

lo spazio
space

lo specchio
mirror

spedire
to send

spegnere
to turn off

spendere
to spend

sperare
to hope

spesso
often

la spiaggia
beach

spiegare
to explain

la spiegazione
explanation

gli spinaci
spinach

spogliarsi
to undress

sporco
dirty

lo sport
sport

sposarsi
to get
married

la squadra
team

lo squarcio
gash

squillare
to ring

sregolato
disorderly

lo stadio
stadium

stamattina
this morning

stampare
to print

stanco
tired

stanotte
tonight

la stanza
room

stare
to be, to stay

stare a cuore
to matter

stare in piedi
to stand

stare per
to be about to

stare zitto
to be quiet

stasera
this evening,
tonight

lo stato
state, condition

la statua
statue

la stazione
station

stendere
to extend, spread

stesso
same

la storia
history

la strada
street

straordinario
extraordinary

stretto
tight

**lo strumento
musicale**
musical
instrument

lo studente
male student

la studentessa
female student

studiare
to study

lo studio
study, studio

studioso
studious

stupido
stupid

su
on

subito
right away

succedere a
to come next

sufficiente
sufficient

suggerire
to suggest

la suocera
mother-in-law

il suocero
father-in-law

suonare
to play (an
instrument)

il supermercato
the supermarket

suppore
to suppose

svedese
Swedish

svegliare
to waken

svegliarsi
to wake up

sviluppare
to develop

la Svizzera
Switzerland

svizzero
Swiss

il tabaccaio
tobacconist

tacere
to be quiet

tanto
so much, so
many

tardi
late

il tassì
taxi

il tavolo
table

il teatro
theater

il tedesco
German

telefonare
to call

la telefonata
telephone call

il telefono
telephone

il telegiornale
TV news

la televisione
television

la tempesta
storm

il tempo
weather, time

il temporale
rainstorm

tenere
to keep

il tennis
tennis

tirare
to pull

togliere
to remove

la tormenta
blizzard

tornare
to return

la torta
cake

tra
between

tradurre
to translate

tranquillamente
peacefully

tranquillo
peaceful

trarre
to pull

il treno
train

la tribù
tribe

triste
sad

tristemente
sadly

troppo
too much, too many

trovare
to find

tu
you (singular, informal)

il/la turista
tourist

ubbidire
to obey

udire
to hear

l'ufficio
office

l'ufficio postale
post office

ultimo
last

l'università
university

l'uomo
man

usare
to use

usato
used

uscire
to go out

la vacanza
vacation

valere
to be worth

il vapore
steam, vapor

variabile
changeable

vario
various

il vaso
vase

vecchio
old

vedere
to see

veloce
quick, fast

velocemente
rapidly

vendere
to sell

venerdì
Friday

venire
to come

il vento
wind

il verbo
verb

verde
green

la verità
truth

vero
true

vestire
to dress

vestirsi
to get dressed

i vestiti
clothes

la via
street

viaggiare
to travel

il viaggio
trip

vicino
close

il vicino di casa
neighbor

il vigliacco
coward

vincere
to win

il vino
wine

la virgola
comma

visitare
to visit

il vitello
veal

vivere
to live

il vocabolario
vocabulary

la voce
voice

voi
you (plural, informal)

volere
to want, owe

il volo
flight

la volta
time, turn

il voto
grade

il vulcano
volcano

vuoto
empty

lo zaino
backpack

la zebra
zebra

lo zero
zero

la zia
aunt

lo zio
uncle

lo zoo
zoo

lo zucchero
sugar

gli zucchini
zucchini

la zuppa
soup

English-to-Italian Glossary

a lot
parecchio;
molto

about
di

to accompany
accompagnare

actor
l'attore

**to address some-
one formally**
dare del Lei

**to address some-
one informally**
dare del tu

adjective
l'aggettivo

advice
il consiglio

to advise
consigliare

African
africano

after
dopo

afternoon
il pomeriggio

again
ancora

agency
l'agenzia

aggressive
agressivo

agreeable
simpatico

air
l'aria

airplane
l'aeroplano

airport
l'aeroporto

already
già

always
sempre

American
americano

anchovy
l'acciuga

anniversary
l'anniversario

answer
la risposta

to apologize
scusarsi

to appear
comparire

apple
la mela

appointment
l'appuntamento

April
aprile

aranciata
l'aranciate

to arrange
disporre

to arrive
arrivare

as soon as
appena

to ask
chiedere

to ask a question
domandare

to ask a question
fare una
domanda

astrology
l'astrologia

at
a, in

to attend
assistere

to attend
frequentare

to attend
assistere

attention
l'attenzione

attentive
attento

attentively
attentamente

attitude
l'atteggiamento

August
agosto

aunt
la zia

Australian
australiano

author
l'autore

authority
l'autorità

autumn
l'autunno

baby food
la pappa

backpack
lo zaino

bad
cattivo, male

badly
male

bar
il bar

base
la base

to be
essere

to be able
potere

to be about to
stare per

to be afraid (of)
avere paura (di)

to be at stake
essere in gioco

to be born
nascere

to be broke
essere al verde

to be cold
avere freddo

**to be cold
(weather)**
fare freddo

to be full
essere sazio

to be hot
avere caldo

**to be hot
(weather)**
fare caldo

to be hungry
avere fame

to be in a hurry
avere fretta

**to be pleasing,
please**
piacere

to be quiet
stare zitto

to be quiet
tacere

**to be right,
correct**
avere ragione

to be thirsty
avere sete

to be tired, sleepy
avere sonno

to be worth
valere

to be wrong
sbagliarsi

**to be wrong,
incorrect**
avere torto

to be, stay
stare

beach
la spiaggia

beautiful
bello

beauty
la bellezza

because
perché

to become
diventare

bed
il letto

beer
la birra

before
prima

to begin
cominciare

to begin
incominciare

to believe
credere

to belong
appartenere

beneath
sotto

best
migliore

better
meglio

between
fra, tra

beyond
oltre

bicycle
la bicicletta

big
grosso

big
grande

bill
il conto

birth
la nascita

birthday
il compleanno

black
nero

to bless
benedire

blizzard
la tormenta

blonde
biondo

blue
azzurro

blue
blu

boarding school
il collegio

book
il libro

bookstore
la libreria

bored
annoiato

boring
noioso

boss
il capo

bottle
la bottiglia

bottom
il fondo

boy, boyfriend
il ragazzo

Brazilian
brasiliano

breakfast
la colazione

to bring
portare

brother
il fratello

brown
marrone

brunette
castagno

to build
costruire

building
l'edificio

bus
l'autobus

butter
il burro

to buy
comprare

cake
la torta

calendar
il calendario

to call
chiamare

to call
telefonare

to call oneself, be called
chiamarsi

can
potere

Canadian
canadese

capable
bravo

car
l'automobile, la macchina

card
la scheda

to carry
portare

cart
il carro

casino
il casinò

cat
il gatto

to celebrate
celebrare

to celebrate
festeggiare

century
il secolo

certain
sicuro

certainly
sicuramente

to challenge
sfidare

to change
cambiare

changeable
variabile

chapel
la cappella

to chatter
chiaccherare

check
il conto

cheese
il formaggio

chestnut
castagno

children
i bambini

Chinese
cinese

chocolate
il cioccolato

choice
la scelta

to choose
scegliere

Christmas
Natale

church
la chiesa

cigar
il sigaro

cigarette
la sigaretta

cinema
il cinema

city
la città

civilization
la civiltà

class
la classe

classic
classico

classroom
l'aula

to clean
pulire

clear
chiaro

climate
il clima

to climb
salire

to close
chiudere

close
vicino

clothes
i vestiti

clothes dryer
l'asciugatrice

cloud
la nuvola

cloudy
nuvoloso

coffee
il caffè

cold
freddo

colleague
il/la collega

color
il colore

to comb one's hair
pettinarsi

to come
venire

to come next
succedere a

comma
la virgola

compact disc
il CD

company, companionship
la compagnia

company
la ditta

to complain
lamentarsi

to complete
compiere

to compose
comporre

computer
il computer

concert
il concerto

condominium
il condominio

conference
la conferenza

to contradict
contraddire

conversation
la conversazione

to cook
cucinare

to cook
cuocere

cookie
il biscotto

cool
fresco

correct
corretto

to cost
costare

country soup
la pappa

country, countryside
la campagna

course
il corso

to cover oneself
coprirsi

coward
il vigliacco

cream
la panna

creation
la creazione

credit card
la carta di credito

to crumble to pieces
sgretolarsi

to crush, squish
schiacciare

cure
la cura

currently
attualmente

to curse
maledire

customer
il cliente

dad, daddy
il papà

to dance
ballare

dark
il buio

date
la data

daughter
la figlia

day
la giornata

day
il giorno

to daydream
essere nelle nuvole

dear, expensive
caro

December
dicembre

to decide
decidere

to declare
indire

to descend, climb off
scendere

desk
la scrivania

desperate
disperato

desperately
disperatamente

dessert
il dolce

to detain
ritenere

to develop
sviluppare

diagnosis
la diagnosi

diary
il diario

dictionary
il dizionario

to die
morire

difficult
difficile

difficultly
difficilmente

diligent
diligente

diligently
diligentemente

dinner
la cena

dirty
sporco

to discover
scoprire

to discuss
discutere

disdain
lo sdegno

dish
il piatto

to dislocate
slogarsi

disorderly
sregolato

to displease
dispiacere

to dissuade
sconsigiare

to do, make
fare

doctor
il dottore

doctor
il medico

dog
il cane

dollar
il dollaro

door
la porta

dormitory
il dormitorio

to doubt
dubitare

downtown
in centro

to dream
sognare

dream
il sogno

to dress
vestire

to drink
bere

to drive
guidare

driver's license
la patente di guida

to dry
asciugare

during
durante

dusk
il crepuscolo

Dutch
olandese

each time
ogni volta

each
ogni

early
in anticipo

early
presto

to earn
guadagnare

easily
facilmente

easy
facile

to eat
mangiare

economical
economico

economically
economicamente

Egyptian
egiziano

election
l'elezione

electronic
elettronico

elegant
elegante

e-mail
l'email

empty
vuoto

to encourage
incoraggiare

energy
l'energia

English
l'inglese

enough, rather
abbastanza

European
europeo

evening
la sera

every
ogni

everyone
ognuno

exam
l'esame

excellent
eccellente

excuse
la scusa

exercise
l'esercizio

to exhibit
esporre

expensive
caro

to explain
spiegare

explanation
la spiegazione

to extend
stendere

extraordinary
straordinario

eye
l'occhio

fabulous
favoloso

fabulously
favolosamente

face
la faccia

factory
la fabbrica

fairy
la fata

to fall
cadere

to fall asleep
addormentarsi

to fall in love
innamorarsi

fall, autumn
l'autunno

false
falso

family
la famiglia

famous
famoso

fast
rapido; veloce

fat
grasso

father
il padre

father-in-law
il suocero

favor
il favore

fear
la paura

February
febbraio

to feel
sentirsi

to feel bad
aversela a male

to feel like
avere voglia di

female child
la bambina

female cousin
la cugina

female doctor
la dottoressa

female friend
l'amica

female student
la studentessa

few
poco

fiance
il fidanzato

fiancee
la fidanzata

file
la scheda
film
il film

final
finale

to find
trovare

fingernail polish
lo smalto

to finish
finire

fire
il fuoco

firm
la ditta

first
il primo

fish
il pesce

flight
il volo

floor
il piano

flour
la farina

flower
il fiore

foam
schiuma

fog
la nebbia

to follow
seguire

following
seguente

foolish
sciocco

foot
il piede

for
per

to foresee
prevedere

free
libero

freely
liberamente

French
il francese

Friday
venerdì

**friend,
companion**
il/la compagno/a

from
da, di

frost
il gelo

fruit
la frutta

fun
divertente

future
il futuro

gallery
la galleria

game
il gioco

game
la partita

garage
il garage

garden
il giardino

garlic
l'aglio

gash
lo squarcio

to gather
raccogliere

generous
generoso

genius
il genio

gentleman
il signore

German
il tedesco

to get angry
arrabbiarsi

to get bored
annoiarsi

to get dressed
vestirsi

to get lost
perdersi

to get married
sposarsi

to get up
alzarsi

ghetto
il ghetto

gift
il regalo

girl, girlfriend
la ragazza

to give
dare

to give a gift
fare un regalo

to give a gift
regalare

to give back
restituire

to give back
rendere

to go
andare

to go
recarsi

to go crazy
impazzire

to go food shopping
fare la spesa

to go for a ride
fare un giro

to go out
uscire

to go shopping
fare le spese

good
buono

good
bravo

governor
il podestà

grade
il voto

to graduate
laurearsi

granddaughter
la nipote

grandfather
il nonno

grandmother
la nonna

grandparents
i nonni

grandson
il nipote

Greek
il greco

green
verde

to greet (one another)
salutarsi

grey
grigio

guide
la guida

guitar
la chitarra

habit, practice
l'abitudine

hail
la grandine

hair
i capelli

hand
la mano

happy
contento

happy
felice

to harm
nuocere

hat
il cappello

to have
avere

to have breakfast
fare colazione

to have dinner
cenare

to have fun, enjoy oneself
divertirsi

to have lunch
pranzare

to have to
dovere

he
lui

health
la salute

healthy
sano

to hear
sentire

to hear
udire

heavy
pesante

hello
salve

to help
aiutare

help
l'aiuto

here
qui, qua

Here it is!/Here they are!
Ecco!

hero
l'eroe

highway
l'autostrada

history
la storia

holiday
la feria

the homeless
i senzatetto

homework
il compito

honest
onesto

to hope
sperare

horse
il cavallo

hospital
l'ospedale

hotel
l'albergo

hotel
l'hotel

hour
l'ora

house
la casa

how much, how many
quanto

how
come

How?/What?
Come?

husband
il marito

I
io

ice
il ghiaccio

ice cream
il gelato

idea
l'idea

to imagine
immaginare

important
importante

to impose
imporre

impossible
impossibile

improbable
improbabile

in
a, in

in front of
davanti a

incorrect
incorretto

Indian
indiano

independence
l'indipendenza

to inflate
gonfiare

information
l'informazione

inhabitant
l'abitante

to inspire
indurre

intelligent
intelligente

intelligently
intelligentemente

interesting
interessante

to introduce
introdurre

to invent
inventare

to invite
invitare

Irish
irlandese

island
l'isola

jacket
la giacca

January
gennaio

Japanese
il giapponese

joke
lo scherzo

July
luglio

June
giugno

to keep
tenere

key
la chiave

**to know a fact,
know how to do
something**
sapere

to know
conoscere

to lack
mancare

lady
la signora

lake
il lago

language
la lingua

large
grande

lasagna
le lasagne

last
ultimo

last
scorso

late
in ritardo

late
tardi

later
dopo

lawyer
l'avvocato

lazy
pigro

to lead
condurre

leaf
la foglia

to learn
imparare

to leave
lasciare, partire

lecture
la conferenza

to lend
prestare

lesson
la lezione

letter
la lettera

library
la biblioteca

lie
la bugia

to lie down
giacere

to light
accendere

light
leggero

lightning
il lampo
like
come

lion
il leone

to listen (to)
ascoltare

little brother
il fratellino

little sister
la sorellina

to live
abitare

to live
vivere

living room
il salotto

long
lungo

to look at
guardare

to look for
cercare

to loosen
sciogliersi

to lose
perdere

love
l'amore

luggage
il bagaglio

lunch
il pranzo

luxurious
lussuoso
machine
la macchina

madam
la signora

magazine
la rivista

magnificent
magnifico

magnificently
magnificamente

to maintain
mantenere

**to make a
mistake**
fare un errore

**to make a tele-
phone call**
fare una
telefonata

male child
il bambino

male cousin
il cugino

male friend
l'amico

male student
lo studente

man
l'uomo

many
molto

March
marzo

mass
la messa

match
la partita

to matter
stare a cuore

May
maggio

mayor
il sindaco

meat
la carne

mechanic
il meccanico

to meet
incontrare,
conoscere

meeting
la riunione

to melt
sciogliersi
message
il messaggio

Mexican
messicano

middle
medio

midnight
mezzanotte

milk
il latte

mirror
lo specchio

misfortune
sfortuna

miss
la signorina

to miss
mancare

mist
la foschia
mister
il signore

Monday
lunedì

money
i soldi

monkey
la scimmia

month
il mese

monument
il monumento

morning
la mattina

Moroccan
marocchino

most
più

mother
la madre

mother-in-law
la suocera

motorcycle
la moto

mountain
la montagna

movie
il film

movie theater
il cinema

much
molto

museum
il museo

mushroom
il fungo

music
la musica

**musical
instrument**
lo strumento
musicale

must
dovere

name, noun
il nome

Neapolitan
napoletano

necessary
necessario

necktie
la cravatta

to need
bisognare

**to need, have
need (of)**
avere bisogno (di)

neighbor
il vicino di casa

nephew
il nipote

never
mai

new
nuovo

New Zealander
neozelandese

news
la notizia

newspaper
il giornale

newsstand
l'edicola

next
prossimo
niece
la nipote

nice
simpatico

night
la notte

no longer
più

no one
nessuno

nocturnal
notturno

noise
chiasso

noise
il rumore

noon
mezzogiorno

normal
normale

nose
il naso

nostalgia
la nostalgia

notebook
il quaderno

nothing
niente

to notice
accorgersi

novel
il romanzo

November
novembre

now
adesso

number
il numero

to obey
ubbidire

object
l'oggetto

to obtain
ottenere

ocean
il mare

October
ottobre

odor
l'odore

of
di

to offer
offrire

office
l'ufficio

office manager
il capoufficio

often
spesso

oil
l'olio

old
vecchio

on
su

one hundred
cento

one thousand
mille

to open
aprire

to oppose
opporre

orthodox
ortodosso

other
altro

out, outside
fuori

oven
il forno
to owe
volere

package
il pacco

page
la pagina

painful
doloroso

painfully
dolorosamente

pair
il paio

paper
la carta

parade, show
sfilata

parents
i genitori

to park
parcheggiare

park
il parco

parking lot
il parcheggio

to participate
partecipare

particular
particolare

particularly
particolarmente

party
la festa
past
scorso

patience
la pazienza

to pay
pagare

to pay attention
fare attenzione

peaceful
tranquillo

peacefully
tranquillamente

pen
la penna

percent, percentage
il percento

period
il punto

person
la persona

pharmacy
la farmacia

philosophy
la filosofia

photograph
la foto

to pick
cogliere

piece
il pezzo

pizza
la pizza

pizza maker
il pizzaiolo

place
il locale

place
il luogo, il posto

to place
porre

plan
il piano

plate
il piatto

play
la commedia

to play (a sport or game)
giocare a

to play (an instrument)
suonare

plaza
la piazza

point
il punto

police
la polizia

Polish
polacco

polite
educato

politician
il politico

politics
la politica

pool
la piscina

poor
povero

pope
il papà

Portuguese
portoghese

possible
possibile

post office
l'ufficio postale

to prefer
preferire

to prepare
preparare

to prepare oneself
prepararsi

present
il regalo

president
il presidente

to pretend
fingere

to print
stampare

probable
probabile

probably
probabilmente

to produce
produrre

professor
il professore

to prohibit
interdire

to promote
promuovere

pronoun
il pronome

to propose
proporre

prosciutto
il prosciutto

psychology
la psicologia

public
pubblico

to pull
tirare

to pull
trarre

punctual
puntuale

punishment
la pena

to put
porre

to put after
posporre

to put back
riporre

to put on (oneself)
mettersi

to put
mettere

question
la domanda

quick
veloce

quickly
rapidamente

to quit
smettere

to rain
piovere

rain
la pioggia

rainstorm
il temporale

rapidly
velocemente

rare
raro

rarely
raramente
rather
abbastanza

raw
crudo

to read
leggere

to reason
ragionare

reason
la ragione

reasonable
ragionevole

to receive
ricevere

recent
recente

recently
recentemente

record album
il disco

red
rosso

to reduce
ridurre

to remain
rimanere, restare

to remove
togliere

to rent
affittare

to rent (a car)
noleggiare

to repeat
ripetere

to report
riferire

representative
il rappresentante

to resemble
assomigliare

to respect
rispettare

to respond, answer
rispondere

to rest
riposarsi

restaurant
il ristorante
to restore
rendere

to retract
disdire

to return
ritornare

to return
tornare

rich
ricco

right away
subito

to ring
squillare

roast
l'arrosto

room
la camera

room
la stanza

roommate
la compagna di stanza

roommate
il compagno di stanza

row
la fila

rude
sgarbato

rule
la regola

to run
correre

Russian
russo

sad
triste

sadly
tristemente

safe
la cassa

safe
salvo; sicuro

salad
l'insalata

salami
il salame

same
stesso

sandwich
il panino

Saturday
sabato

saxophone
il sassofono

to say
dire

scarf
la sciarpa

scene
la scena

scheme, pattern
lo schema

school
la scuola

science
la scienza

scientific
scientifico

scientist
lo scienziato

Scottish
scozzese

sculptor
lo scultore

second
secondo

to search
cercare

to see
vedere

to seem
parere

to seem
sembrare

to sell
vendere

semester
il semestre

to send
mandare

to send
spedire

sensible
sensibile

September
settembre

serene, nice
sereno

to serve
servire

to shave
farsi la barba

to shave
radersi

shawl
lo scialle

she
lei

shelf
lo scaffale

shell
il guscio

to shine
scintillare

shoe
la scarpa

short
basso

short story
il racconto

show
la sfilata

to show
mostrare

shrewd
furbo

sin
il peccato

synagogue
la sinagoga

sincere
sincero

to sing
cantare

singer
il cantante

single woman
nubile

sister
la sorella

to sit
sedersi

situation
la situazione

to ski
sciare

slave
lo schiavo

to sleep
dormire

slice
la fetta

slow
lento

slowly, softly
piano

small
piccolo

to smile
sorridere

smile
il sorriso

to smoke
fumare

snow
la neve

to snow
nevicare

so
così

so much, so many
tanto

soccer
il calcio

something
qualcosa

sometimes
a volte

son
il figlio

song
la canzone

soon, early
presto

soup
la minestra

soup
la zuppa

space
lo spazio

Spanish
lo spagnolo

to speak
parlare

speech
il discorso

to spend
spendere

spicy
piccante

spinach
gli spinaci

to spoil, to reduce, to lose weight
sciupare

sport
lo sport

to spread
stendere

springtime
la primavera

stadium
lo stadio

stairs
le scale

to stand
stare in piedi

state
lo stato

station
la stazione

statue
la statua

to stay
restare

to stay
rimanere

steam
il vapore

still
ancora

stingy
avaro

to stop
fermare

to stop (oneself)
fermarsi

store
il negozio

storm
il temporale, la tempesta

street
la strada

street
la via

stretched out
sdraiato

strike
lo sciopero

string
lo spago

studious
studioso

to study
studiare

study, studio
lo studio

stupid
stupido

subject
argomento

subtitles
i sottotitoli

to succeed
riuscire

sufficient
sufficiente

sugar
lo zucchero

to suggest
suggerire

summer
l'estate

sun
il sole

Sunday
domenica

supermarket
il supermercato

to support
sostenere

to suppose
suppore

sweater
il maglione

Swedish
svedese

to swim
nuotare

swimming pool
la piscina

Swiss
svizzero

Switzerland
la Svizzera

table
il tavolo

to take
prendere

to take a bath
fare un bagno

to take a break
fare una pausa

to take a picture
fare una foto

to take a short trip
fare una gita

to take a shower
fare la doccia

to take a trip
fare un viaggio

to take a walk
fare una passeggiata

tall
alto

tavern, public house
l'osteria

taxi
il tassì

to teach
insegnare

teacher
il maestro

team
la squadra

telephone
il telefono

telephone call
la telefonata

telephone number
il numero di telefono

television
la televisione

to tell
raccontare; dire

tennis
il tennis

that
quello

theater
il teatro

then
poi

there
lì, là

they
loro

thin
magro

thin
snello

to think
pensare

to think about (doing something)
pensare di

to think about (someone or something)
pensare a

this
questo

this evening
stasera

this morning
stamattina

to throw
gettare

Thursday
giovedì

ticket
il biglietto

to tie
legare

tight
stretto

time
la volta; l'ora; il tempo

tip
la mancia

tired
stanco

to
a, in

tobacconist
il tabaccaio

today
oggi

tomato
il pomodoro

tomorrow
domani

tongue
la lingua

tonight
stanotte; stasera

too much, too many
troppo

tourist
il,la turista

toy
il giocatolo

train
il treno

to translate
tradurre

to travel
viaggiare

travel agency
l'agenzia di viaggi

tree
l'albero

tribe
la tribù

trip
il viaggio

true
vero

to trust
fidarsi

truth
la verità

to try
provare

t-shirt
la maglietta

Tuesday
martedì
turn
la volta

to turn off
spegnere

TV news
il telegiornale

ugly
brutto

uncle
lo zio

under
sotto

to understand
capire

to undo
scogliere

to undress
spogliarsi

university
l'università

unpleasant
antipatico

to untie
slegare

to untie
snodare

until
fino a

to use
usare

used
usato

usually
di solito

vacation
la vacanza; la feria

vapor
il vapore

various
vario

vase
il vaso

veal
il vitello

verb
il verbo

to visit
visitare

vocabulary
il vocabolario

voice
la voce

volcano
il vulcano

to wage war
fare la guerra

to wait
attendere

to wait (for)
aspettare

waiter
il cameriere

waitress
la cameriera

to wake up
svegliarsi

to waken
svegliare

to walk
camminare

to want
desiderare

to want
volere

war
la guerra

warm
caldo

to wash
lavare

to wash up
lavarsi

to watch
guardare

water
l'acqua

watermelon
il cocomero

we
noi

to wear
portare

weather
il tempo

Wednesday
mercoledì

week
la settimana

weight
il peso

to welcome
accogliere

well
bene

what
che, cosa

What?
Che (cosa)?
Come?

when
quando

When?
Quando?

where
dove

Where?
Dove?

which
quale

while
mentre

white
bianco

white lie
la bugia di
convenienza

who, whom
chi, cui
Who?, Whom?
Chi?

why
perché

wife
la moglie

to win
vincere

wind
il vento

window
la finestra

wine
il vino

winter
l'inverno

witch
la maga

with
con

without
senza

word
la parola

to work
lavorare

to worry
preoccuparsi

worry
la preoccupazi-
one

worst
pessimo

wristwatch
l'orologio

to write
scrivere

**wrong,
incorrect**
sbagliato

to yawn
sbadigliare

year
l'anno

yellow
giallo

yesterday
ieri

**you (plural,
formal)**
Loro

**you (plural,
informal)**
voi

**you (singular,
formal)**
Lei

**you (singular,
informal)**
tu

young
giovane

youth
la gioventù

zebra
la zebra

zero
lo zero

zoo
lo zoo

zucchini
gli zucchini

APPENDIX C

Verb Tables

ESSERE (TO BE) — auxiliary verb

	present		subjunctive
io	sono		sia
tu	sei		sia
lui, lei, Lei	è		sia
noi	siamo		siamo
voi	siete		siate
loro, Loro	sono		siano
	passato prossimo		**imperfect**
io	sono stato/a		ero
tu	sei stato/a		eri
lui, lei, Lei	è stato/a		era
noi	siamo stati/e		eravamo
voi	siete stati/e		eravate
loro, Loro	sono stati/e		erano
	future		**conditional**
io	sarò		sarei
tu	sarai		saresti
lui, lei, Lei	sarà		sarebbe
noi	saremo		saremmo
voi	sarete		sareste
loro, Loro	saranno		sarebbero
	imperative		**imperfect subjunctive**
io	—		fossi
tu	sii		fossi
lui, lei, Lei	sia		fosse
noi	siamo		fossimo
voi	siate		foste
loro, Loro	siano		fossero
	gerund		**past participle**
	essendo		stato

AVERE (TO HAVE) AUXILIARY VERB

	present	subjunctive	
io	ho	abbia	
tu	hai	abbia	
lui, lei, Lei	ha	abbia	
noi	abbiamo	abbiamo	
voi	avete	abbiate	
loro, Loro	hanno	abbiano	
	passato prossimo	**imperfect**	
io	ho avuto	avevo	
tu	hai avuto	avevi	
lui, lei, Lei	ha avuto	aveva	
noi	abbiamo avuto	avevamo	
voi	avete avuto	avevate	
loro, Loro	hanno avuto	avevano	
	future	**conditional**	
io	avrò	avrei	
tu	avrai	avresti	
lui, lei, Lei	avrà	avrebbe	
noi	avremo	avremmo	
voi	avrete	avreste	
loro, Loro	avranno	avrebbero	
	imperative	**imperfect subjunctive**	
io	—	avessi	
tu	abbi	avessi	
lui, lei, Lei	abbia	avesse	
noi	abbiamo	avessimo	
voi	abbiate	aveste	
loro, Loro	abbiano	avessero	
	gerund	**past participle**	
	avendo	avuto	

RICEVERE (TO RECEIVE) REGULAR –ERE VERB

	present	subjunctive	
io	ricevo	riceva	
tu	ricevi	riceva	
lui, lei, Lei	riceve	riceva	

noi	*riceviamo*		*riceviamo*
voi	*ricevete*		*riceviate*
loro, Loro	*ricevono*		*ricevano*
	passato prossimo		**imperfect**
io	*ho ricevuto*		*ricevevo*
tu	*hai ricevuto*		*ricevevi*
lui, lei, Lei	*ha ricevuto*		*riceveva*
noi	*abbiamo ricevuto*		*ricevevamo*
voi	*avete ricevuto*		*ricevevate*
loro, Loro	*hanno ricevuto*		*ricevevano*
	future		**conditional**
io	*riceverò*		*riceverei*
tu	*riceverai*		*riceveresti*
lui, lei, Lei	*riceverà*		*riceverebbe*
noi	*riceveremo*		*riceveremmo*
voi	*riceverete*		*ricevereste*
loro, Loro	*riceveranno*		*riceverebbero*
	imperative		**imperfect subjunctive**
io	—		*ricevessi*
tu	*ricevi*		*ricevessi*
lui, lei, Lei	*riceva*		*ricevesse*
noi	*riceviamo*		*ricevessimo*
voi	*ricevete*		*riceveste*
loro, Loro	*ricevano*		*ricevessero*
	gerund		**past participle**
	ricevendo		*ricevuto*

DORMIRE (TO SLEEP)   **REGULAR *–IRE* VERB**

	present		**subjunctive**
io	*dormo*		*dorma*
tu	*dormi*		*dorma*
lui, lei, Lei	*dorme*		*dorma*
noi	*dormiamo*		*dormiamo*
voi	*dormite*		*dormiate*
loro, Loro	*dormono*		*dormano*

	passato prossimo	imperfect	
io	ho dormito	dormivo	
tu	hai dormito	dormivi	
lui, lei, Lei	ha dormito	dormiva	
noi	abbiamo dormito	dormivamo	
voi	avete dormito	dormivate	
loro, Loro	hanno dormito	dormivano	
	future	conditional	
io	dormirò	dormirei	
tu	dormirai	dormiresti	
lui, lei, Lei	dormirà	dormirebbe	
noi	dormiremo	dormiremmo	
voi	dormirete	dormireste	
loro, Loro	dormiranno	dormirebbero	
	imperative	imperfect subjunctive	
io	—	dormissi	
tu	dormi	dormissi	
lui, lei, Lei	dorma	dormisse	
noi	dormiamo	dormissimo	
voi	dormite	dormiste	
loro, Loro	dormano	dormissero	
	gerund	past participle	
	dormendo	dormito	

ANDARE (TO GO) IRREGULAR –ARE VERB

	present	subjunctive	
io	vado	vada	
tu	vai	vada	
lui, lei, Lei	va	vada	
noi	andiamo	andiamo	
voi	andate	andiate	
loro, Loro	vanno	vadano	

	passato prossimo	imperfect
io	sono andato/a	andavo
tu	sei andato/a	andavi
lui, lei, Lei	è andato/a	andava
noi	siamo andati/e	andavamo
voi	siete andati/e	andavate
loro, Loro	sono andati/e	andavano
	future	conditional
io	andrò	andrei
tu	andrai	andresti
lui, lei, Lei	andrà	andrebbe
noi	andremo	andremmo
voi	andrete	andreste
loro, Loro	andranno	andrebbero
	imperative	imperfect subjunctive
io	—	andassi
tu	va, vai, va'	andassi
lui, lei, Lei	vada	andasse
noi	andiamo	andassimo
voi	andate	andaste
loro, Loro	vadano	andassero
	gerund	past participle
	andando	andato

BERE (TO DRINK)   IRREGULAR *–ERE* VERB

	present	subjunctive
io	bevo	beva
tu	bevi	beva
lui, lei, Lei	beve	beva
noi	beviamo	beviamo
voi	bevete	beviate
loro, Loro	bevono	bevano

	passato prossimo	imperfect	
io	ho bevuto	bevevo	
tu	hai bevuto	bevevi	
lui, lei, Lei	ha bevuto	beveva	
noi	abbiamo bevuto	bevevamo	
voi	avete bevuto	bevevate	
loro, Loro	hanno bevuto	bevevano	
	future	conditional	
io	berrò, beverò	berrei, beverei	
tu	berrai, beverai	berresti, beveresti	
lui, lei, Lei	berrà, beverà	berrebbe, beverebbe	
noi	berremo, beveremo	berremmo, beveremmo	
voi	berrete, beverete	berreste, bevereste	
loro, Loro	berranno, beveranno	berrebbero, beverebbero	
	imperative	imperfect subjunctive	
io	—	bevessi	
tu	bevi	bevessi	
lui, lei, Lei	beva	bevesse	
noi	beviamo	bevessimo	
voi	bevete	beveste	
loro, Loro	bevano	bevessero	
	gerund	past participle	
	bevendo	bevuto	

CERCARE (TO LOOK FOR)   –ARE VERB (C>CH)

	present	subjunctive	
io	cerco	cerchi	
tu	cerchi	cerchi	
lui, lei, Lei	cerca	cerchi	
noi	cerchiamo	cerchiamo	
voi	cercate	cerchiate	
loro, Loro	cercano	cerchino	

	passato prossimo	imperfect
io	*ho cercato*	*cercavo*
tu	*hai cercato*	*cercavi*
lui, lei, Lei	*ha cercato*	*cercava*
noi	*abbiamo cercato*	*cercavamo*
voi	*avete cercato*	*cercavate*
loro, Loro	*hanno cercato*	*cercavano*
	future	**conditional**
io	*cercherò*	*cercherei*
tu	*cercherai*	*cercheresti*
lui, lei, Lei	*cercherà*	*cercherebbe*
noi	*cercheremo*	*cercheremmo*
voi	*cercherete*	*cerchereste*
loro, Loro	*cercheranno*	*cercherebbero*
	imperative	**imperfect subjunctive**
io	—	*cercassi*
tu	*cerca*	*cercassi*
lui, lei, Lei	*cerchi*	*cercasse*
noi	*cerchiamo*	*cercassimo*
voi	*cercate*	*cercaste*
loro, Loro	*cerchino*	*cercassero*
	gerund	**past participle**
	cercando	*cercato*

DARE (TO GIVE) IRREGULAR *–ARE* VERB

	present	subjunctive
io	*do*	*dia*
tu	*dai*	*dia*
lui, lei, Lei	*dà*	*dia*
noi	*diamo*	*diamo*
voi	*date*	*diate*
loro, Loro	*danno*	*diano*

	passato prossimo	imperfect	
io	avevo dato	davo	
tu	avevi dato	davi	
lui, lei, Lei	aveva dato	dava	
noi	avevamo dato	davamo	
voi	avevate dato	davate	
loro, Loro	avevano dato	davano	
	future	conditional	
io	darò	darei	
tu	darai	daresti	
lui, lei, Lei	darà	darebbe	
noi	daremo	daremmo	
voi	darete	dareste	
loro, Loro	daranno	darebbero	
	imperative	imperfect subjunctive	
io	—	dessi	
tu	dà, dai, da'	dessi	
lui, lei, Lei	dia	desse	
noi	diamo	dessimo	
voi	date	deste	
loro, Loro	diano	dessero	
	gerund	past participle	
	dando	dato	

DIRE (TO SAY, TO TELL)   IRREGULAR –*IRE* VERB

	present	subjunctive	
io	dico	dica	
tu	dici	dica	
lui, lei, Lei	dice	dica	
noi	diciamo	diciamo	
voi	dite	diciate	
loro, Loro	dicono	dicano	

	passato prossimo	imperfect
io	ho detto	dicevo
tu	hai detto	dicevi
lui, lei, Lei	ha detto	diceva
noi	abbiamo detto	dicevamo
voi	avete detto	dicevate
loro, Loro	hanno detto	dicevano
	future	conditional
io	dirò	direi
tu	dirai	diresti
lui, lei, Lei	dirà	direbbe
noi	diremo	diremmo
voi	direte	direste
loro, Loro	diranno	direbbero
	imperative	imperfect subjunctive
io	—	dicessi
tu	dì, di'	dicessi
lui, lei, Lei	dica	dicesse
noi	diciamo	dicessimo
voi	dite	diceste
loro, Loro	dicano	dicessero
	gerund	past participle
	dicendo	detto

DOVERE (TO HAVE TO, MUST)   IRREGULAR –ERE VERB

	present	subjunctive
io	devo	debba
tu	devi	debba
lui, lei, Lei	deve	debba
noi	dobbiamo	dobbiamo
voi	dovete	dobbiate
loro, Loro	devono, debbono	debbano

	passato prossimo	imperfect	
io	ho dovuto	dovevo	
tu	hai dovuto	dovevi	
lui, lei, Lei	ha dovuto	doveva	
noi	abbiamo dovuto	dovevamo	
voi	avete dovuto	dovevate	
loro, Loro	hanno dovuto	dovevano	
	future	conditional	
io	dovrò	dovrei	
tu	dovrai	dovresti	
lui, lei, Lei	dovrà	dovrebbe	
noi	dovremo	dovremmo	
voi	dovrete	dovreste	
loro, Loro	dovranno	dovrebbero	
	imperative	imperfect subjunctive	
io	—	dovessi	
tu	—	dovessi	
lui, lei, Lei	—	dovesse	
noi	—	dovessimo	
voi	—	doveste	
loro, Loro	—	dovessero	
	gerund	past participle	
—	dovendo	dovuto	

FINIRE (TO FINISH)   IRREGULAR –IRE VERB (–IRE>–ISC)

	present	subjunctive	
io	finisco	finisca	
tu	finisci	finisca	
lui, lei, Lei	finisce	finisca	
noi	finiamo	finiamo	
voi	finite	finiate	
loro, Loro	finiscono	finiscano	
	passato prossimo	imperfect	
io	ho finito	finivo	
tu	hai finito	finivi	
lui, lei, Lei	ha finito	finiva	

	present	subjunctive
noi	*abbiamo finito*	*finivamo*
voi	*avete finito*	*finivate*
loro, Loro	*hanno finito*	*finivano*
	future	**conditional**
io	*finirò*	*finirei*
tu	*finirai*	*finiresti*
lui, lei, Lei	*finirà*	*finirebbe*
noi	*finiremo*	*finiremmo*
voi	*finirete*	*finireste*
loro, Loro	*finiranno*	*finirebbero*
	imperative	**imperfect subjunctive**
io	—	*finissi*
tu	*finisci*	*finissi*
lui, lei, Lei	*finisca*	*finisse*
noi	*finiamo*	*finissimo*
voi	*finite*	*finiste*
loro, Loro	*finiscano*	*finissero*
	gerund	**past participle**
	finendo	*finito*

FARE (TO DO, TO MAKE)   IRREGULAR *–ARE* VERB

	present	subjunctive
io	*faccio*	*faccia*
tu	*fai*	*faccia*
lui, lei, Lei	*fa*	*faccia*
noi	*facciamo*	*facciamo*
voi	*fate*	*facciate*
loro, Loro	*fanno*	*facciano*
	passato prossimo	**imperfect**
io	*ho fatto*	*facevo*
tu	*hai fatto*	*facevi*
lui, lei, Lei	*ha fatto*	*faceva*
noi	*abbiamo fatto*	*facevamo*
voi	*avete fatto*	*facevate*
loro, Loro	*hanno fatto*	*facevano*

	future	conditional	
io	*farò*	*farei*	
tu	*farai*	*faresti*	
lui, lei, Lei	*farà*	*farebbe*	
noi	*faremo*	*faremmo*	
voi	*farete*	*fareste*	
loro, Loro	*faranno*	*farebbero*	
	imperative	**imperfect subjunctive**	
io	—	*facessi*	
tu	*fa, fai, fa'*	*facessi*	
lui, lei, Lei	*faccia*	*facesse*	
noi	*facciamo*	*facessimo*	
voi	*fate*	*faceste*	
loro, Loro	*facciano*	*facessero*	
	gerund	**past participle**	
	facendo	*fatto*	

MANGIARE (TO EAT)   IRREGULAR *–ARE* VERB *(IA > E)*

	present	subjunctive	
io	*mangio*	*mangi*	
tu	*mangi*	*mangi*	
lui, lei, Lei	*mangia*	*mangi*	
noi	*mangiamo*	*mangiamo*	
voi	*mangiate*	*mangiate*	
loro, Loro	*mangiano*	*mangino*	
	passato prossimo	**imperfect**	
io	*ho mangiato*	*mangiavo*	
tu	*hai mangiato*	*mangiavi*	
lui, lei, Lei	*ha mangiato*	*mangiava*	
noi	*abbiamo mangiato*	*mangiavamo*	
voi	*avete mangiato*	*mangiavate*	
loro, Loro	*hanno mangiato*	*mangiavano*	

	future	conditional
io	*mangerò*	*mangerei*
tu	*mangerai*	*mangeresti*
lui, lei, Lei	*mangerà*	*mangerebbe*
noi	*mangeremo*	*mangeremmo*
voi	*mangerete*	*mangereste*
loro, Loro	*mangeranno*	*mangerebbero*
	imperative	imperfect subjunctive
io	—	*mangiassi*
tu	*mangia*	*mangiassi*
lui, lei, Lei	*mangi*	*mangiasse*
noi	*mangiamo*	*mangiassimo*
voi	*mangiate*	*mangiaste*
loro, Loro	*mangino*	*mangiassero*
	gerund	past participle
	mangiando	*mangiato*

MORIRE (TO DIE)   **IRREGULAR –*IRE* VERB *(O > UO)***

	present	subjunctive
io	*muoio*	*muoia*
tu	*muori*	*muoia*
lui, lei, Lei	*muore*	*muoia*
noi	*moriamo*	*moriamo*
voi	*morite*	*moriate*
loro, Loro	*muoiono*	*muoiano*
	passato prossimo	imperfect
io	*sono morto/a*	*morivo*
tu	*sei morto/a*	*morivi*
lui, lei, Lei	*è morto/a*	*moriva*
noi	*siamo morti/e*	*morivamo*
voi	*siete morti/e*	*morivate*
loro, Loro	*sono morti/e*	*morivano*

	future	conditional	
io	morirò, morrò	morirei, morrei	
tu	morirai, morrai	moriresti, morresti	
lui, lei, Lei	morirà, morrà	morirebbe, morrebbe	
noi	moriremo, morremo	moriremmo, morremmo	
voi	morirete, morrete	morireste, morreste	
loro, Loro	moriranno, morranno	morirebbero, morrebbero	
	imperative	imperfect subjunctive	
io	—	morissi	
tu	muori	morissi	
lui, lei, Lei	muoia	morisse	
noi	moriamo	morissimo	
voi	morite	moriste	
loro, Loro	muoiano	morissero	
	gerund	past participle	
	morendo	morto	

PAGARE (TO PAY) **IRREGULAR *–ARE* VERB (G > GH)**

	present	subjunctive	
io	pago	paghi	
tu	paghi	paghi	
lui, lei, Lei	paga	paghi	
noi	paghiamo	paghiamo	
voi	pagate	paghiate	
loro, Loro	pagano	paghino	
	passato prossimo	imperfect	
io	ho pagato	pagavo	
tu	hai pagato	pagavi	
lui, lei, Lei	ha pagato	pagava	
noi	abbiamo pagato	pagavamo	
voi	avete pagato	pagavate	
loro, Loro	hanno pagato	pagavano	

	future	conditional
io	*pagherò*	*pagherei*
tu	*pagherai*	*pagheresti*
lui, lei, Lei	*pagherà*	*pagherebbe*
noi	*pagheremo*	*pagherebbero*
voi	*pagherete*	*paghereste*
loro, Loro	*pagheranno*	*pagherebbero*
	imperative	imperfect subjunctive
io	—	*pagassi*
tu	*paga*	*pagassi*
lui, lei, Lei	*paghi*	*pagasse*
noi	*paghiamo*	*pagassimo*
voi	*pagate*	*pagaste*
loro, Loro	*paghino*	*pagassero*
	gerund	past participle
	pagando	*pagato*

PIACERE (TO PLEASE)

	present	subjunctive
io	*piaccia*	*piaccia*
tu	*piaci*	*piaccia*
lui, lei, Lei	*piace*	*piaccia*
noi	*piaciamo*	*piacciamo*
voi	*piacete*	*piaciate*
loro, Loro	*piaccione*	*piacciano*
	passato prossimo	imperfect
io	*sono piaciuto/a*	*piacevo*
tu	*sei piaciuto/a*	*piacevi*
lui, lei, Lei	*è piaciuto/a*	*piaceva*
noi	*siamo piaciuti/e*	*piacevamo*
voi	*siete piaciuti/e*	*piacevate*
loro, Loro	*sono piaciuti/e*	*piacevano*

	future	conditional	
io	*piacerò*	*piacerei*	
tu	*piacerai*	*piaceresti*	
lui, lei, Lei	*piacerà*	*piacerebbe*	
noi	*piaceremo*	*piaceremmo*	
voi	*piacerete*	*piacereste*	
loro, Loro	*piaceranno*	*piacerebbero*	
	imperative	imperfect subjunctive	
io	—	*piacessi*	
tu	*piaci*	*piacessi*	
lui, lei, Lei	*piaccia*	*piacesse*	
noi	*piacciamo*	*piacessimo*	
voi	*piacete*	*piaceste*	
loro, Loro	*piacciano*	*piacessero*	
	gerund	past participle	
	piacendo	*piaciuto*	

POTERE (TO BE ABLE TO, CAN)   IRREGULAR *–ERE* VERB

	present	subjunctive	
io	*posso*	*possa*	
tu	*puoi*	*possa*	
lui, lei, Lei	*può*	*possa*	
noi	*possiamo*	*possiamo*	
voi	*potete*	*possiate*	
loro, Loro	*possono*	*possano*	
	passato prossimo	imperfect	
io	*ho potuto*	*potevo*	
tu	*hai potuto*	*potevi*	
lui, lei, Lei	*ha potuto*	*poteva*	
noi	*abbiamo potuto*	*potevamo*	
voi	*avete potuto*	*potevate*	
loro, Loro	*hanno potuto*	*potevano*	

	future	conditional
io	*potrò*	*potrei*
tu	*potrai*	*potresti*
lui, lei, Lei	*potrà*	*potrebbe*
noi	*potremo*	*potremmo*
voi	*potrete*	*potreste*
loro, Loro	*potranno*	*potrebbero*
	imperative	imperfect subjunctive
io	—	*potessi*
tu	—	*potessi*
lui, lei, Lei	—	*potesse*
noi	—	*potessimo*
voi	—	*poteste*
loro, Loro	—	*potessero*
	gerund	past participle
	potendo	*potuto*

STARE (TO STAY, TO FEEL)   IRREGULAR *–ARE* VERB

	present	subjunctive
io	*sto*	*stia*
tu	*stai*	*stia*
lui, lei, Lei	*sta*	*stia*
noi	*stiamo*	*stiamo*
voi	*state*	*stiate*
loro, Loro	*stanno*	*stiano*
	passato prossimo	imperfect
io	*sono stato/a*	*stavo*
tu	*sei stato/a*	*stavi*
lui, lei, Lei	*è stato/a*	*stava*
noi	*siamo stati/e*	*stavamo*
voi	*siete stati/e*	*stavate*
loro, Loro	*sono stati/e*	*stavano*

	future	conditional	
io	starò	starei	
tu	starai	staresti	
lui, lei, Lei	starà	starebbe	
noi	staremo	staremmo	
voi	starete	stareste	
loro, Loro	staranno	starebbero	
	imperative	imperfect subjunctive	
io	—	stessi	
tu	sta, stai, sta'	stessi	
lui, lei, Lei	stia	stesse	
noi	stiamo	stessimo	
voi	state	steste	
loro, Loro	stiano	stessero	
	gerund	past participle	
	stando	stato	

VENIRE (TO COME)   IRREGULAR –IRE VERB

	present	subjunctive	
io	vengo	venga	
tu	vieni	venga	
lui, lei, Lei	viene	venga	
noi	veniamo	veniamo	
voi	venite	veniate	
loro, Loro	vengono	vengano	
	passato prossimo	imperfect	
io	sono venuto/a	venivo	
tu	sei venuto/a	venivi	
lui, lei, Lei	è venuto/a	veniva	
noi	siamo venuti/e	venivamo	
voi	siete venuti/e	venivate	
loro, Loro	sono venuti/e	venivano	

	future	conditional
io	*verrò*	*verrei*
tu	*verrai*	*verresti*
lui, lei, Lei	*verrà*	*verrebbe*
noi	*verremo*	*verremmo*
voi	*verrete*	*verreste*
loro, Loro	*verranno*	*verrebbero*
	imperative	imperfect subjunctive
io	—	*venissi*
tu	*vieni*	*venissi*
lui, lei, Lei	*venga*	*venisse*
noi	*veniamo*	*venissimo*
voi	*venite*	*veniste*
loro, Loro	*vengano*	*venissero*
	gerund	past participle
	venendo	*venuto*

VOLERE (TO WANT)   **IRREGULAR –ERE VERB**

	present	subjunctive
io	*voglio*	*voglia*
tu	*vuoi*	*voglia*
lui, lei, Lei	*vuole*	*voglia*
noi	*vogliamo*	*vogliamo*
voi	*volete*	*vogliate*
loro, Loro	*vogliono*	*vogliano*
	passato prossimo	imperfect
io	*ho voluto*	*volevo*
tu	*hai voluto*	*volevi*
lui, lei, Lei	*ha voluto*	*voleva*
noi	*abbiamo voluto*	*volevamo*
voi	*avete voluto*	*volevate*
loro, Loro	*hanno voluto*	*volevano*

	future	conditional	
io	*vorrò*	*vorrei*	
tu	*vorrai*	*vorresti*	
lui, lei, Lei	*vorrà*	*vorrebbe*	
noi	*vorremo*	*vorremmo*	
voi	*vorrete*	*vorreste*	
loro, Loro	*vorranno*	*vorrebbero*	
	imperative	**imperfect subjunctive**	
io	—	*volessi*	
tu	—	*volessi*	
lui, lei, Lei	—	*volesse*	
noi	—	*volessimo*	
voi	—	*voleste*	
loro, Loro	—	*volessero*	
	gerund	**past participle**	
	volendo	*voluto*	

Answer Key

Chapter 3

Exercise 3-1
1. feminine
2. masculine
3. feminine
4. feminine
5. masculine

Exercise 3-2
1. masculine
2. feminine
3. masculine
4. masculine
5. feminine

Exercise 3-3
1. masculine, plural
2. feminine, plural
3. feminine, plural
4. masculine, singular and plural
5. feminine, singular

Exercise 3-4
1. definite article
2. indefinite article
3. definite article
4. definite article
5. indefinite article

Exercise 3-5
1. *buone studentesse*
2. *buoni ragazzi*
3. *una buon'amica*
4. *un buon vino*
5. *un buon albergo*

Exercise 3-6
1. *Che bella casa!*
2. *Che bel giorno!*
3. *Che bei ragazzi!*
4. *Che belle amiche!*
5. *Che begli uffici!*

Exercise 3-7
1. *il loro libro*
2. *i nostri amici*
3. *la Sua casa*
4. *il vostro compleanno*
5. *i suoi libri*

Exercise 3-8
1. *il mio libro*
2. *la loro sorella*
3. *i nostri amici*
4. *nostro cugino*
5. *il suo ragazzo*

Chapter 4

Exercise 4-1

1. *noi*
2. *lui*
3. *loro*
4. *voi*
5. *loro*
6. *lei*

Exercise 4-2

1. *Io e Davide abbiamo una nuova macchina.*
2. *Tu ed Eugenio avete molti amici in Italia.*
3. *Michele e Mario hanno fame.*
4. *Tu hai una buon'idea.*
5. *Io ho caldo.*

Exercise 4-3

Answers may vary.

1. *Sono di Providence.*
2. *Sì, ho molti amici.*
3. *Sì, gli amici sono simpatici.*
4. *Ho una VW.*
5. *Sì, è nuova.*

Exercise 4-4

*Maria è di Roma. Io non **sono** di Roma. Marco e suo fratello **sono** di Roma. Anche noi **siamo** di Roma. Paola **è** di Napoli. E tu, di dove **sei?** Voi **siete** di Venezia.*

*Tu sei americana. Giuseppe **è** americano? Io e mia moglie **siamo** americani, ma Massimo non **è** americano: **è** italiano.*

Exercise 4-5

Answers may vary.

1. *Sì, c'è un ristorante cinese a Boston.*
2. *Ci sono molti abitanti a Boston.*
3. *Sì, c'è un'università a Boston.*
4. *Ci sono ristoranti italiani a Boston.*
5. *C'è una biblioteca pubblica a Boston.*

Chapter 6

Exercise 6-1

1. *regna*
2. *marciamo*
3. *assaggio*
4. *avvinghi*
5. *invecchia*
6. *noleggiate*
7. *parcheggia*
8. *racconciano*

Exercise 6-2

1. *giocare*
2. *telefonare*
3. *pensare*
4. *abitare*
5. *pensare*

Exercise 6-3

1. *Imparo a parlare italiano.*
2. *Cominciano a lavorare venerdì.*
3. *Pensiamo di mangiare nel nuovo ristorante.*
4. *I ragazzi vogliono spiegare la situazione.*
5. *Il professore parla con uno studente.*
6. *John abita a Boston.*
7. *Giochi a tennis?*

8. *Ha paura degli altri bambini.*

9. *Abbiamo voglia di mangiare la pizza.*

10. *Tu e John non avete bisogno del computer oggi.*

Exercise 6-4

1. *Come **stanno** Loro oggi?*
2. *Che cosa **fai**, tu?*
3. *Io **vado** a mangiare in un ristorante.*
4. *La madre **dà** soldi a suo figlio.*

Exercise 6-6

1. *Noi **facciamo** attenzione quando parla.*
2. *Tu e Mario **andate** a casa oggi?*
3. *Dove **andiamo** noi per le vacanze?*
4. *Loro **danno** informazioni ai turisti.*
5. *Come **stanno** Loro oggi?*
6. *Che cosa **fai**, tu?*
7. *Io **vado** a mangiare in un ristorante.*
8. *La madre **dà** soldi a suo figlio.*

Exercise 6-8

1. ***Come** stai?*
2. ***Dove** vai stasera?*
3. ***Quanti** libri desideri comprare?*
4. ***Perché** fai così?*
5. ***Quale** film desideri vedere questo fine settimana?*

Chapter 7

Exercise 7-1

1. *Tu ed Elena **rispondete** alle mie lettere.*
2. *Giovanni e Mario **discutono** di sport nel bar.*

3. *Io **prendo** la mia macchina.*
4. *Mia sorella **perde** sempre le chiavi di casa.*
5. *Lui **chiude** la porta perché tira vento.*

Exercise 7-4 Answers will vary.

1. *Tu non puoi comprare una nuova Mercedes perché devi comprare una nuova casa.*
2. *Davide e Maria non possono fare un viaggio in Inghilterra perché devono andare in Germania.*
3. *I miei amici non possono andare al cinema perché devono studiare.*
4. *Lui non può ascoltare la musica perché deve andare in biblioteca.*
5. *Io ed Elena non possiamo visitare Venezia perché piove troppo.*

Exercise 7-6

1. *Facilmente*
2. *Raramente*
3. *Disperatamente*
4. *Recentemente*
5. *difficilmente*

Exercise 7-7

1. *Andrea Bocelli canta <u>molto bene.</u>*
2. *Noi ascoltiamo <u>attentamente.</u>*
3. *Mio fratello parla <u>poco.</u>*
4. *Giovanni cerca <u>disperatamente</u> le chiavi della macchina.*

Chapter 8

Exercise 8-1

valere (to be worth)

io valgo	noi valiamo
tu vali	voi valete
lui vale	loro valgono
lei vale	Loro valgono
Lei vale	

Exercise 8-2

1. *Marco non tiene l'anello.*
2. *Tutti i miei amici si siedono al banco.*
3. *Davide e Maria vanno al mare.*
4. *Tu, come stai?*
5. *Mi dà dei consigli?*

Exercise 8-4

1. *io sostengo*
2. *tu sostieni*
3. *Elena sostiene*
4. *noi sosteniamo*
5. *voi sostenete*
6. *tutti i ragazzi sostengono*

Exercise 8-5

1. *Giovanni non **sa** che io vengo alla festa.*
2. *Matteo ed Elena **conoscono** bene la città di Boston.*
3. *Massimo vuole **conoscere** la mia amica.*
4. *Io **so** sciare ma non **so** giocare a tennis.*
5. *Tutti gli studenti **sanno** parlare inglese.*

Exercise 8-6

1. *Io e Marco usciamo stasera.*
2. *Gabriella viene alla festa.*

3. *I ragazzi dicono la verità.*
4. *Loro escono insieme.*
5. *Tu non vieni con noi.*

Exercise 8-7

1. *Tu e Marco udite il grido.*
2. *I ragazzi riempiono il vaso di acqua.*
3. *Io muoio dalla voglia di sapere la verità.*
4. *Noi due saliamo le scale.*

Exercise 8-8 Answers will vary.

1. *Preferisco il ristorante italiano.*
2. *Leggo un libro o ascolto la musica.*
3. *Sì, capisco l'italiano.*
4. *Posso suggerire "La vita è bella."*
5. *Finisco di lavorare alle 5.00.*

Chapter 9

Exercise 9-2

1. *Marcello abita **a** Roma.*
2. *Il fratello **di** Massimo si chiama Adriano.*
3. *Gli studenti studiano **in** biblioteca.*
4. *Telefono **a** mia madre ogni domenica.*
5. *Non mi piace la pizza **con** acciughe.*

Exercise 9-4

1. *Ho dato delle rose **a** mia moglia.*
2. *Partiamo **da** Boston.*
3. *Pensano **di** fare un viaggio.*
4. *Studio **in** biblioteca.*
5. *Lascio un messaggio **per** mia moglie.*

Chapter 10

Exercise 10-1
1. *Marco scrive <u>una lettera.</u>*
2. *Voglio mangiare <u>la pizza.</u>*
3. No direct object
4. No direct object
5. *Mio figlio ha molti <u>amici.</u>*

Exercise 10-2
1. *Do il libro <u>al mio amico.</u>*
2. *Puoi telefonare <u>a mio padre</u> stasera.*
3. *Non vuole chiedere soldi <u>a suo padre.</u>*
4. *Restituisco la penna <u>a Lei.</u>*
5. *Tommaso dice bugie <u>a noi.</u>*

Exercise 10-3
1. Not reflexive
2. Reflexive
3. Not reflexive
4. Not reflexive
5. Reflexive

Exercise 10-4
1. *Ci* = reciprocal pronoun
2. *le* = indirect object pronoun
3. *Gli* = indirect object pronoun
4. *ti* = direct object pronoun
5. *Mi* = reflexive pronoun

Exercise 10-5
1. *Se si studia molto, si impara molto.*
2. *Si parlano molte lingue straniere.*
3. *Si va a teatro stasera?*
4. *Si dice che Roma sia bella.*
5. *Si parte alle otto.*

Chapter 11

Exercise 11-1
1. *io ho*   *io sono*
2. *tu hai*   *tu sei*
3. *lui/lei/Lei ha*   *lui/lei/Lei è*
4. *noi abbiamo*   *noi siamo*
5. *voi avete*   *voi siete*
6. *loro/Loro hanno*   *loro/Loro sono*

Exercise 11-2
1. *preso*
2. *mangiato*
3. *andato*
4. *sceso*
5. *detto*

Exercise 11-3
1. *Io li ho letti.*
2. *Noi l'abbiamo mangiata.*
3. *Gli studenti li hanno fatti.*
4. *Maria ci ha visti.*
5. *Vi abbiamo cercati.*

Exercise 11-4
1. *Gliel'abbiamo portata.*
2. *Gliel'hai restituito.*
3. *Gliel'ho data.*
4. *Ce li avete mandati.*
5. *Mio padre ve li ha portati.*

Exercise 11-5
1. *Io **guardavo** la televisione.*
2. *Noi **facevamo** attenzione.*
3. *Tutti i ragazzi **giocavano** a calcio.*
4. *Voi **aspettevate** l'autobus.*
5. *Marco non **rispondeva** alle mie domande.*

Exercise 11-6

1. *Avevo visto il mio amico.*
2. *Eravamo andati a teatro.*
3. *Ci eravamo conosciuti anni fa.*
4. *Il signor Gori aveva comprato una Moto Guzzi.*
5. *Tu avevi saputo la verità.*

Exercise 11-7

1. *Non aveva visto il film.*
2. *Mi ero alzato tardi.*
3. *Avevi già letto quel libro.*
4. *Avevamo ascoltato la musica.*
5. *Si erano innamorati.*

Chapter 12

Exercise 12-1

1. *È il film di **cui** ti ho parlato.*
2. *Il libro **che** ho letto è molto interessante.*
3. ***Chi** studia, impara.*
4. *La persona a **cui** scrivo è mio fratello.*
5. *La città **nella quale** sono nato è molto bella.*

Exercise 12-2

1. *Abito a Boston.*
2. *Ci abito.*
3. *Ho delle mele.*
4. *Ne ho.*
5. *Ho cinque fratelli.*
6. *Ne ho cinque.*

Exercise 12-3 Answers will vary.

1. *Studio l'italiano dall'anno scorso.*
2. *Ho la patente da sette anni.*
3. *Lavoro da un mese.*
4. *Sono in vacanza da dieci giorni.*
5. *Guardo il telegiornale da venti minuti.*

Exercise 12-4

1. *io sto dormendo*
2. *tu stai mangiando*
3. *Marco sta partendo*
4. *noi stiamo leggendo*
5. *voi state andando*
6. *loro stanno cantando*

Exercise 12-5

Answers will vary.

1. *Sto leggendo il giornale.*
2. *Sto guardando un film.*
3. *No, non stavo dormendo.*
4. *Sì, mi sto divertendo molto.*

Chapter 13

Exercise 13-1

1. *tu dormirai*
2. *io vorrò*
3. *loro saranno*
4. *lui pagherà*
5. *voi farete*

Exercise 13-2

1. *Tu imparerai l'italiano.*
2. *Domani sera io starò a casa.*
3. *Mio figlio sarà famoso.*
4. *Non verremo a casa tua.*
5. *Balleremo tutta la sera.*

Exercise 13-3

1. *Saranno le otto di sera.*
2. *Giovanni sarà stanco.*
3. *Mangerà appena sarà pronta la pastasciutta.*
4. *Appena finirà di mangiare, andrà a letto.*
5. *Domani mattina si alzerà presto.*
6. *Si farà la doccia, farà colazione, e partirà per la stazione.*
7. *Prenderà il treno delle otto e venti, e arriverà in ufficio per le nove.*

Exercise 13-4

1. *Mangia la frutta!*
2. *Non fare così!*
3. *Prendi le chiavi!*
4. *Non bere quell vino!*
5. *Di' la verità!*
6. *Non aprire la finestra!*

Exercise 13-5

1. *Mangialo!*
2. *Leggetela!*
3. *Dammi un po' di vino!*
4. *Digli la verità!*
5. *Non lo fare!*
6. *Non parliamole!*

Chapter 14

Exercise 14-1

1. *io leggerei*
2. *tu leggeresti*
3. *lui leggerebbe*
4. *noi leggeremmo*
5. *voi leggereste*
6. *loro leggerebbero*

Exercise 14-2

1. *io partirei*
2. *tu partiresti*
3. *lui partirebbe*
4. *noi partiremmo*
5. *voi partireste*
6. *loro partirebbero*

Exercise 14-3

	potere	vedere
io	potrei	vedrei
tu	potresti	vedresti
lui, lei, Lei	potrebbe	vedrebbe
noi	potremmo	vedremmo
voi	potreste	vedreste
loro, Loro	potrebbero	vedrebbero

Exercise 14-4

1. *io berrei*
2. *loro farebbero*
3. *noi saremmo*
4. *io direi*
5. *tu puliresti*

Exercise 14-5

1. *Marco **darebbe** la mancia al cameriere, ma è al verde.*
2. *Che cosa **penserebbe** tuo padre?*
3. *Noi **vorremmo** un arrosto di vitello.*
4. *Loro **partirebbero** alle otto, se avessero i biglietti.*
5. *Mio figlio **si sveglierebbe** presto.*

Exercise 14-6

1. *Voi non **avreste dovuto** mangiare prima delle otto.*
2. *Anna e Carlo **avrebbero aiutato** il figlio.*
3. *Mi **sarei vestito** in fretta.*
4. *Gaetano **avrebbe mangiato** gli spaghetti.*
5. *Tu e Marcello **sareste tornati** presto.*

Exercise 14-7

1. *Marco canta meglio di Luigi.*
2. *Marco è così intelligente come Angela.*
3. *Nuotare è tanto difficile quanto sciare.*
4. *Elena è bella come un fiore.*
5. *Ho tanta pazienza quanto te.*

Exercise 14-8

1. *È arrivato molto tardi.*
2. *Elena è la mia miglior amica.*
3. *Matteo è il più piccolo dei tre fratelli.*
4. *Giovanni e Marco sono molto simpatici.*
5. *Il signor Gates è assai ricco!*
6. *La pizza è buonissima!*
7. *La moto andava velocissimo!*
8. *Giovanni è un ottimo falegname, ma usa materiali di pessima qualità.*
9. *Lei parla piano piano.*
10. *È un ragazzo buono buono.*

Chapter 15

Exercise 15-1

1. *io capii*
2. *tu capisti*
3. *lui capí*
4. *noi capimmo*

5. *voi capiste*
6. *loro capirono*

Exercise 15-2

1. *io lessi*
2. *tu leggesti*
3. *lui lesse*
4. *noi leggemmo*
5. *voi leggeste*
6. *loro lessero*

Exercise 15-3

	parlare	leggere	partire
io	parli	legga	parta
tu	parli	legga	parta
lui, lei, Lei	parli	legga	parta
noi	parliamo	leggiamo	partiamo
voi	parliate	leggiate	partiate
loro, Loro	parlino	leggano	partano

Exercise 15-4

1. *Credo che Maria venga oggi.*
2. *È necessario che tu legga l'articolo.*
3. *Pare che lui parta stasera.*
4. *È un peccato che Marco sia triste.*

Exercise 15-5

1. *Speravamo che tu arrivassi in orario.*
2. *Speravo che Marco venisse.*
3. *Non sapevo che loro partecipassero alla conferenza.*
4. *Ero contento che tu facessi la spesa.*
5. *Pensava che io prendessi il caffè.*

Index